Bewitching
Betsy Bonaparte

ALICE CURTIS DESMOND

ILLUSTRATED

WITH PHOTOGRAPHS

DODD, MEAD & COMPANY

NEW YORK, 1958

Library of Congress Catalog Card Number: 58-5671

Printed in the United States of America
by The Cornwall Press, Inc., Cornwall, N. Y.

To

my husband

THOMAS C. DESMOND

Acknowledgments

I T IS A PLEASURE to be able to express my gratitude to people who assisted me in writing this book. Foremost was Dorothy M. Bryan, of Dodd, Mead and Company, my dear friend and able editor, who, acting as godmother of this volume, patiently edited several drafts.

I am especially grateful to Dorothy Mackay Quynn, whom I consulted in regard to factual material for this book, and who graciously permitted me to make use of some material that was available only because of her own competent research. Mrs. Quynn, an expert on Betsy Bonaparte, was tireless in providing information, and in rescuing me from possible errors.

Dorothy M. Quynn and Frank F. White, Jr., formerly of the manuscript division, Library of Congress, Washington, D. C., were also kind enough to permit me to borrow what I wished from their account of the Bonapartes' trip to Portugal on the *Erin,* published in the *Maryland Historical Magazine* of September, 1953.

Kimball C. Elkins, senior assistant in the Harvard University Archives, Harvard College Library, Cambridge, Massachusetts, was also helpful. He sent me information about Mr. Patterson's request for his grandson to receive his degree *in absentia;* Jerome's admonition for a "festive entertainment," and later suspension for the same reason. Poor boy! His escapades, after more than a hundred years, are still in the Harvard files.

I also wish to acknowledge the kindness of the following executives of museums and historical associations, who gave me the benefit of clippings, manuscripts and portraits belonging to their organizations: James W. Foster, director, Francis C. Haber, librarian, Garner Ranney, genealogist of the Maryland Historical Society, Baltimore, Maryland, and Fred Shelley, formerly of the staff; James D. Breckenridge, curator, The Baltimore Museum of Art; Eleanora V. Lynn, Maryland Department, Enoch Pratt Free Library, Baltimore; Mrs. Marmaduke Wolfe, curator, and Mrs. H. L. Reisenweber of the Flag House, Baltimore; Louis Nauman, manager, and the officers of The Maryland Club, Baltimore; R. W. G. Vail, director of the New York Historical Society; the staff of the Frick Art Reference Library, New York; and Elydeeth G. McPherson, Library of Congress Manuscript Division, Washington, D. C.

The following people made available to me original source material: Charles Francis Gosnell, state librarian, Mrs. Edna L. Jacobsen, associate librarian, and Miss Marian P. Wiltsie, head researcher in the history section, New York State Library, Albany, furnished me with a map of New York State in 1805, and made it possible for me to read John Maud's account of his visit to Niagara Falls in 1800, invaluable to me in writing about the Bonapartes' honeymoon journey. Miss Jacobsen also showed me pencil sketches, now owned by the State library, done by Princess Charlotte Bonaparte, while traveling up the Hudson to her father's estate in northern New York.

My thanks also go to Mrs. Patterson Tidrick of Phoenix, Arizona, who allowed me to use as an illustration the portrait of her great-great-great-grandmother, Mrs. William Patterson, with daughter Betsy; and to W. H. Dorrance of Dorrance & Company, for permission to reproduce the photograph of Jerome Bonaparte IV from *The Bonapartes in America* by C. E. MacCartney and Gordon Dorrance, published by his firm; to Captain William W. Evans, of Baltimore, for information concerning the old Patterson graveyard; to Miss Reba Shevin for research material; to Mrs. Benton Ten-Broeck, Mrs. Roy H. Weir, and Mrs. Irving Rudolph, who typed the manuscript; and last, but not least, to my husband, Thomas C. Desmond, for his constant aid and encouragement while this book was being written.

                                                              —ABCD

Newburgh, New York.

Contents

BEWITCHING BETSY BONAPARTE

THE BONAPARTE FAMILY

Carlo Bonaparte
1746-1785

Letizia Ramolino
1750-1836

- **Joseph** 1768-1844 m. Julie Clary
  - Zenaide m. Charles (Son of Lucien Bonaparte)
  - Charlotte m. Napoleon (son of Louis Bonaparte)

- **Napoleon** 1769-1821 m. 1. Josephine de Beauharnais — m. 2. Marie Louise of Austria
  - King of Rome

- **Lucien** 1775-1840 m. 1. Christine Boyer — m. 2. Alexandrine Jouberthou
  - Charlotte (by his first wife) m. Prince Gabrielli
  - Charles m. Zenaide dau. of Joseph Bonaparte
  - Letitia m. Sir Thos. Wyse
  - Paul
  - Jeanne m. Marquis Honorati
  - Lucien
  - Pierre
  - Antione
  - Maria m. Viscount Valentini
  - Constance

- **Elisa** 1777-1820 m. Felix Bacciochi
  - Elisa m. Count Camarata
  - Charles

- **Louis** 1778-1846 m. Hortense de Beauharnais
  - Napoleon, Chas.
  - Napoleon, Louis m. Charlotte, dau. of Joseph Bonaparte
  - Charles Louis (Napoleon III) m. Eugénie de Montijo de Guzman
    - Eugene Napoleon Louis (The Prince Imperial)

- **Pauline** 1780-1825 m. 1. Victor Leclerc — m. 2. Prince Borghese
  - Dermide (by her first husband)

- **Caroline** 1782-1839 m. Joachim Murat
  - Nap. Achille m. Catherine Willis of Pensacola, Florida (grand-niece of George Washington)
  - Lucien m. Caroline Fraser of South Carolina
  - Letitia m. Count Pepoli
  - Louise m. Count Rasponi

- **Jerome** 1784-1860 m. 1. Eliz. Patterson
  - Jerome Nap. m. Susan May Williams
    - Jerome Nap. m. Caroline Edgar
    - Chas. Joseph m. Ellen Day
      - Louise Eugénie m. Count Moltke-Hintfeldt
      - Jerome Nap. m. Blanche Strebeigh
  - m. 2. Catherine of Wurtemberg
    - Jerome Nap. Mathilde m. Count Demidov
    - Nap. Joseph (Prince Nap.) m. Clothilde of Savoy
      - Victor Nap. m. Clementine of Belgium
        - Louis Napoleon (Present claimant to the Imperial throne of France)
      - Louis Napoleon
      - Letizia m. Duke of Aosta

1. Teen-Age Rebel of 1803

THE GIRL SLIPPED OUT of the big brick house with white shutters, two blocks from the Baltimore waterfront, and ran to the wall that hid the garden from curious eyes on South Street.

"Henri!" she called.

The tanned sailor, his hair in a pigtail, had already scrambled onto the low brick wall from the street. He sat astride it, waiting eagerly, as he had on other nights. Betsy climbed up beside him. But as the young man leaned to kiss her, she turned her cheek.

"Sweetheart, just once, a real kiss on your lips?" Henri begged. Betsy shook her head and laughed. "I make love to you, and you laugh," he complained.

Through the still July night there came a sound from the candlelit mansion across the dark garden. A Negro girl darted out from under a huge, pale-barked sycamore. "Someone's comin', Missy! If yer pa catches you out here wit' a fella—" But Betsy interrupted her young maid, "Hush, you'll give us away! I told you, stand guard."

"Oh, if we git caught, my boss man'll have me whipped fer not tellin' him, and as fer you—" Magnolia glared up at the sailor astride the wall "—you'll git fired."

"Yes, Mr. Skipper," Betsy said, "you wouldn't be the captain of the *Sea Witch,* or in Papa's employ for long, after he caught you making love to his daughter in the moonlight."

"Bah! It's worth the risk," cried the pigtailed sailor recklessly. "Do you love me, pretty Betsy?"

Another sound came from the house. "Honey, come down!" Magnolia pleaded, as Henri whispered, "Tomorrow night? Same time?"

He jumped nimbly down to the street; and on the garden side of the wall, Betsy dropped into Magnolia's brown arms. As the girls started back toward the house, along a path bordered with boxwood, the moon rose, mellow and round, over the trees. Betsy dropped onto a bench, "It's too nice a night to go in," she sighed.

"Honey, Massa William be wonderin' where you be—" Magnolia looked apprehensively at the house, where, through a lighted window, the family of William Patterson of Baltimore, Maryland, could be seen in the parlor. Mrs. Patterson was embroidering. Her white-wigged husband sat, quill in hand, scowling at the ledger before him. William, twenty-three, stood behind him. Then Betsy saw Robert and John, twenty-two and twenty, come to join William. The three brothers, all in the family shipping firm, stood looking down at what their father had written.

The eleven Patterson children were present, or accounted for, all but Betsy. Seventeen-year-old Joseph passed the window; and she knew that, at a table, Edward fourteen, Peggy ten and George seven were doing their lessons for the next day. Upstairs in the nursery, Mammy Belle was putting

Caroline five and Henry three to bed. One-year-old Octavius had been placed in his cradle hours ago.

Out in the garden, Magnolia was pleading, "Honey, don't fool 'round with dat no-count sailor no more!" The little maid had been Betsy's Christmas gift from her parents ten winters ago; now the eighteen-year-old girls were like sisters. Magnolia was allowed to speak freely. "What you doin' it fer? You ain't goin' to marry him—"

"Don't be so sure, Magnolia. Henri's going to own his own fleet of ships some day, like Papa, he says. Papa was poor like Henri once, when he came from Ireland, a boy of fourteen. Now look at him, the second richest man in Maryland."

Elope with Henri—because Papa would never consent to her marrying one of his skippers—why not, Betsy asked herself. Henri's family lived in squalor down by the docks, but he was good-looking and part French. Frenchmen fascinated her. Married to Henri, she would sail the seven seas and see France, about which Madame Lacombe talked so much.

"Run 'way wit' dat sailor man?" Magnolia looked puzzled. "But, honey, you don't lub him?"

"Well, there's magic for that! Come on, Magnolia, let's go see Mammy July. She'll give me a love potion that will make me lose my heart to the first man I meet."

Betsy didn't believe such nonsense; but, bored, she was wild for any excitement. Magnolia's eyes rolled with delight under her red bandanna. She knew she shouldn't lead Miss Betsy into mischief. Mr. Patterson was strict with his pretty daughter. His orders were: Betsy must never go out unless chaperoned by her parents or one of her brothers; she must always wear a hat. But the moon was making Magnolia even more giddy and reckless than usual, for this was her chance to get a charm to keep High Flier faithful. She caught Betsy's hand. "Come on, honey!" Magnolia cried.

On South Street, a grilled iron gate had been set into the brickwork. Mr. Patterson locked it at nightfall. But it was only a matter of minutes for the agile girls to scramble over the wall and drop to the street below.

The moon was hidden by gathering storm clouds, as they hurried toward the waterfront. At the foot of Gay Street, the Patterson warehouses stretched impressively along the docks, a thicket of masts rising behind them. Even at night, this section of Baltimore was busy. Hogsheads of tobacco waited to be shipped abroad; while, to the chant of Negro voices, molasses and sugar from the West Indies were being loaded into covered Conestoga wagons, to roll off, whips cracking over six-horse teams, headed for inland towns.

Across the street from the wharves were dives and taverns, frequented by sailors of every race. In the doorway of a ramshackle hut squatted Mammy July. She was tiny, wrinkled as a dried prune and bald, but she managed to look like an African queen by wearing four men's hats, telescoped together and tied on with a red necktie.

Magnolia reminded the turbanned witch of the promised love charm. A ragged child was sent into the evil-smelling shack to fetch the bone of a bull frog. The toothless hag handed this to Magnolia with a torrent of jumbled words.

"She say," the girl translated, "when I git a chance, I must step up to High Flier and scratch him somewhere on de bare skin with dis bone. Den dat good-fer-nothin' is certain to lub me. He won't run 'round wit' dat no-count Susie no more."

The Negro woman held out her gnarled claw. "She wants money," Magnolia sighed. Betsy hadn't thought of needing money. After a moment's hesitation, she took off a small locket and handed it to the aged crone. "Give me a fetish, too, to make me love someone," she said.

Mammy July took from her rags a tiny bag filled with the bones of a black cat. As Betsy, with a shudder, hung the dirty thing about her neck, the old woman went into a fit of jerks, mumbling at her and pointing a long, bony finger.

"Old One say, you don't need no magic to make you lub de man you is to marry," Magnolia explained. "Give de bones back to her, honey. Dey is powerful medicine, might make you sick. Instead, Mammy'll tell yer fortune. But first she wants money—"

Betsy didn't believe in fortunetellers, but curious to hear what the old woman had to say, she handed over her cameo pin. It was hard to understand what Mammy July said above the wheeze of an accordian in a sailor's dive next door, but Betsy caught something about "a trip across de water . . . you be fine lady . . ."

"But first she sees fer you a grand marriage," Magnolia interrupted. "Not to no Baltimore boy, but with folks known de world over. She say youse is to be related to an emperor, because—Mercy me—" the Negro girl gasped incredulously. "She say, you is to marry a *king!*"

The world whirled about Betsy. "I'm to marry a king. Then I'll be a *queen?* Oh, I don't believe it!"

The fortuneteller held out her hand, palm up. "She wants money," Magnolia sighed.

Telling herself sternly that there was no truth to this nonsense, yet eager to hear more, Betsy ripped the bracelet from her wrist. "I'm to be queen of what country?" she demanded. But clutching her loot, the aged Negro settled back among her rags and closed her eyes. Her turban of hats toppled forward, her chin sank on her chest, she snored. In the doorway of the dark, odoriferous hut behind her loomed the figure of a huge man, who glared at the girls menacingly.

There was a roll of thunder. It began to rain. "Honey, let's go," begged Magnolia nervously.

In the big Georgian house of red brick with white trim, number 20, on the east side of South Street, near Water Street, the clock on the parlor mantel struck nine. William Patterson closed his ledger; he pushed his spectacles up onto his wig. "Bedtime," he announced. The family hastened to obey. Mrs. Patterson put down her embroidery. William, Robert and John carried their father's account books to a highboy and stored them away. Joseph, Edward, Peggy and George, picking up their candles, went obediently off to bed.

"Where's Betsy?" Papa demanded.

"In bed, I think, Mr. Patterson," his wife, Dorcas, candle in hand, replied from the stairs. "She spoke at supper of having a headache."

At the thought of each member of his household safely tucked away for the night, a pleased smile lighted William's stern face, for he kept a watchful eye on his family. Especially, he insisted that the children go to bed early, by nine o'clock.

Taking his candle, Mr. Patterson set about his nightly ritual of seeing that all fires and lights were out before he went to bed. In the kitchen, where in a wide brick fireplace, hung with long-handled toasting forks and iron pots, a big wood blaze had burned all day, he poked among the ashes to make sure that Mammy Lu had put out any hot coals before she went off to the Negro quarters in the garden. Then he locked the back door and put the key in his pocket.

He returned through the dining room, where portraits in heavy gold frames looked down at him from the walls.

They were not of William's parents. His father, a small farmer of Fanat, Donegal County, in northern Ireland, had been too burdened with poverty and a large family to sit to a limner for his likeness. The distinguished gentleman over the sideboard was Dorcas' father, Samuel Spear, who had come to Baltimore from Lancaster, Pennsylvania.

William Patterson mounted the stairs, a sturdy man in a brown velvet coat and knee breeches. He didn't stop on the second floor, where Dorcas waited for him in a huge canopied four-poster, but climbed to the Captain's Walk, to which he came each night to take a look through a telescope for his ships, the world-wide fleet of clippers that were Patterson's pride and joy.

It was raining when William stepped out onto the Captain's Walk, but from the roof of his house, he could look down on all of Baltimore. In 1803, it was but a small town. He saw his warehouses and the Bank of Maryland, of which he was the first president. Pretty good for a boy with little education, whose parents had sent him to America when he was but fourteen, William thought. He had arrived at Philadelphia in 1766, and had become the clerk of Samuel Jackson, an Irish shipping merchant; but by the time he was twenty-one, Patterson was in business for himself, with a good West Indian trade.

William remembered how, during the Revolution, he had daringly put every shilling he had into two ships and, sailing on one of them himself, went to France to fetch the arms and gunpowder the Colonies needed. The ammunition he sent to America arrived barely in time, George Washington told him; the Patriot army at Boston had hardly powder enough left to fire a salute.

On the way back from France, William had one of his boats drop him off at the Caribbean Island of St. Eustatius.

He returned to America in 1778, after two years of trading at St. Eustatius and Martinique in the West Indies, the owner of several ships and with $100,000, a fortune for those days. Half of his wealth Patterson put into the shipping business. The rest he invested in real estate, for he had decided to live in Baltimore and marry Dorcas Spear, the daughter of a local merchant. His fortune grew with the town, until within a few years the boy who had come to America penniless was the wealthiest man in Maryland—perhaps in the United States—except for Charles Carroll of Carrollton.

William Patterson also became a friend of Lafayette's, when, in 1781, the British began pillaging in Chesapeake Bay, and General Lafayette was sent to defend Maryland.

The people of Baltimore gave a ball for the French general, but, even in the midst of the gaiety, the Marquis looked depressed. "General Lafayette, why are you sad?" Dorcas Patterson asked.

"Madam, how can I help being sad, with my soldiers in rags?"

"They shall have new uniforms, General!"

The next day Dorcas and her friends turned the Assembly ballroom into a sewing room. The ladies cut out shirts and trousers, and stitched busily, until Lafayette's troops were properly clad. Mr. Patterson gave the Marquis $450 for blankets and shoes for his men. Lafayette never forgot all William Patterson did to help finance the Revolution and the struggling early days of the young Republic. He still wrote to him from France.

Now, training his telescope upon Federal Hill, William saw that signal lights were run up, denoting the approach down the bay of some graceful, sailing ship. Perhaps it was his own *Pride of Baltimore,* due from Havre, bringing him a letter from Lafayette.

He would have liked to see the ship sail up the bay, but a drenching deluge descended suddenly on his head. Afraid he would ruin his white wig, if he got it wet, Mr. Patterson went below. He left the roof only a few minutes before two ghost-like forms climbed over the garden wall and ran to the back of the house. Fortunately, William, on his way downstairs, did not see them.

On the second floor, he passed the doors behind which his children lay sleeping. Mr. Patterson thought of his eldest daughter, who had gone to bed with a headache. Betsy, with her high spirits and sweet smile, was his favorite child, although she was the most disobedient of his children. He found her hard to manage, for Betsy was determined and stubborn—like him in so many ways.

William Patterson had always wanted a daughter. When, after three boys, a girl was born to Dorcas, he had lost his heart to the pretty, lively child and loved her as much as it was in his stern nature to love anybody. Now he said to himself, "I'll sleep better if I see how Betsy is—"

Softly, William opened the door of her room. The light of his candle fell upon a bed on which no one had slept.

Meanwhile, the two girls were frantically trying to get in the back door. They were locked out. "Now we's goin' to catch it!" Magnolia began to cry. Betsy trembled with fright. What were they going to do? The terrified girls jumped as a dark form loomed out of the shadows. Chill fear gripped them before they recognized the kindly face of the Patterson gardener, Uncle Remus, Magnolia's grandfather.

Sympathetic eyes had been watching. Everyone in the quarters, from Mammy Lu, queen of the kitchen, to her youngest grandchild, loved Miss Betsy. From his pocket Uncle Remus took a homemade pass key, that Mr. Patterson would be very much surprised to know existed, and un-locked the door.

"Now don't do this agin', Little Miss; and you, Cream Puff—" he cuffed Magnolia lightly "—git to bed out in de quarters befor' yer Grandpappy takes de hide off you!"

"Oh, thank you, Uncle Remus—" With a sigh of relief, Betsy slipped into the house and heard the door locked be-hind her.

She hung up her wet cape to dry and shook the rain from her brown curls. As she tiptoed through the silent house, there was a blinding flash of lightning and a clap of thunder so loud that she stuck her fingers in her ears. Another roll of thunder muffled the sound of her footsteps, as she crept up the stairs. A second flash came, lighting up the upper hall. Betsy froze, for it revealed her father, standing, candle in hand, frowning down at her.

"I thought you were in bed. Where have you been?" he demanded, as Betsy reached the top of the stairs.

"Out in the garden with Magnolia."

"What were you doing?"

"Looking at the moon, Papa."

Such a frivolous reason for going outdoors at night, when he wished his children safe in the house under his stern eye, so upset Mr. Patterson that he failed to wonder how the two girls had managed to get back into a house he had care-fully locked.

"Well, never go out after dark again, without my permis-sion. Do you understand, Betsy? You know I insist that all the family be in bed by nine-thirty. And where is your hat? You know that I forbid you to leave the house without a bonnet. Now hasten to your room, and tomorrow you'll remain indoors all day. Looking at the moon, eh? I'll cure you of such romantic notions."

Was she never to have any fun? Betsy flounced off to her room, her heart in hot revolt against her father. She kicked off her wet shoes and quickly undressed, but she had hardly hopped into bed, when the door opened. It was Mama, carrying a cup and a piece of flannel dipped in turpentine and warm melted lard.

"Betsy, Papa says you were out in the garden. It's raining; you must be wet. Did you rub your feet dry, dear, so you won't catch cold?" Dorcas, sitting down on the bed, held out a cup of hyssop tea. "First, drink this. It's bitter, but the bitterer the medicine, the swifter the cure."

Betsy gulped down the vile-tasting brew. Then she submitted gratefully while her mother wrapped the flannel strip about her neck. "It will burn, but it should keep you from getting a sore throat," Dorcas said, kissing her daughter. "Now go to sleep, my precious."

But Betsy couldn't sleep. As her anger against her father subsided, she lay staring into the darkness, reliving every moment of her exciting evening. "I'm to marry a king and be a queen!" she whispered incredulously. Of course, she didn't *really* believe such nonsense, that Mammy July or anyone else could peer into the future. Betsy was too intelligent. Still, the old seeress' prophecies were certainly exciting. Wouldn't they impress the girls at Madame Lacombe's, when Betsy told them. What would her best friends at school, Henriette Pascault, Maria Burns and the Caton sisters, say to that—a *queen!*

2. *Exit the Pigtailed Sailor*

MONDAY WAS MISS MAY'S DAY at the Pattersons'. A birdlike little woman in a shabby bonnet and shawl, she hurried up the white marble steps that led into the big brick house, built in true Baltimore fashion, flush with the street. Her eyes sparkled behind her spectacles, for she was bubbling over with news.

Miss May was the town gossip. Many families who had no sewing to be done had the seamstress come to their house anyway, just to hear the latest scandal. This morning Miss May knew she would cause a sensation; and in her excitement, she pounded the brass sea-horse knocker loudly. The door under the fanlight opened. An old Negro in livery stood smiling at her.

"Good morning, Moses."

"Mornin', Miss May."

The dressmaker entered the wide hall, her eyes darting about, trying to take in everything. Miss May loved elegant homes, and at night, in her shabby room down by the docks,

12

she dreamed of the mansions of the rich in which she spent her days—the William Pattersons on Monday, the Samuel Smiths on Tuesday, the John Eager Howards on Wednesday, the Samuel Chases on Thursday, the Robert Gilmors on Friday, and on Saturday, the Richard Catons.

"Miss Dorcas's waitin'," Moses reminded her from the stairs, for the seamstress had stopped to feast her eyes on a carved teakwood screen. "Brought from China in the Patterson's *Bonny Flora,* no doubt," Miss May said to herself, thrilled, as she mounted the curving staircase.

The butler led the way into a room where two ladies sat sewing. Dorcas Patterson, a woman of forty-two, frail and pretty in mauve taffeta, had just cautioned her younger sister, "Be careful what you say in front of Miss May, Nancy. You might as well put it in the *Maryland Gazette.*" Now Dorcas looked up from the lace she was mending to greet the dressmaker. Then she called to her daughter in the next room, "Betsy!"

The seamstress caught her breath in admiration as the girl hastened into the room. She was slim and petite; her brown hair, a mass of short curls, like the head on a Greek sculpture. She was a little beauty. But there was a tragic expression in her large hazel eyes.

"Mama, must I have this old rag made over a third time? Can't I pass it on to Peggy and have something new?"

"No, dear, Papa said—"

"All the other girls at the Assembly will have new dresses."

Her white muslin dress, with a blue sash up under Betsy's arms, a modest neckline and long bishop sleeves, was certainly old; Miss May had made it four years ago. Too bad that Mr. Patterson, who was so rich and loved his family dearly, loved his money even more, the dressmaker thought. Feeling sorry for Betsy, she patted her shoulder comfortingly.

"You'll be the belle of the Assembly ball in whatever you wear, honey. Beside any other girl in Baltimore, you're a queen."

At the word "queen" Betsy opened her mouth to speak, then shut it tightly. Tall, angular Miss Spear's knitting needles clicked faster, a sign she was annoyed. "Tut, tut, Miss May! Don't flatter Betsy so, you'll make the child more conceited than she is."

Rebuked, the dressmaker took up her scissors and began to snip the faded trimming from Betsy's gown. Had the time come to speak about the exciting visitors? Anxious to relish a little longer the moment when she would be the focus of all eyes, Miss May decided to wait. But, unable to be silent long, her tongue rattled on.

"I'm making Henriette Pascault's wedding dress; when am I going to make yours, Betsy? Who's the lucky man to be? John Yardley? But then half the young men in Baltimore are in love with you."

The girl before the mirror lifted her nose disdainfully. "I wouldn't have one of them. They bore me to death."

What a sensation she would cause, Betsy thought, if she told them a grander fate was in store for her then a hum-drum marriage with some local boy. That she was to marry a king! But she wasn't going to say anything so foolish. Even jokingly. Miss May would tell it all over Baltimore. People would laugh at her. Instead, Betsy said airily, "I'd like to marry a titled Frenchman like Henriette's father, the Marquis de Poléon."

Mrs. Patterson and Sister Nancy exchanged glances. "Always admiring the French," Dorcas sighed. "Mr. Patterson and I made a mistake sending Betsy to Madame Lacombe's. She fell so in love with *la belle France,* she has not been the same girl since."

"Oh, Mama—" Betsy protested, for Madame Lacombe, a sad-eyed Frenchwoman, dressed always in black, a silver cross suspended from a chain about her neck, had opened up a new world to her.

Her brothers had tutors; but Betsy, at first, was educated at home by her mother, who had taught her little. She was gay and wild and quite unmanageable, until her parents sent her to Madame Lacombe, a refugee from the Saint-Domingue horrors, who had opened a School for Young Ladies in Baltimore. Betsy was to be taught exquisite manners and turned into a proper little lady. She scorned the usual female accomplishments, such as playing the harpsichord, singing, drawing and needlework, however, but took readily to mathematics, learned to dance gracefully and was soon chattering in French like a native.

Delighted, Madame Lacombe opened her lonely heart to the exquisite child, who sat spellbound, listening for hours to stories of her beloved Paris. She taught her eager pupil to love everything French.

Betsy admired her teacher extravagantly. She imitated Madame's French accent, copied her walk, her gestures, her manners. Especially, she believed as gospel truth everything Madame Lacombe said about France being the only civilized country in the world. So when Nancy Spear exclaimed in a shocked voice, "Surely, Betsy, you wouldn't marry a Frenchman!" her niece retorted, "Wouldn't I? They're the only men who can talk of art and literature"—a remark Betsy had heard Madame make.

The conversation was taking just the turn that Miss May hoped it would. Biting off her thread, she said, "Betsy, if you're so stuck on foreigners, you'd better set your cap for one of the Frenchmen coming to visit the Barneys." Then the little dressmaker sat back to relish her triumph. It was even better than she had anticipated. Dorcas dropped her handful of lace; the clatter of Nancy's needles stopped; Betsy's eyes grew big and round.

"What Frenchmen?" Mrs. Patterson asked.

"Well, there's Lieutenant Reubell, the French officer Henriette Pascault is going to marry, who's his aide . . . Le Camus, the secretary . . . and Dr. Garnier, he's the doctor . . . oh, and a valet . . ."

"Whose aide? Whose secretary? Whose doctor? Whose valet?" Questions were hurled at Miss May from all sides.

"They're part of his suite. Whose? Why, didn't I tell you? Jerome Bonaparte's, the brother of the First Consul."

Betsy could hardly believe it. "Miss May, you don't mean to say that a brother of the great Napoleon is actually coming to Baltimore?"

Yes, the dressmaker assured her, she had heard the exciting news the Saturday before, at the Catons. Jerome Bonaparte was coming to stay at the Barneys' over the August and September races. It seemed that Joshua Barney had met Napoleon's brother when the American had served as commander in the French navy.

"Mrs. Caton is highly elated over Bonaparte's visit," the dressmaker confided. "She wed an Englishman, you know. I fancy she'd like to see her daughters, Mary, Louisa, Elizabeth and Emily, each capture a titled foreigner."

Betsy listened eagerly. . . . When she decided that Miss May had imparted all the gossip she knew, she glanced at the clock. "I must go to market," she announced. Since Mrs. Patterson was occupied with a new baby each year, it was her eldest daughter who ran the house and managed the large staff of Negro servants. Betsy disliked her housekeeping tasks. But she loved to go to market, if only to escape from the house.

This morning, however, Betsy wasn't going to the Marsh Market, five blocks away, where she usually did her shopping. When Miss Patterson and the family butler left the house, with Moses carrying a large basket, Betsy surprised the old Negro by announcing that they were going clear across Baltimore to the new Center Market. Her household errands done, she intended to get rid of Moses, go call upon Henriette Pascault, who lived in that section of town, and hear more about the French visitors.

Amid indignant protests from Moses, who wailed that his feet hurt him too much to walk so far, they set out.

Her face hidden from bold, admiring male eyes by a big scoop bonnet (the reason that William Patterson forbade his pretty daughter to go hatless), Betsy tripped along the cobbled streets, breathing deeply of the salt air from the bay that always reminded the people of Baltimore they lived on the seacoast. All the shops had signs hung before them, swinging over the heads of the passers-by—big keys, boots, bells and anchors. She had stopped before a store, where, beyond small, square panes, the latest goods from England were displayed, when she heard, "Betsy!"

It was Henri. Catching sight of his love through a tavern window, the pigtailed sailor had dropped his mug of ale and come bounding after her. "Sweetheart, tonight—" He caught her hand.

Betsy drew back. She saw Henri needed a shave. "What do you mean, tonight?" she asked coldly.

The seaman looked hurt. "We're to meet in the garden tonight. Had you forgotten?" Yes, all about him. "You mustn't come again," Betsy said hurriedly. "Papa suspects."

"But I'm sailing for Havre on Saturday. It'll be a dangerous trip, with France and England at war. We're not carrying arms, but neutrals are forbidden to trade with French ports. British cruisers are stopping and searching American merchantmen on the flimsiest excuses and impressing our crews. Betsy, meet me in the garden before I go. I may be dumped into the hold of a prison ship to rot and never come back."

In 1803, only twenty years after the signing of the peace with Britain that ended the Revolution, the troubles that brought on the War of 1812 were already brewing. Betsy knew the dangers Henri faced. She felt sorry for him, but shook her head nevertheless.

"You're different this morning." Henri looked at Betsy sadly. She *was* different. Mammy July's prophecy, silly as it was, had changed her outlook on life. With her head full of the exciting possibility of meeting the brother of Napoleon, Betsy had no time for this thickheaded yokel. How could she ever have dreamed of eloping with him?

"I must go to market," Betsy said primly.

"Not 'til you kiss me good-bye—"

Henri pulled her roughly toward him, his lips brushed hers. Angrily, Betsy pushed him away. Straightening her bonnet, she spoke sharply, "Come, Moses," and, followed by the grinning Negro, Miss Patterson flounced off down the street.

In those days before telephones and store deliveries, housewives went daily to market, to select their own food. Betsy moved from stall to stall at the Center Market, choosing the freshest vegetables and fruit, picking out the plumpest chickens, watching the cutting of her beef with a critical eye. Moses followed with his basket, to carry home her purchases.

Betsy had stopped at the cheese stall and was paying the rosy-cheeked woman who peered out from behind the mounds of cheese for a slice of Swiss, when she saw, coming

from the flower stall, the person she most wished to see—Mrs.
Joshua Barney.

There were none of her father's cronies, with whom he
drank a glass of ale and exchanged the news at the Fountain
Inn, that Betsy liked better than Joshua Barney. She loved
to hear the gay Irishman tell how, during the Revolution,
he had served as the youngest officer in the infant American
navy, at first consisting of but eight old converted merchant
ships. A sloop, the *Hornet,* was placed under his command.
To raise a crew, Barney stood on a Baltimore street corner
with fife and drums and unfurled the first Continental flag
seen in Maryland.

Betsy's younger brothers, Joseph and Edward, could never
hear enough of Barney's adventures. "John Paul Jones claims
he was the first to fly the American flag," Joshua had told
them. "But I hoisted the first flag of the American union
a month before, right here in Baltimore. And I saw it saluted
for the first time by a foreign power, the Dutch, at St.
Eustatius, in the West Indies."

For the parade that took place when the Constitution was
adopted, Barney had built a three-masted ship, fifteen feet
long. This was mounted on wheels and drawn through the
streets of Baltimore by four horses. Aboard were Barney
and his crew, who pretended to hoist the sails, to the delight
of the crowd. The celebration over, the Commodore sailed
his miniature ship down Chesapeake Bay and up the Potomac
to Mt. Vernon, where he presented it to George Washington.

This had been a proud moment for Joshua Barney. But
Betsy liked best to hear him tell how he kissed Marie Antoinette. The end of the Revolution had found the gallant
captain engaged in secret trans-Atlantic missions for the
American government. Benjamin Franklin took him out
to Versailles, where the gay young queen was so charmed

with the breezy seaman that, instead of her hand, Marie Antoinette offered him her cheek to be kissed.

"Then all her ladies in waiting must be similarly saluted." Barney laughed his jolly laugh. "But don't tell Anne!"

Now it was his wife, Anne, who came over to the cheese stall to greet Betsy. "Have you heard about our distinguished visitor?" she asked. "Lieutenant Bonaparte's coming to Baltimore for the fall races; and I'm afraid that entertaining Napoleon's brother in our little house for two months is going to be quite a problem. His secretary, Monsieur Le Camus, wrote that Bonaparte is bringing with him two aides, a doctor, a valet, six servants and a monkey!" Anne Barney shuddered.

A monkey! Betsy was impressed. She couldn't imagine any of her Baltimore beaux—for instance, proper John Yardley—with such an exotic pet.

A half hour later, Moses was induced to go home with the groceries and Betsy slipped away to visit her best friend, Henriette Pascault. Henriette lived nearby, in a house guarded by impressive wrought-iron gates imported from France. Baltimore had a large French population—Arcadians, exiled from Nova Scotia before the French and Indian War; aristocrats, who had come from France to escape the Terror; and Saint-Domingue refugees, who had fled to Baltimore, driven by the uprising on the Caribbean island which followed close upon that in France.

Before the French Revolution, Saint-Domingue, as Haiti was then called, was France's richest colony. Its plantations at Cap Français supplied Europe with most of its sugar and coffee, raised by slave labor, until the news of the fall of the Bastille reached the Negroes. The National Assembly of France had proclaimed equality between whites and blacks, and the refusal of the French planters in Saint-Domingue to

WILLIAM PATTERSON
by Thomas Sully

COMMODORE JOSHUA BARNEY
by Rembrandt Peale

MRS. WILLIAM PATTERSON WITH HER
DAUGHTER, ELIZABETH

ELIZABETH PATTERSON AND JEROME NAPOLEON
WITH THEIR SIGNATURES

CHARLES CARROLL OF CARROLLTON

GENERAL SAMUEL SMITH

by Rembrandt Peale

ELIZABETH PATTERSON BONAPARTE

by Georges D'Almaine (after Stuart)

NAPOLEON BONAPARTE AND HIS BROTHERS
(center) Napoleon, *(upper left)* Joseph, *(upper right)* Lucien
(lower left) Louis, *(lower right)* Jerome

VIEW OF BALTIMORE, MARYLAND, IN 1801
by G. Beck

COLDSTREAM IN 1919, ITS GLORY GONE

MME. JEROME BONAPARTE

Painted by Firmin Massot in Geneva, Switzerland, in 1823

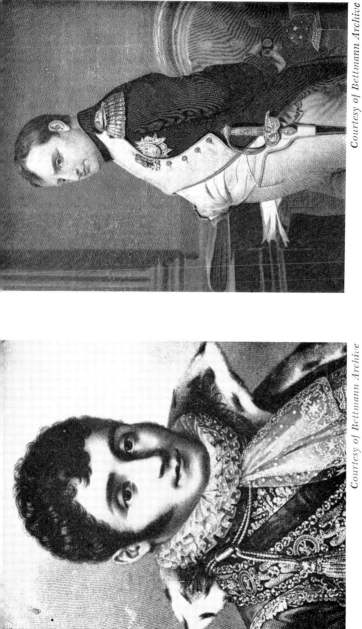

NAPOLEON I
by Paul Delaroche

JEROME BONAPARTE
by Mme. Kinson

CATHERINE OF WURTEMBERG

Louis Joseph Elisa Josephine Napoleon Mme. Mère Jerome Catherine Pauline Caroline Murat

MARRIAGE OF JEROME BONAPARTE AND PRINCESS CATHERINE OF WURTEMBERG

by Regnault (British Museum)

MME. JEROME BONAPARTE
by Kinson

JEROME BONAPARTE
by A. J. Gros

LETIZIA RAMOLINO BONAPARTE (MADAME MÈRE)
after Gérard

PAULINE BONAPARTE, PRINCESS BORGHESE
by Lefèvre

MRS. ROBERT PATTERSON (MARY CATON)
by Sir Thomas Lawrence

PRINCESSES CHARLOTTE AND ZENAIDE,
JOSEPH BONAPARTE'S DAUGHTERS
by Jacques Louis David

JEROME BONAPARTE
by Mme. Kinson

JEROME NAPOLEON BONAPARTE II, SON OF THE
KING OF WESTPHALIA

MRS. JEROME NAPOLEON BONAPARTE II (SUSAN MAY WILLIAMS)
by Georges D'Almaine

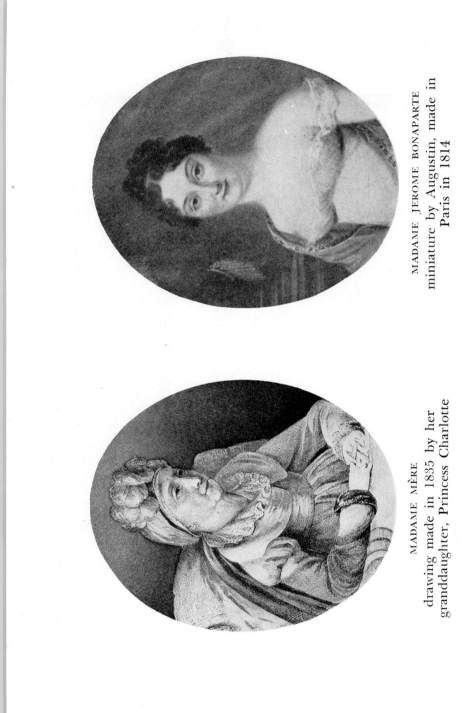

MADAME JEROME BONAPARTE
miniature by Augustin, made in
Paris in 1814

MADAME MÈRE
drawing made in 1835 by her
granddaughter, Princess Charlotte

Photographed by The Hughes Company

BETSY BONAPARTE'S GRAVE IN GREENMOUNT CEMETERY,
BALTIMORE, MARYLAND

Courtesy of Maryland Historical Society
and Frick Art Reference Library

JEROME NAPOLEON BONAPARTE III

Courtesy of Enoch Pratt Free Library

CHARLES J. BONAPARTE
by Thomas C. Corner

JEROME BONAPARTE AT SEVENTY

HIS SON, PRINCE NAPOLEON

Courtesy of Bettmann Archive

From "The Bonapartes in America" by
C. E. MacCartney and Gordon Dorrance, Dorrance & Company, publishers

JEROME NAPOLEON BONAPARTE IV,

Courtesy of Maryland Historical Society

GEORGE PATTERSON (BETSY'S BROTHER)

recognize the decree led to a terrible revolt of the slaves. Waves of them poured down from the hills, burning planta-tions at Cap Français and murdering white people.

The French fled in terror to the ships in the harbor, their only refuge. Thirteen boatloads of white planters with their families arrived in Baltimore during July, 1793. The exiles struggled to make a living. They became hairdressers and milliners; they taught dancing, music and French; they opened schools, like Madame Lacombe.

Henriette's father, Louis Pascault, the Marquis de Poléon, had barely escaped with his family from Saint-Domingue during the massacre. Two of his children and their nurse had been killed. But, financially, he was better off than most of the refugees. The sale of his family jewels alone enabled him to live comfortably without working.

The Pascaults were people of culture and artistic tastes. At noon, when William Patterson and his sons, like all Amer-ican merchants, were in their counting-houses at work, Betsy found the Marquis playing a flute, while his round little lady accompanied him on the harpsichord. The prints of the Tuileries gardens on the walls; the latest French books on the table; the strong black coffee that the Marquise served in thin china cups, while the Marquis, tapping an exquisite gold snuffbox, conversed about art and literature—here was the gracious living for which Betsy yearned. As much as Madame Lacombe, the Pascaults had taught her to admire everything French.

Yet, even in 1803, Maryland was far from being the "bar-barous country" poor, homesick Madame Lacombe called it. The interior of America was still crude. But the towns along the eastern seaboard, such as Philadelphia, Annapolis and Baltimore, amazed sophisticated travelers. Baltimore's streets were lined with charming brick houses. Its harbor was filled

with ships that brought to the shops the same goods as the
fashionable Bond Street stores showed. At the routs in the
Assembly Rooms, the wines were as choice, the stakes at
the card tables as high, and the ladies' fashions as extreme
as in London. Baltimore's coffee-houses served the best food
in the United States. It had for years supported a theater,
and the gentry from as far away as New York and Virginia
flocked to Maryland's spring and fall race meetings.

People called Baltimore the gayest town in America. Fed-
eralist in sympathy, it was a London in miniature. But Betsy
longed for culture, with a French accent.

She was gazing in rapture at the Marquis de Poléon—
courtly, charming and, my dear, a title besides!—when her
friend Henriette, a pretty girl dressed in blue, with a cap of
ribbon and lace on her blonde curls, rushed into the room
to kiss Betsy rapturously.

"At last, my sweetheart has arrived!" Henriette cried.
"Jean had no idea when he could get leave, until Jerome
Bonaparte decided to come to America. They're in Wash-
ington, but they are coming to Baltimore to stay with the
Barneys over the fall races, and Jean and I can be married."

Betsy listened enviously. The two girls went out to sit on
the porch steps, where Henriette had more to tell her friend.

"Betsy, what d'you think Jean writes? He says that Jerome
Bonaparte is coming to Baltimore, just to meet you. Down
in Saint-Domingue, Jean told him that you were the prettiest
girl in town. Napoleon ordered his brother home when war
broke out, but Jerome insisted on coming to America first.
Jean declares it's to see you! Jerome's so positive you're going
to fall in love with him, he already calls you *ma jolie épouse*."

Betsy tossed her head. "Lieutenant Bonaparte sounds
pretty sure of himself!"

"Oh, Jerome's terribly attractive. All the girls fall in love with him."

"Then, perhaps he's my fate, Henriette. Magnolia and I went to a fortuneteller last night, for some excitement. She said I was going to marry into a family known the world over. Doesn't that sound like the Bonapartes? And that I was to marry a king. Oh, Henriette, just think, I'll be a *queen!* Mammy July didn't exactly say so, but she said I was to marry a king, and a king's wife is a queen, isn't she? Of course, I don't believe a word of it. Mammy July's just a crazy old crone the Negroes all go to with their troubles. But some of the things she told me were pretty startling. They set me thinking—"

Henriette wasn't as impressed as Betsy had hoped she would be. "Well, if you want to be a queen, dear, don't throw yourself away on Jerome Bonaparte. He isn't a king, only a mere lieutenant. Napoleon has come up fast. He has made himself First Consul. But Papa says he's due for a fall. Likely by the next packet we'll hear there has been another revolution in France, and someone else has seized power. Without Napoleon, what'll Jerome be? Nothing."

Betsy was already sorry she'd told Henriette about the glorious future Mammy July had said was in store for her. Henriette would tell Maria Luther, who would tell the Catons, Mary Chase and Maria Burns. Her friends would have a good laugh at her expense. Betsy hoped they didn't think she believed such nonsense.

"Well, even if Lieutenant Bonaparte isn't a king, married to him, I'd get to Paris," Betsy hastened to say, for Napoleon's brother had taken the place of the pigtailed sailor in her hopes of some day seeing Madame Lacombe's beloved France. "Henriette, you'll meet Napoleon's brother before I do,"

Betsy added wistfully. "Oh dear, I wish just as something exciting is going to happen, I wasn't leaving town!"

The entire Patterson household was moving next day to Springfield, their largest Maryland plantation, twenty miles inland, to escape Baltimore's unhealthy August. But they would be back in September, for the races out on Whetstone Point. There, she and Lieutenant Bonaparte would meet, Betsy vowed to herself. He'd fall in love with her—

But wasn't she, as much as Bonaparte, taking a great deal for granted? Betsy's eyes clouded. Jerome Bonaparte had been in the navy. He had seen the world, while she had never been further from home than Annapolis—not even to Philadelphia or Washington. Papa didn't believe in travel. He seldom left Baltimore. What could she talk to a man like Napoleon's brother about? He would find her stupid and prefer Mary Caton. Oh, it was all so hopeless! He might hardly deign to notice her.

But men seldom failed to notice Betsy Patterson. She knew that. So perhaps—Then Betsy's hopes were dashed, as Henriette said, "Well, I wouldn't count on marrying Jerome Bonaparte, Betsy. Jerome was only joking of course, when he called you *ma jolie épouse*. Because he told Jean that he would never marry an American girl, he doesn't like them."

3. *A. W. O. L.*

J EROME WAS THE ONLY ONE of the eight Bonaparte children who never knew the poverty the family endured during their early days in Corsica. In 1796, when his youngest brother was twelve years old, Napoleon became world-famous by his victory over the Austrians in Italy. A true Corsican in his devotion to the clan, Napoleon thought first of how he could help his family. Jerome was sent at his expense to the Collège Irlandis, at Saint Germain, outside Paris, then to the Collège of Juilly.

On his return from Egypt, Napoleon overthrew the Directory, with the help of his brother Lucien, president of the Senate, and made himself dictator of France. Jerome left school. He went to live with the First Consul at the Tuileries, where Napoleon called his young brother with tolerant amusement *"petit polisson"* (little rascal). If Jerome saw anything in the shops he liked, he bought it; even a gold-fitted traveling case with razors, combs for mustaches and beards, and shaving-pots, which could be of no possible use to a youth so young he had only fuzz for a beard.

Napoleon scolded him, "So it's you, sir, who indulge in traveling cases costing 10,000 francs?" "Oh," replied Jerome, unconcerned, "I only care for beautiful things." Napoleon, amused, paid the bill. He was fifteen years older than Jerome. Their relationship was more like that of an indulgent father and son, than that between brothers.

A year later, a duel the hotheaded boy fought made Napoleon realize the baby of the family was growing up. Jerome, although only sixteen, was put into the navy. A squadron under Admiral Gantheaume was sailing to carry supplies to the French army in Egypt. The recruit reported at Brest, on board the *Indivisible,* with orders from Napoleon that Midshipman Jerome Bonaparte mustn't be shown any favoritism.

Admiral Gantheaume knew better. Napoleon's brother was given a seat at the Admiral's table; and on June 24, 1801, when the French fleet came upon the *Swiftsure,* and, after a brief fight, she struck her flag, it was pampered young Bonaparte who—to the astonishment and disgust of veteran officers —was given the honor of going on board the captured warship to receive the captain's sword. He returned to Paris, to be given a hero's welcome that would have turned the head of any youth, not already spoiled.

Jerome was indignant when Napoleon sent him to sea again, this time to the West Indies, with the fleet of Admiral Villaret-Joyeuse. It was going to Saint-Domingue, to try to restore French authority there. The Negro slaves, who had revolted in 1792, had since then been in control of the island.

In January, 1802, the squadron helped the French army capture Port-au-Prince, after which, Jerome went ashore at Cap Français, to visit his sister Pauline, whose husband, General Victor Leclerc, was in command of the land forces.

Gay, frivolous Pauline could sympathize with Jerome at

being banished from Paris. She had only come to the West Indies because Napoleon, shocked by Pauline's scandalous love affairs, insisted she accompany her husband. But, in Saint-Domingue, Pauline was behaving admirably. Yellow fever had broken out among the French troops. Faced with the danger of contagion, Pauline remembered she was Napoleon's sister, she must be worthy of him. She refused to return to France. Instead, she kept up the spirits of the frightened colonists by giving concerts and balls, at which the survivors of the military band played, while people danced and tried to forget, for a few hours, that they might soon be among the dead in the seemingly unending line of carts going to the cemetery.

It was enough to dampen even Jerome's high spirits. But the fun-loving young man managed to amuse himself.

"Enjoy yourself, you'll soon have to go back to France and behave," Pauline told him. "Napoleon is fond of us, but he thinks his family only live to help him climb in the world. Elisa and Joseph married before he was important enough to rule the clan. But look how Napoleon married Caroline to Murat, me to Leclerc and Louis to Hortense, his stepdaughter. Louis dislikes Hortense. And I still love Stanilas Fréron."

"I'll never let Napoleon choose a wife for me. Why should I?" retorted Jerome. "Did Napoleon marry to please his family, when he wed Josephine, whom we all hate? No, he married for love, as I shall do."

Pauline shrugged. "Try it, *mon cheri,* and see what happens to you. Your own happiness has nothing to do with it. Napoleon will marry you off to someone useful to him."

In instant revolt, Jerome thought, had Napoleon asked the consent of his mother or of Joseph, as the eldest brother, when he wed Josephine? He had not, so his marriage was

illegal by Corsican law. Signora Letizia Bonaparte could
have had it annulled by issuing a protest. But then, Napoleon gave himself liberties he did not allow the rest of
the family.

Jerome had had enough of Saint-Domingue, where any day
he might come down with yellow fever. He persuaded Admiral Villaret in March, 1802, to send him back to France
with dispatches. At Brest Jerome amused himself in ways
that made Napoleon anxious to send his seventeen-year-old
brother to sea as soon as possible.

Lieutenant Bonaparte was shipped off to the West Indies
again, second-in-command of the *Epervier,* under Captain
Halgan, who allowed him to do as he pleased. Not liking
the quiet naval uniform, Jerome brought along a hussar
uniform and strode about the deck of the warship in the
scarlet vest of a cavalry captain.

On reaching Martinique, Halgan was taken ill, so Bonaparte was put in command of the *Epervier.* Napoleon's
brother had risen rapidly from midshipman to lieutenant,
due to his name, along with a little lecture from Admiral
Villaret that Jerome should take his profession more se-
riously. It was known in navy circles, Villaret told him,
that Napoleon intended to make his youngest brother Admiral of the Fleet. Surely, Lieutenant Bonaparte wished to
be a credit to the navy.

In May, 1803, war broke out between France and England.
Napoleon ordered his brother home at once, before the
British navy made the Atlantic unsafe. Jerome refused to
return on the *Epervier.* He predicted the French ship would
be captured by the enemy. It was safer for him to wait, he
said, and take passage under a neutral flag.

So Lieutenant Bonaparte disobeyed orders: allowing the
Epervier to sail without him, he remained at Martinique,

visiting Mme. Tascher de la Pagerie, Josephine's mother. General Leclerc having died of yellow fever in Saint-Domingue, Pauline had returned to France and taken up her gay life in Paris once more.

With Jerome at Martinique were his aides, Ensign Meyronnet and Lieutenant Reubell; Garnier, a doctor from the *Epervier;* and Alexander Le Camus. The November before, on visiting the volcano, Bonaparte had been taken ill with sunstroke. He was nursed back to health in the home of a Martinique planter, whose son Alexander had become Jerome's secretary.

Jean-Jacques Reubell, son of Jean-François Reubell, one of the five Directors who ruled France until Napoleon seized power, often spoke to Lieutenant Bonaparte of Henriette Pascault, the American girl he was to marry. "She's lovely, but then so are all Baltimore girls. It's a town noted for its horses, food and pretty women. Jerome, if you saw Mademoiselle Patterson, you'd lose your heart!"

Bonaparte replied that he could never marry an American girl. No manners, veritable hoydens, he had heard.

"Oh, don't be so sure!" Lieutenant Reubell exclaimed. "You haven't met Betsy Patterson!"

After that, Jerome, half in jest, half in earnest, always spoke of Miss Patterson as *ma jolie épouse,* for the more he thought of the marriage plans Napoleon might have in mind for him, the more resentful he grew.

The spoiled child of the Bonaparte family had never taken kindly to discipline, naval or otherwise. Jerome decided to kick over the traces. He would return to France as his brother ordered, but by way of the United States, and see if this American girl was as lovely as they said. He would spend a few days in Baltimore. Napoleon would never know about it.

As Jerome predicted, the *Epervier* sailed and was promptly captured by the British, who were sadly disappointed to lose so rich a prize as Napoleon's brother. Meanwhile, Bonaparte, his suite and a monkey Jerome had bought in Martinique, reached Norfolk, Virginia, safely, on July 20, 1803, aboard a neutral American ship. Lieutenant Bonaparte had left the French fleet without asking permission. But as the brother of the ruler of France, he didn't consider himself under a mere admiral's orders.

From Norfolk, Jerome, with his entourage, went on to Washington. He sent Le Camus to inform Louis André Pichon, the French chargé d'affaires, of his arrival.

Pichon was surprised at the sudden appearance in Washington of the First Consul's brother. He had received no letter from Talleyrand, the French foreign minister, announcing his visit. Pichon went to see Bonaparte; he advised him to move to a more respectable hotel, and—at a cost of $10,000—chartered the *Clothier* to take Jerome and his party to Europe on the 3rd of August.

On the 24th of July, to Louis Pichon's consternation, Lieutenant Bonaparte, his suite and pet monkey, drove off in a stylish yellow curricle Jerome had purchased, not to Philadelphia for the return voyage to France, but to Baltimore. The bewildered chargé d'affaires, whose troubles were only beginning, was left with a bill for $10,000 to pay for the chartering of the *Clothier,* on which Bonaparte refused to sail, because he had received an invitation from Joshua Barney to be his guest for the August and September races. Jerome had known Barney in Paris when Joshua, disgusted with the treatment handed out to him in the American navy, served for several years as commodore under the French flag.

The two friends visited York, Lancaster and Philadelphia, and on the way back to Baltimore, took in the races at

Havre de Grace, on the Susquehanna. Jerome, gazing over
the crowded race course, asked, as he had several times before,
"Do I meet *ma jolie épouse* today?"

"No, the Pattersons are still at their Springfield plantation," Barney replied. "But they'll be back when cold
weather makes Baltimore safe from yellow fever. You'll see
Betsy in September, I promise."

When the day of the September meet out on Whetstone
Point came, all Baltimore seemed to be going to the races.
Bonaparte's yellow curricle was only one of a long procession
of cabriolets and landaus, more humble gigs, hacks and
farmer's carts overflowing with people, girls and boys on
horseback and on foot, that poured out of Baltimore on
the road that led to the track, which was located near Fort
McHenry, guarding the harbor.

A band in red coats played gaily, as they led the parade
of horses before the grandstand. Mr. Harrison's Hamlet was
the favorite to win. Jerome, his monkey Jocco perched on
his shoulder, raised his small telescope to inspect the horses.
Barney seized his arm. "There's Betsy!"

Jerome focused his spyglass on the girl. She rode side-
saddle, her tan riding habit, with its lace jabot, tight jacket
and long, divided draped skirt, outlined her slender figure.
A sweeping black ostrich feather trimmed her leghorn hat.

A shout from the crowd, the horses were off. Wee Admiral
was first, Knockdown next, Patriot third. The latter moved
to second place in the run down the stretch for the first
time, as Tidy Bid took over the lead, with Hampden fourth.
Hamlet was sixth, running in a slow lope, as though he
knew he could easily outdistance the field, so was in no
hurry now.

The stands were shouting themselves hoarse, but Jerome
kept his spyglass on the girl he had come from the West

Indies to meet. He saw that she resembled someone he knew. "Pauline!" he murmured, pleased. His sister was considered the most beautiful woman in Europe.

Betsy was only outwardly serene, as she sat her horse Lightning with easy grace. Her hands on the reins trembled. With Bonaparte's eyes on her, she told herself excitedly, "Every woman here is looking at him, and he's looking only at me, not even at the horses!" And Betsy had planned it that way. She knew she looked well on a horse, so she had refused to drive to the races with Mama and Aunt Nancy in a carriage spilling over with young Pattersons. She had ridden out on horseback instead, escorted by her three brothers.

William had dismounted to chat with a friend. Betsy turned to Robert. "We can't see well from here. Let's ride closer."

"Fine!" His gaze turned eagerly to where the Caton cabriolet was parked down the track, beside Bonaparte's yellow curricle. Betsy smiled. Poor Robert! He would always go where he might catch a glimpse of Mary Caton, eldest granddaughter of Charles Carroll of Carrollton. Robert had loved Mary since childhood.

John came, too. Betsy made a charming picture as she rode her sleek black mare, between Robert's Dancer and John's Happy Time, to within ten yards of where Jerome Bonaparte and Joshua Barney stood by the rail, the Frenchman in his hussar's blue coat and scarlet vest, the American in his blue Navy uniform with red lapels.

Betsy reined in her horse. So Bonaparte didn't like American girls? Better not go nearer. It wouldn't do to appear too eager. How presumptuous of him to call her *ma jolie épouse!* Her eyes fixed straight ahead, Betsy saw Tidy Bid was done in the back-stretch, Patriot had moved to the lead. Then the stand went wild with excitement, for Hamlet made up his mind to begin to run. He was ahead at the half-mile pole, and around the turn, widened out on the field. Patriot dropped back as Lord Boswell, having come from behind, took up the chase. At the furlong pole, the race was between Hamlet and Lord Boswell, running neck and neck.

Betsy, stealing a glance, saw perched on the Frenchman's shoulder an animal with a small, wistful face. A long tail was wrapped about his neck. "A monkey! Oh, I love pets!" A girl in the crowd moved closer to the flock of ladies surrounding the good-looking hussar in blue and scarlet. By Robert's jealous expression, Betsy knew that Mary Caton was under one of the bonnets.

"Come!" she ordered her brother, and they rode closer to where the Frenchman was standing. The crowd was screaming excitedly as Hamlet galloped across the finish line, the winner, but Jerome never saw that exciting climax. Within a few feet of him, Betsy pulled her mare up sharply. It was theatrical, but necessary, if she would lay siege to her quarry. She made Lightning rear and, front hoofs pawing the air, walk forward a few steps on her hind legs.

"Bravo, *ma jolie épouse!*" Jerome cried.

Betsy saw that he was exceedingly handsome, slim, dark and curly-haired. Then she realized she was staring at the Frenchman like a bold minx. Blushing furiously, with a wave of her crop at him, Betsy galloped away between Robert and John.

Jerome stood looking after Elizabeth Patterson, wishing with all his heart that he could make her his *épouse* in earnest.

Next morning, Betsy lay on her bed, absorbed in *The Dutchess' Lover*. There was a kiss or a murder on every page. She hardly glanced up as Peggy, sturdy and pink-cheeked, with two chestnut braids down her back, came into the room carrying Octavius. *The Dutchess' Lover* had been lent to Betsy by Maria Luther. Mary Chase was promised the thriller next.

Peggy stood at the window. "Blow, Sweetie," she said, holding a handkerchief to Octavius' nose.

Why, Peggy actually enjoys blowing noses and changing diapers, Betsy thought in disgust. She didn't yearn for romance and adventure in far-off places, as Betsy did. Her sister liked housekeeping chores; she asked for nothing better than to marry a local boy and raise a flock of children. Until ten-year-old Peggy had babies of her own, she liked to help Mammy Belle keep the younger children under some control. It was no easy task. There were so many small Pattersons, that Betsy had grown to consider all squalling, soggy babies as troublesome brats. She hoped she would never have any.

"See the pretty birdie?" Peggy asked Octavius, pointing out of the window. "Why, there's the Barney's gig, Betsy! I wonder why it's stopping here?"

"Jerome Bonaparte!"

With a cry of joy, Betsy sprang off the bed. After yesterday's splendid beginning, she knew he would come. Hiding *The Dutchess' Lover* under her pillow, Betsy dashed to a shelf where she kept Rochefoucauld's *Maxims* and Young's *Night Thoughts,* books Madame Lacombe had given her. Betsy liked to be seen reading them. Choosing the Frenchman's cynical proverbs as more suitable to the occasion than the Englishman's sad poetry, Miss Patterson tucked Rochefoucauld's *Maxims* under her arm as a conversation piece, to impress her caller, and hurried downstairs.

To her surprise, Betsy didn't find Lieutenant Bonaparte

below in the hall, only Moses with a letter the Barneys'
coachman had handed him to give to Mr. Patterson.

Betsy saw the flourishing handwriting on the envelope.
She wanted to seize it. But the old Negro butler, holding
the letter firmly, shuffled into the study, where Mr. Patterson
was going over bills with Captain Burns, who had brought
in his *Flying Cloud* that morning from Lisbon. Joseph, Edward and George had been to the waterfront, to see the crew
haul down the sails.

Captain Burns sat at Mr. Patterson's right at dinner. As
they ate, the family listened while the sea captain told what
a dangerous crossing he had had, dodging the British fleet.

"We were stopped and made to show our papers three
times. Each time, I thought we'd be towed off to an English
port, but I talked the blighter out of it—"

Betsy, seated between Caroline and Henry, thought how
her father's skippers all talked alike. They had always overcome pirates and storms, and now, in wartime, the British
fleet, and brought their ship safely home only by their remarkable skill and bravery. What was in that letter from
the Barneys? Had Papa read it? She believed he had, he
looked cross enough.

The hearty midday meal of fish, roast duck and rice pudding ended with fruit and nuts. Mr. Patterson rose, a signal
for his family to return to their tasks. Captain Burns, William, Robert and John went back to the warehouse. Joseph
and Edward trudged off to school. George, Henry and Caroline dashed out into the garden to play Blind Man's Bluff.
Mama, picking up her sewing, sat down by Betsy and Peggy
at their tapestry frames.

Papa usually went straight to his big leather account books.
His income was enormous, but his sharp eyes accounted for
every penny. Today, however, he said sternly, "Betsy, come

into my study, I want to talk to you." She entered the room
to find him seated at his desk. The letter lay before him.

"This is most unpleasant," he said. "That Frenchman at
the Barneys' has written to ask if he may call on you. Naturally, I've no intentions of allowing him to do so."

Fury flamed in her. "Why not, Papa?"

"Because he's just the type to turn your foolish head,
Miss. You're always mooning over foreigners. You haven't
the brains you were born with, Betsy. If you had any sense,
you'd fall in love with some fine American, like—"

"John Yardley?" Betsy made a face.

They were on a sore point. Even gentle Mama, who never
found fault with anybody, reproached Betsy for turning up
her nose at "nice John Yardley." Betsy thought him a dim-
witted fellow, who, she declared, talked of nothing but
horses and smelt of horses. In comparison with Jerome
Bonaparte's cock-of-the-walk manner, John seemed to her
to be more prosaic and dull than ever.

"I shall write this Frenchman a curt refusal," her father
announced. At which Betsy cried out, "Oh, Papa, please
don't! I want to meet him so much!" She knew at once
she had made a mistake. His face turned purple.

"So what I heard about your actions yesterday at the
races is true, Miss." His cold, gray eyes shot a sharp look
at his daughter's flushed, pleading face. "Then you'll certainly *not* see that Frenchman again! Go to your room and
pack for Springfield. You and your mother are going back
to the country tomorrow, to stay there until this foreigner
leaves town."

"Oh, Papa, listen—" In tears, Betsy ran to fling her arms
about his neck. "Darling, please—" She planted a kiss on
his severe countenance. "The Howards, the Martins, the
Gilmors, the Catons, are all giving parties for Lieutenant

Bonaparte. You wouldn't have me miss them, would you?"
But her father couldn't be wheedled. He flung off her clinging arms.

"No member of my family is going to be seen at a party
for Napoleon's brother! Napoleon's a blackguard, a disturber
of the peace of Europe! I shall also forbid William, Robert
and John to attend. Now do as I say, Betsy." He looked as
though, if she didn't, he would box her ears. "No more
crying now. Go wash your face and get ready to leave for
Springfield."

Betsy packed for the journey in paroxysms of tears and despair. Magnolia sobbed too, because she wasn't to be allowed
to go with Little Miss. Nor was a groom to ride Lightning
behind the Patterson barouche, although Betsy always took
her mare to Springfield. Papa feared Betsy might escape on
the horse. "The girl's capable of it," he muttered.

The rest of the family were asleep when, the next morning
at sunrise, Betsy drove off along the Frederick Pike with her
mother. Her eyes swam as the spires of Baltimore sank
below the hills. Each turn of the wheels took her further
away from the town from which she had often longed to escape
and see the world. Now, all she wanted was just to be back
there!

Betsy rode along wondering which one of her brothers
had told Papa about the ardent glances she exchanged with
Lieutenant Bonaparte at the races. Robert, in love himself,
would never inform on her. It must have been John. She
would never forgive that tattletale, never!

4. House Arrest

SPRINGFIELD, stretching for two thousand acres over the rolling countryside, was one of the finest plantations in Maryland. Back of the mansion with its columned portico was a kitchen, stables, the estate office and quarters for the help. It was a small town in itself. But what was there to do? Without Lightning to ride, Betsy, bored and unhappy, took to driving about with Jones, the overseer. She was seated in his chaise one afternoon, waiting outside a log cabin where slaves were weaving cloth, when a neighbor rode in through the gate.

"I've been to Baltimore," he said. "Here's a letter Mary Chase asked me to give you."

Betsy tore it open to read of the good times she was missing. The French colony had outdone itself in hospitality to Napoleon's brother. But Mary also wrote of balls and dinners being given for him at the Howards' Belvedere, the Carrolls' Doughoregan, the Catons' Brooklandwood, the Gilmors'

Beach Hill. Mary and her father, Judge Samuel Chase, were to give a dance in Bonaparte's honor. Betsy's girl friends missed her, Mary remembered to say.

Betsy smiled. "I'm sure they're brokenhearted!" Well, Mary Chase, Maria Luther and the Catons weren't going to rob her of Jerome Bonaparte as easily as that! She was twenty miles from Baltimore, with no horse to ride, but she would be at the Chase ball tomorrow night.

At daybreak, Betsy was dressed in a boy's shirt, breeches and boots. A blue cotton dress she kept for parties in the country, satin slippers, a fan and some sandwiches under her arm, she climbed out of the window and down a wisteria vine to the ground. She ran to the stable, only to find it locked. Standing, wondering what to do, Betsy caught sight of a work mule under a shed. Luckily, he had a saddle on him. A field hand had brought the animal in the night before and lazily walked away, leaving him saddled.

Her scarlet riding cape over her ballgown to protect it from the dust, Betsy had several times ridden with her brothers the twenty-five miles between Baltimore and Annapolis, to attend a dance. But twenty miles on a mule! She went over and patted the rough mane of the big ugly brute, then, before he could jump aside, Betsy was in the saddle. The mule kicked and tried to shake her off. Then he was galloping, bucking as he galloped, along the drive and out the gate.

His hard-footed gait was enough to shatter her spine, but she stuck on. Betsy talked to the mule and gradually quieted him. When he slowed down to a trot, she was able to slip her dress, shoes, fan and sandwiches into the saddle bag and get two hands on the reins.

The sun rose, and with it the girl's courage. Hour after

hour, she rode. She stopped at noon to let the mule graze, while she lunched. Then, at a kick of her heels, he broke into a canter again that ate up the miles.

As she neared Baltimore, the pike was crowded with Conestoga wagons loaded with grain. The teamsters thought Betsy to be a boy. "Hi, lad!" they shouted. She waved back. But both girl and mule were tiring. Betsy tried to cheer herself by singing. The mule seemed to like it, he jogged along faster.

In a wooded tract, on the outskirts of town, Betsy rolled off the mule's back and threw herself on the ground, exhausted. She slept until dark, bathed in a brook; then, refreshed, she dressed in her blue cotton gown and rode in triumph through Baltimore to the Chases.

Betsy tied the mule to a picket fence, and as she removed his saddle, she whispered in his ear, "Good old fellow! Lightning couldn't have brought me here any better!"

Silken-clad ladies and gentlemen were entering a house ablaze with candles, where, in the hall, Mary and her father, big, florid Judge Samuel Chase, member of the Supreme Court and a signer of the Declaration of Independence, stood receiving their guests. When Betsy walked in, she had to smile at Mary's crestfallen expression.

"Why, Betsy," Mary exclaimed, "I thought you were at Springfield!"

Betsy's back ached, she was stiff from her long ride; she had bathed in a brook and dressed in the bushes; but she looked as radiant as if she had napped all afternoon, and Magnolia had dressed her for the party. The blue cotton dress was simple, but becoming, and Betsy's beautiful hazel eyes were aglow at the thought of meeting *him* tonight.

She was quickly surrounded by young men. The minuet

was promised to Edward Fottrel, the quadrille to John
Yardley, the country dance to Timothy Paca, the reel to
George Wedgewood, the cotillion to John Comegys. Couples
formed for the minuet; hands touched hands, the violins
sang. But even as Betsy pointed her dainty foot, whirled
under Edward's lifted arm and sank to the floor before his
bow in a curtsy, her eyes sought the door. Where was
Bonaparte?

Along the wall sat a row of matrons, among them, Betsy's
Aunt Margaret, Dorcas Patterson's elder sister. Betsy was
aware of her aunt's shocked gaze. When the music stopped,
Mrs. Samuel Smith greeted her niece coldly. "Where are
your parents, Betsy? And your brothers? Surely, you're not
here without an escort!"

"I'll be her escort. My dear, may I have this dance?"

A blue-veined hand tucked Betsy's under a protective arm.
She was led out onto the polished floor, under the crystal
chandeliers, by no less a person than the Mr. Carroll, who,
by adding "of Carrollton" to his name—"so the British will
know which Carroll it is"—risked his neck and several million
dollars, when he signed the Declaration. Mr. Carroll was
not only rich, but venerated; he was Baltimore's First Citizen.
Mrs. Smith's pleased smile followed her niece. John Yardley,
who had been promised the quadrille, stood respectfully
aside.

Carroll had been a good dancer in his youth. But that was
forty-odd years ago. He trod upon Miss Patterson's toes.
"I'm a little out of practice—pray forgive me—" The music
stopped. Relieved and a bit breathless, he suggested, "Shall
we join my daughter, dear? I want to introduce you to the
guest of honor."

Betsy's heart pounded, not with the exertion of the dance,

for *he* had entered the ballroom with a laughing group, having dined at Brooklandwood with the Richard Catons.

"Lieutenant Bonaparte, may I present you to the loveliest girl in America?" Mr. Carroll said.

Jerome bowed. "I've been living for this moment, sir. Miss Patterson, shall we dance?"

Without asking if the next figure of the quadrille was promised, he led her out onto the floor. John Yardley, who had come to claim the remainder of his dance, stood sick at heart, watching Betsy go off with the foreigner.

They joined three other couples, making a square. Betsy danced with her eyes half closed, her lips parted. She made no attempt to conceal the thrill that ran through her whenever Lieutenant Bonaparte touched her. John saw the Frenchman bend his head to catch something Betsy said. As he did so, a gold chain he wore became entangled in her hair. Gently Bonaparte untangled it, while Betsy looked up at him meltingly from behind her fan. She has never looked at me like that, John thought. Unable any longer to watch Betsy and the foreigner making love to each other, right on the dance floor, he turned away bitterly and went to ask Mary Chase to dance.

Jerome, who spoke little English, was pleased to discover Miss Patterson spoke French. When the music stopped, he took her arm. "Come out into the garden, I want to kiss *ma jolie épouse.*"

"Oh, no, the next dance is promised."

"Then I'll kiss you, right here."

They laughed. He started to pull her toward the door. She protested, but wanting to go, not very hard. They were hardly aware of the disapproving eyes that followed them out onto the porch and down the garden path. Nor did they

care. Nothing was of any importance but each other and
the fact that they were alone in the darkness.

An hour later, under the stars, Betsy remembered Mrs.
Samuel Smith, sitting sternly among the dowagers. "I must
go in," she murmured against Bonaparte's lips. "I don't
know what Aunt Margaret will say. I promised the cotillion
to John Comegys. They must be dancing the cotillion now—"

Jerome's arms tightened about her. "*Chérie,* you'll not
dance with any other man but me again, ever!"

As they sat on a marble bench, half hidden behind fat
boxwoods, other couples wandered by, arm in arm. Once
Betsy caught a flash of red. She remembered that Mrs. Caton
was wearing red satin, then thought no more about it.

"Wait here," Jerome said, at suppertime. "Don't move
or speak to anyone while I'm gone." He dashed into the
house and came back with a plate for each of them heaped
with terrapin, pheasant, deviled crab, ices and cake.

After midnight, the moon sank behind the locusts; the
lights in the house went out. The ball was over. Betsy and
Jerome knew they had better go home, not back into the
house to say good night to Judge Chase and his daughter.
Bonaparte who hadn't danced with his hostess, Betsy who
had cut every dance after meeting the Frenchman, wouldn't
be welcomed at the Chases' again.

Hand in hand, they walked to the gate. "I'll take you
home," Jerome said. She explained why she couldn't go
home. "Then we'll go to the Pascaults."

Driving through the dark, deserted streets, Jerome stopped
the curricle frequently and took Betsy's face between his
hands. They kissed, long kisses that left them breathless.
"Why did you run away? You ruined all the parties for

me." His voice trembled. "After I saw you at the races, I couldn't look at another girl."

"You don't like American girls."

"Did I say that, Elise?" he murmured the French equivalent to Betsy. "I'd never seen an American girl, I was just trying to sound smart. You must have thought me a fool."

How sweet Jerome was! If, she suspected, somewhat vain and spoiled. She should keep him guessing. But Betsy threw caution to the winds, whispering how much she loved him, knowing she shouldn't tell him and not caring that she did. It no longer mattered to her that Jerome was Napoleon's brother. The wife of a certain young navy lieutenant was all Betsy wanted to be, not a queen.

The carriage stopped. Afraid, she looked out at the dark house. "The Pascaults have gone to bed. Oh, darling, what shall I do?"

"We'll wake them up." Jerome helped Betsy step out. His arm around her, they walked up the path and pounded the knocker. The door opened. Mme. Pascault, wearing a nightcap and wrapped in a warm robe, stood looking at them in surprise.

"Madame, I bring you *ma jolie épouse*," Jerome announced, and Betsy threw herself into the Frenchwoman's outstretched arms.

Next day, Henriette's mother insisted on notifying Betsy's parents where she was. William, the eldest and most solemn of her brothers, came to fetch his errant sister. He looked as cross and disapproving as Papa. It was raining and not a pleasant journey as they drove to the Patterson's city home.

"How did you get here from Springfield?" William asked. "Mama was frantic when she discovered you'd escaped."

"On a mule. Oh, Willie, he's tied to the Chase fence! You must send and get him."

"Twenty miles on muleback!" Her brother whistled in admiration. Then he remembered his orders. "Papa says I'm not to talk to you." They finished the ride in silence.

The big red brick house on South Street was as quiet as though someone had died there. Dorcas Patterson stood in the hall, her eyes red from weeping. "Your father's waiting to talk to you, Betsy," was all she said.

At the sight of Papa's face, Betsy's knees trembled. His cold, gray eyes glared at her from under frowning brows as she entered his study, closed the door and sat down.

"Well, Papa?" Betsy managed to say.

"So you deliberately disobeyed me?" His voice was dangerously low, his face hard. "You went to a dance I forbade you to attend."

"I'm sorry, Papa." A feeling of relief flooded Betsy. Perhaps this was all her father knew about her actions last night.

"Hold your tongue, Miss. That isn't the worst. Your Aunt Margaret came this morning to tell me about your shocking behavior. You've disgraced the family, Betsy. It's a spectacle you made of yourself, going out in the dark with a stranger you hardly knew, cutting all your dances with old friends! Polly Caton saw that Frenchman kissing you. Of course, she's telling all Baltimore about it today. By gad, girl, I ought to whip you. Letting a man kiss you the first time he meets you!"

Betsy had sat in silence, head bent. She looked up, eyes swimming with tears, into her father's angry face. "I love him, Papa."

"Love? Bah! Did the fellow ask you to marry him? You see what he thinks of you, a cheap hussy! He must be a scoundrel to ruin a girl's reputation like that. All Baltimore is gossiping about you this morning. No respectable young man will call on you again. And this foreigner, don't you see him again—"

Betsy sprang to her feet. "I will see him!" she cried in fury, her eyes enormous with rage.

"Not in my house."

"Then we'll meet elsewhere!" Betsy ran sobbing from the room and up the stairs. Her bedroom door slammed. It shook the house.

That Papa had ordered her to give up seeing Jerome Bonaparte merely made Betsy the more rebellious. Clandestine meetings followed, Magnolia being skillful at delivering notes. Jerome continued his passionate wooing. He quoted the most tender passages of Petrarch's sonnets; they exchanged locks of hair. One day, Bonaparte fastened about Betsy's neck a garnet necklace. Engraved on its clasp was a single French word, *Fidélite*.

"Always faithful?" she whispered. "Do you mean that?"

"Forever!" Jerome promised, with a kiss.

Are we engaged? Betsy wondered, nearly out of her mind with bliss and doubt. Did men always say formally, "Will you marry me?" Or had Jerome asked the question, and she answered him, in their first delirious kiss? He continued to call her *ma jolie épouse*. But was it merely an endearment? He never mentioned marriage.

One afternoon, the lovers snatched a stolen rendezvous, strolling in the shadows of a huge Spanish elm at Belmont, on the Campbell estate, that had become a favorite trysting place. Betsy was depressed. The French frigate *Poursuivante* was anchored in the Patapsco. People were saying Napoleon had sent the warship to bring his disobedient brother home. Trying to sound casual, she forced herself to say, "Well, are you returning to France on the frigate?"

"Captain Willaumez says I am—in fact, he commands me to do so, as my superior in rank—but I've refused." Jerome drew himself up proudly. "Willaumez doesn't outrank the brother of the First Consul. He has no right to give me orders. But I'll have to return home soon. Dear little Elise, I cannot go without you. Your father must agree to our marriage."

Fidélite, he meant it then! Betsy almost fainted on Jerome's breast for joy. Her lover held her tenderly, for this was no passing flirtation, he wanted to marry Betsy. The idea startled Jerome. He had never wanted to tie himself down to one girl before.

At the same time that Jerome Bonaparte, forgetting Napoleon and his career, made up his mind that he wanted to marry Elizabeth Patterson because he loved her, Betsy's Aunt Margaret decided they should be married for another reason. All Baltimore was gossiping about the infatuated pair. They were seen kissing behind the curtains of a box at the theater, driving for hours in Bonaparte's yellow curricle along the waterfront and holding hands at Henriette Pascault's wedding, on October 5, 1803, more in love than the bride and groom. Since the affair had gone this far, Mrs. Smith declared, the Frenchman shouldn't be prevented from marrying her niece, but made to do so.

"I'm going to tell Brother William as much," Margaret Smith informed her husband one morning. "Betsy's as headstrong as her father. She'll run off with that man. William must see they're properly married."

At teatime, an elegant landau drove up to the Pattersons' town house. Mrs. Smith stepped out. She found her sister Dorcas and her daughter arranging flowers, Betsy looking pale and unhappy.

"Dorcas, I'll have tea with you later," Margaret said briskly. "First, I want to see William." She marched with determined step into his study.

Dorcas' sister Margaret was married to General Samuel Smith, Revolutionary hero, congressman and owner of Montebello, a magnificent estate, several miles northeast of Baltimore, that impressed even William Patterson. He thought her a smart woman and listened to Margaret Spear Smith, although he never listened to anyone else.

Mrs. Smith returned to the parlor, looking smug. Nancy Spear, on one of her frequent visits to the Pattersons, came downstairs as Moses brought in the silver tea tray. Over the tea cups, the sisters discussed the weather, that they agreed had been awful.

"Dorcas, I'm going back to the counting-house," announced a chastened voice from the doorway.

"Come in, Brother William," Margaret commanded. He obeyed, head bent, shoulders sagging. "You've something to say to Betsy—" she prompted him.

"Young lady," her father said, each word wrung from him, "I see only unhappiness for you in this marriage. But if you insist—on having this—Frenchman, you might—at least— invite him to meet your parents. Why, I've never laid eyes on the fellow!"

Heavens, was Betsy going to faint? Mama and Aunt Nancy were staring at Papa in round-eyed amazement. Betsy flashed her Aunt Margaret a grateful smile. What was her surprise when the General's sedate lady actually winked at her!

Mr. Patterson sent a formal note to Lieutenant Bonaparte, inviting him to call. He came, bringing flowers for Mrs. Patterson and toys for the children. A man of the world, yet boyish, Betsy's family were charmed with him. In a few days, the lieutenant was calling prim Miss Spear "Nancy," pleasing

Mama by praising her turtle soup and thrilling Joseph and
George with tales of his naval adventures in the West Indies.
Even Papa conceded the Frenchman wasn't a bad sort, as
foreigners go.

Jerome sent the Marquis d'Yrujo, the Spanish minister,
who, having married an American girl himself, was sympathetic, to Mr. Patterson to ask formally for Miss Betsy's hand.
Meanwhile, her lover went to Washington to pay his belated
respects to the President.

Jefferson, who had recently negotiated with the First Consul the purchase of Louisiana, felt friendly toward France.
He gave a dinner for Napoleon's brother on the 23rd of
October, at which the unhappy Pichon, who had heard
why Bonaparte lingered in America, tried to persuade him
that "the very unhealthy town of Baltimore" was dangerous
for his health. He urged Jerome to return to France. Bonaparte as good as told Pichon to mind his own business.
He was going to marry Miss Patterson on November 13th,
he said, and invited the French chargé d'affaires to come to
the wedding.

Poor, harassed Louis Pichon, who felt himself responsible
for the First Consul's impulsive young brother, didn't know
what to do. He agreed to be present. Then, aware that
Napoleon wasn't likely to approve, he refused to come, and
wrote to Pierre Sotin, the French consul at Baltimore, to
Mr. Patterson and to Jerome. He pointed out to them that,
by the laws of France, no Frenchman could marry before
the age of twenty-five without the consent of his parents.
Jerome was only eighteen.

Young Bonaparte replied with an angry letter. He knew
as well as Pichon that Napoleon might not approve of this
marriage. But he didn't let it worry him. When his brother
saw Betsy, he would fall in love with her. Hadn't Napoleon

always humored him? When the commander-in-chief returned from the campaign of Marengo, and Jerome had begged for the sword his brother wore in the battle, hadn't Napoleon good-naturedly unbuckled the precious trophy and given it to him?

At fourteen, Jerome wanted a sword to swagger around with; at eighteen, he wanted Betsy Patterson. He was sure he could get around the First Consul, who found it hard to deny his family anything. So on the 29th of October, the lovers went to the Baltimore Court House to get a marriage license.

Just as things seemed to be going well for Betsy, her father received several anonymous letters, warning him that, from Jerome's actions in the navy, he wasn't likely to prove a faithful husband. They advised Mr. Patterson, if he cared for his child's happiness, to stop the marriage.

"Will he marry your daughter at the Catholic church before the Bishop, as did his friend Reubell?" one writer asked. "I say no! Because he knows such a marriage would be binding."

Another letter informed Betsy's father that Jerome's conduct in the West Indies made him afraid to return home and face Napoleon. He wished to be married merely "to secure himself a home at your expense until things can be arranged for his return to France, when rest assured he'll be the first to turn your daughter off, and laugh at your credulity!"

William Patterson had only agreed to Betsy's marriage most reluctantly. His worst fears were confirmed. In his careful way, he wrote on the envelope of the last letter "Received this by Penny Post, on Saturday, 5th November 1803, at one o'clock, P.M.," then he called Betsy and Jerome into his study.

Jerome's hot Corsican blood boiled. He shouted angry denials. Then he admitted he might have made love to a girl or two in Martinique. Well, all naval officers went in for gallantry. What else was there to do in those dull West Indies? Besides, that was months ago. He had forgotten even the girls' names.

Betsy wasn't so sure. Wild with jealousy, she burst into tears and flung herself into Papa's arms. "Tell him—I won't marry him!" she sobbed.

Jerome wheeled on Betsy as though she had slapped him. "You aren't going to believe an unsigned letter, written by some political enemy of Napoleon's? Dear little one, what if those accusations are true? Are you cruel enough to break off our engagement because I amused myself a bit, before I met you?"

Betsy refused to be placated. What did he expect her to do? Condone his infidelities? Not she. Angrily she tore off the engagement ring Jerome had given her and flung it at him.

"I never want to see you again!"

"Very well, you won't."

To come to America to be humiliated! He, the brother of the most powerful man in Europe, to be cast aside by the first girl to whom he had given his heart! Clicking his heels in his most impressive military manner, Lieutenant Bonaparte bowed and strode from the room.

Hurrying back to the Barneys', he wrote to Pichon that he had broken off his engagement. Bonaparte informed the French chargé d'affaires he was leaving for New York, to sail for Europe. He asked for a loan of $1,000 and, begging Pichon to return to him all the letters they had exchanged on the subject of his marriage, requested him not to write about it to Paris.

Pichon gasped at advancing another large sum. What

would the First Consul say? But he sent it without a murmur, so overjoyed was he by Jerome's letter.

Even more pleased over Bonaparte's decision to sail was his secretary, Alexander Le Camus, who had been most unhappy over the engagement. The young Creole longed for the glitter of Napoleon's court, the balls at the Tuileries, the fêtes at Fontainebleau. Was he going to have to live in America? Thank heavens, no! Jerome's romance was over.

"I told you it wouldn't last!" Le Camus smiled at Dr. Garnier, as with light hearts Bonaparte's entourage climbed into the stagecoach headed for New York.

5. Madame Eve

In WILLIAM PATTERSON'S EYES, not even Napoleon's brother was good enough for his daughter. He was glad they had seen the last of young Bonaparte. But not Betsy. In a fit of pique, she had given Jerome up, but in the days that followed she declared that nothing would change her love for him. Betsy became so melancholy her mother grew worried.

"The child needs to go to Bath and drink the waters," Dorcas said. It was her cure for everything.

"You'll need new dresses at the Springs, Betsy, perhaps one or two," Papa said, for, pleased with the turn of events, he was feeling unusually generous.

Betsy loved pretty clothes. But not even the new frocks and a plumed bonnet in the little pigskin trunk strapped to the top of the coach succeeded in interesting her, as she and her mother, with Zeke on the carriage box, drove off one chilly November day to Virginia.

The waters of Bath were said to be beneficial for gout and

consumption. But Betsy's ailment couldn't be cured by drinking water. She remembered his eyes, dark under heavy brows; his kisses, Jerome's lips pressed firm and hard against her mouth—and wept. There were plenty of amusements at Bath, whist and loo, horse racing, shooting for bearskins, an occasional duel. Betsy went to the picnics and dances with her face all puffed up, her eyes nearly shut from crying. Her mother was in despair.

One night, wakened by weeping, Dorcas saw Betsy on her knees by the bed, saying a prayer, punctuated by loud hiccuping sobs. "Our Father, Who are in heaven—oh, please, God, send him back to me, don't let him sail—please, God!"

So the next morning, when Betsy wailed, "Mama, take me home, I can't live without him. I'll do something terrible if I can't have him—," her mother, remembering that touching prayer, could deny the girl nothing. To her worried chant of "Gracious Betsy, I don't know what your father will say—," Mrs. Patterson and her daughter left the Springs after two weeks and returned to Baltimore, on the first of December.

"I've changed my mind, Papa, I want Jerome back," Betsy announced. "What if he was a bit wild? Any flirtations Jerome had in the West Indies were before he met me. He loves me. I'm sure I can hold him."

Betsy, to her surprise, found her father less opposed to her marriage. It seemed that, lonely without his wife and daughter, Mr. Patterson had spent several evenings smoking his pipe over a glass of Madeira with Joshua Barney, at the General Wayne Inn. The Commodore was fond of Jerome and of Betsy, whom he had known since childhood. He was sorry their romance had gone on the rocks.

"Why are you such a crotchety old father, Will?" Barney burst out. "What if Bonaparte was a gay dog in the West

Indies? Better a few wild oats before than after marriage. Why, I'll wager you had a few romances yourself when you were in Martinique as a young man!"

Facing his daughter this morning, Mr. Patterson remembered Barney's words, but he made a last try to save her. "What do you know about this fellow, really? Your upbringing and his have been totally different. Betsy, I see nothing but unhappiness for you in this marriage. You and I will live to regret it."

"If my marriage turns out badly, I won't let out a whimper, Papa, I promise you. I'd rather be the wife of Jerome Bonaparte for one hour than of any other man for a lifetime."

William spat out an angry "Bah!" But he saw that nothing would shake Betsy's determination, so he gave a reluctant consent to the marriage. Moses was sent to Joshua Barney, to ask him to try to get a message to Bonaparte in New York that he must come back.

The delighted young man returned to Baltimore by the first stage, leaving the indignant Le Camus and the rest of his protesting suite to pack and trail after him. In New York, Jerome had been unable to forget Betsy. What was she doing? He couldn't know, and it had been torture to him. For the first time in his life, Jerome Banaparte was truly in love.

When the stagecoach stopped at the Fountain Inn, he jumped out and hurried to the Pattersons'. Betsy had been standing at the window for hours. She ran to the door. "Jerome!" And she was in his arms, his lips pressed hungrily against her mouth.

"You're back!" Clinging to him, she forgot all the things she had planned to say. The bliss of the moment was almost too sweet to bear. Life was wonderful again.

"Dear children, I'm so happy for you!" Dorcas cried, when,

hand in hand, Betsy and Jerome came into the parlor. She kissed them and murmured, "We must have the liveliest fiddlers in Maryland—"

Betsy knew that Mama had already begun to plan the wedding, that would take place on Christmas Eve. The Pattersons, being Scotch-Irish, were Protestants, but Bonaparte was a Roman Catholic, so the ceremony was to be performed by the highest dignitary of the Church Mr. Patterson could get, the Right Reverend John Carroll, Archbishop of Baltimore, a cousin of Charles Carroll, the Signer. Betsy's father had done all he could to prevent the wedding. But seeing further objections were useless, he was willing to have it take place, provided the marriage was legal in the eyes of the Catholic Church.

On November 15th, Jerome had become nineteen. But Mr. Patterson, still worried about so youthful a bridegroom, insisted upon another precaution. The night before the wedding, to make the tie more binding, a marriage contract was drawn up by Alexander J. Dallas, and witnessed by Pierre Sotin, the French consul at Baltimore, and by James Calhoun, the mayor. Mr. Dallas, an able lawyer, made sure that Jerome promised to have the marriage made legal in France, and should the incredible happen, and it be annulled, that Betsy would be entitled to one-third of his fortune.

"Our marriage annulled? For heaven's sake, why? Jerome says nothing but death can part us again—"

With lighthearted contempt, Betsy dismissed her father's precautions to safeguard her future. She signed Mr. Dallas' long, legal document without so much as a glance. When at last Christmas Eve arrived, the bride's thoughts were on more immediate matters. Were the mantels trimmed with holly and evergreens? The best French wines decanted? The tall candles lighted on the altar erected in the parlor?

Betsy's younger sisters, Peggy and Caroline, made sweet
bridesmaids, in flowered cambric gowns, with caps to match
and mitts, as they came down the stairs to join the grooms-
men—dapper Le Camus; Sotin, who was disobeying Pichon's
orders by attending the wedding; Joshua Barney; and John
Comegys, who had good-naturedly forgiven the Frenchman
for causing Betsy to cut the cotillion with him.

Jerome's hair was powdered. He wore a coat of purple
satin embroidered in gold, white knee-breeches and diamond
shoe buckles. The bride, in contrast, was simply dressed.
As Betsy entered the parlor on her father's arm, it was the
happiness that shone in her eyes that made her beautiful.
Her gown was not even new. It was a white Indian muslin
trimmed with lace that Betsy chose to be married in because
it was becoming. The string of pearls about her throat was
the bridegroom's wedding gift.

Jerome swore before God and man to love, honor and
cherish Betsy until death, Dr. Carroll lifted his hand in
blessing, and the happy bride and groom turned to receive
the best wishes of their friends. Betsy was kissed and hugged.
Jerome's hand was shaken by the Americans present; he was
kissed on both cheeks by the Frenchmen. Then the older
couples wandered off to the dining room, while the young
people danced.

Betsy moved about the rest of the evening on the arm of
her proud bridegroom in a blissful trance. Alexander Le
Camus condescended to wish them happiness. "I hope it
works out well," he said glumly. Betsy assured him, with a
smile, that it would. She feared Jerome's secretary; she knew
Le Camus detested her. But tonight, not even the sly Creole
could cloud her happiness.

Papa was acting like a lamb, not scowling, but pleasant to
everyone, and the lively Patterson children—Joseph, Edward,

George and Caroline—were models of deportment, Betsy noted with relief. The guests all agreed that it had been a beautiful wedding. All too soon, it was time to go home, candles burned low, and the carriages began rolling away. In the dining room, Alexander Le Camus, the Reubells, Mary Caton and Robert Patterson still lingered, singing around the punch bowl.

Jerome had always had a passion to possess beautiful things. Now he had beauty incarnate, his lovely bride. He raised his glass. "To Madame Bonaparte!"

As the others joined in the toast, Betsy lifted her head and smiled proudly. It was the first time she had heard her new name. It gave her a thrill of pride and a sense of superiority, difficult, if not impossible, to resist. With flushed cheeks, the entranced girl realized that she was a Frenchwoman now and a Bonaparte, the sister-in-law of Napoleon, the most powerful man in the world.

No invitation had been sent this time to Louis Pichon. Next day, Alexander Le Camus wrote to the unsuspecting chargé d'affaires, to inform him that Lieutenant Bonaparte's marriage to Miss Patterson had taken place. He asked for a loan of $4,000, explaining that Jerome, who needed it to pay for his wedding, was "awaiting with impatience."

The news was a shock to Pichon, who thought he had put an end to the affair. He was disgusted with Jerome. He believed Napoleon would be furious over the marriage, for his star was rising fast, and he could have married his brother to a princess. Pichon replied stiffly that, since the deed was done, Jerome had better take his American wife abroad as soon as possible and try to make peace with the First Consul.

The frigate *Poursuivante* still lay at anchor off Baltimore, ready, when Jerome wished, to take him to France over the sea now swept by English cruisers. But the young man was in no hurry to sail. Before returning to Paris, he wanted to show off his lovely Elise to the French colonies in Philadelphia, New York and Washington.

Since his arrival in America, through Pichon, the extravagant Jerome had drawn on Napoleon for large sums of money. He had bought carriages and horses and a gaudy red sleigh that was the talk of Baltimore. He had also sent to Leroy, the fashionable Paris *couturière,* for a lavish trousseau for his bride. While they awaited the clothes suitable for a queen, in which Betsy would dazzle Washington society, the Bonapartes went for their honeymoon to Coldstream, a 115-acre estate near the village of Homestead, two miles northeast of Baltimore, that Betsy's father had recently acquired. In the Georgian house there, or strolling by the stream that flowed through the grounds, giving Coldstream its name, Betsy and Jerome spent happy days. It was late in January before they returned to Baltimore.

One day they were sleighing on Market Street, part of a gay cavalcade of sleighs that had turned out to enjoy the crisp air and winter sunshine. Jerome cracked his whip over a pair of high-stepping grays, driven tandem, and Betsy nestled cozily beside him under the bearskin rug, until some boys throwing snowballs struck her on the cheek.

At the sight of the blood trickling down his wife's face, Jerome cried, "Elise, you're hurt!" He jumped out of the sleigh and, whip in hand, started after the boys. They ran, pelting with snowballs the foreigner shouting at them in broken English.

Jerome came back to the sleigh caked with snow and still angry. "I'd give five hundred dollars to catch the boy that did that to you!" He touched the cut on Betsy's cheek tenderly.

She laughed. "It's nothing, forget it." His boyish anger was very sweet.

In early February, the ship bringing Bonaparte's purchases from Paris sailed up the Patapsco. Betsy could hardly wait for Magnolia to open the boxes. Dresses, cloaks, hats, shawls, slippers, lingerie and gloves were unpacked, all the most elegant that money could buy. She tried on several of the new style Directoire costumes with a gasp of dismay. Women were dressing like Greek goddesses, clad in clinging draperies. But these low-cut, high-waisted gowns, with narrow skirts of sheer materials, were almost transparent. They left little to the imagination. Betsy blushed. Papa had never allowed her to wear anything immodest.

"Stays and a slip are all you need under them," Jerome said. "Josephine doesn't wear stays, sometimes not even a slip."

Betsy tossed her head. "Then neither shall I."

Jerome had told her of his sister-in-law's exquisite taste. Napoleon's wife, a West Indian from Martinique, had gone to Paris to become the Viscountess de Beauharnais. Her first husband had died on the scaffold during the Revolution. Napoleon's family were jealous of Josephine; an aristocrat, she made the upstart Corsicans feel inferior. But Jerome conceded that Napoleon's wife dressed beautifully. Betsy longed to be like her.

She sat down at the dressing table, and Jerome picked up a blue velvet bonnet with lace edging the brim. "You'll look nice in this. Try it on."◆

Betsy put on the hat, snatched it off and took out of another handbox a white satin toque, trimmed with green ostrich feathers. "That's even more becoming," Jerome said. How pretty Betsy was! With some guidance from him, she would outshine all the beauties of Napoleon's court. She had a natural flair for clothes. Her tight-fisted father had never dressed the girl properly. Now he would give his little wife everything her heart desired, Bonaparte thought fondly.

"Look, dearest, this darling lace cap! I'll wear it when we go to the White House," Betsy turned from the mirror to say. "Oh, Magnolia, open another box, quick!"

Out came a green riding habit, designed by Leger, the most expensive tailor in Paris; underwear of the finest lace and muslin, headbands, turbans, reticules, parasols and a sumptuous pelisse of velvet trimmed with sable and a sable muff. "Beautiful!" Betsy stroked the rich fur, as Magnolia draped the coat about her shoulders.

"You must wear that with your red velvet dress and the ruby necklace I gave you, when we dine at the French legation," Jerome said. "I'll wear my gaudiest uniform and try to outshine you."

Nor were clothes all Bonaparte thought of. To appear at her best in Paris, for which Washington was just a rehearsal, Betsy must be trained in court etiquette. He taught her how to sink gracefully to the floor in a slow curtsy, as Betsy would have to do at the Tuileries when she was presented to Napoleon and Josephine.

Then one day the giddy young pair set out for Washington in a gleaming new red coach with yellow wheels. Jerome had bought new horses too, with silver-plated harness. Betsy was uneasy as the large traveling carriage, piled high with trunks, valises and bandboxes—all the paraphernalia Jerome took with him wherever he went—sped out of Baltimore. The spirited horses were very different from the staid old bays that Zeke drove hitched to the Patterson carriages.

With loud "Whoas!" Toby, Jerome's coachman, reined in at a tavern at noon. But when they went on again the horses seemed more lively than ever. Entering Washington, they plunged down a hill. Before Toby could avoid a mudhole, the horses sank into the soft ooze, dragging the heavy coach after them. Toby cracked his whip over the backs of the horses to make them pull hard and free the wheels from the mud. They plunged. The top-heavy vehicle swayed; Toby was thrown from his seat on the box.

Jerome sprang from the carriage. He ran to the head of one of the horses and tried to catch its bridle. The frightened animal jerked away, and free of control, the pair bolted. They ran off with the coach and Betsy alone inside. But she kept her head. She waited until the carriage came to a snowdrift, then, opening the door, jumped out. When her anxious husband came running up, he found her lying in the snow, laughing and unhurt. Danger and trouble always found Betsy courageous. It brought out the best in her.

The horses were stopped some distance away. With Toby back on the box, the honeymooners drove up in style, if somewhat shaken, to the home of the Samuel Smiths. That night, the General, writing to Mr. Patterson about the runaway, complimented his niece on her presence of mind.

Now life opened intoxicatingly to Betsy. Washington was still little more than scattered buildings along muddy, unpaved streets. But the party in power, Jefferson and his Republicans, were Francophiles. Everyone wanted to entertain for Napoleon's brother. Then it did Betsy no harm socially that her Aunt Margaret's Sam was now in the Senate; his brother Robert, Jefferson's Secretary of the Navy. Congressman and Mrs. John Van Ness gave a ball for the Bonapartes; the rich Washington heiress, Marcia Burns Van Ness, having been to school with Betsy at Madame Lacombe's. At balls in the legations or at parties in Georgetown, the Bonapartes danced the nights away, while the violins played. They were the most elegant, the most sought-after young couple in Washington.

But the town buzzed with chatter, that February of 1804, about Mme. Bonaparte's low-cut dresses that displayed, some said, far too much of her beautiful rounded shoulders and tapering arms. At every function the men crowded around her. The ladies were not so admiring.

"If you wish us to attend Mme. Pichon's luncheon for you, my dear Betsy," Mrs. Robert Smith said bluntly, "you must promise to have more clothes on."

Betsy was being a bad example. The young girls of Washington were begging their Mamas to let them discard their chemises, petticoats and stays. But none of the girls had Mme. Bonaparte's figure or such a back and shoulders.

The Washington wits had nicknamed her Madame Eve, Betsy's gowns were but fig leaves, they said. She hoped Papa wouldn't hear of it. He had never allowed her to have a low-cut gown or a dress without sleeves. But encouraged by Jerome, who found shocking stodgy people amusing, Betsy was enjoying her new freedom like a giddy schoolgirl. So Mrs. Smith's reprimand didn't curb her behavior. She knew how elated the Smiths were over her marriage. Uncle Sam, now that he was related to Napoleon, hoped to be made minister to France.

Aaron Burr is quoted as saying he could have put all the clothes worn by Mme. Bonaparte in his pocket. Certainly the Vice President made no objection. Burr was one of Betsy's most ardent admirers. So was Thomas Jefferson. The President was a widower. Dolly Madison, the wife of the Secretary of State, was Jefferson's official hostess, whom he always took in to dinner. But when the Jerome Bonapartes dined at the White House, the President offered his arm to nineteen-year-old Mme. Bonaparte and escorted her to the table.

Betsy sat on Jefferson's right, regal in white satin, a smile on her lips. How could she help smiling? She was so in love with her husband and elated with her new sense of importance. The President was treating her, not as the daughter of his old friend, William Patterson, but with all the respect due the sister-in-law of the great Napoleon.

Jerome, seated next to Dolly Madison, was proud of his wife. Already Betsy had that air of a little queen she retained all her life. She'll grace the Tuileries, he thought.

Down the table, Louis Pichon looked at the honeymooners, misty-eyed. So young and in love! Their romantic marriage was like a real-life fairy tale. But how would it end? No word had been received from Napoleon since the marriage. Now the deed was done, the kindly Pichon wanted to see Betsy and Jerome live happily ever after, like the prince and princess in the fairy tale. But would Napoleon let them?

Older and wiser heads worried about the young Bonapartes while they went their gay, thoughtless way. Jerome had written to Madame Mère about his wedding and asked his mother to break the news to Napoleon. It was strange they hadn't heard from her.

But when Betsy remarked on the fact one afternoon, Jerome only shrugged and replied, "Oh, we'll hear from Mama soon. Hurry, Elise, we're due at the White House for tea." He never worried much about anything.

They found Thomas Jefferson wearing his usual old coat and carpet slippers, his sandy hair tousled. But Jerome liked Mr. Jefferson. Under his informal attire he recognized the scholar Jefferson was and the gentleman. Besides, the President was someone with whom Bonaparte could speak French, while Betsy chatted with Dolly Madison and laughed at little Mr. Madison's jokes.

Jefferson took a letter from his pocket. "Read this, Betsy

dear. It's a copy of what I wrote to Robert Livingston, our minister in Paris. I urged him to see Napoleon and try to reconcile him to Jerome's marriage. As Livingston has never met your father, I've written him some facts he should know about your family, before he talks with Napoleon."

It seemed that Vice President Burr had asked his good friend, Dolly Madison, to persuade Jefferson to write the American minister to France in Betsy's behalf. Livingston was to explain to Napoleon that his brother, far from marrying beneath him in America, had made a fine marriage. Mr. Patterson was very wealthy, the president of the Bank of Maryland; Betsy's mother, the sister-in-law of Senator Samuel Smith. The Pattersons of Baltimore were one of the best families in the United States.

"Thank you, Mr. President." Betsy returned Jefferson's letter to him with a blush of pleasure. So her marriage had become an international problem! It gave the teen-age girl a thrill to think that she was now important enough to have the President of the United States concerning himself about her affairs.

"I'll have James, as Secretary of State, also write to Napoleon about you, Betsy," Dolly Madison promised.

Why, Dolly's sorry for me! So is Mr. Jefferson! Well, they needn't be, Betsy thought. Any day now, Jerome will hear from Napoleon. Then they would go to Paris and take their place there as the brother and sister of the most powerful man in the world, while people said that Mr. Madison, Jefferson's protégé, would have to go out of politics and retire to Virginia, when Jefferson's term as president was over. Thinking of the dull plantation life in store for her, Betsy thought, poor Dolly!

6. *Royalty Roughs It*

JOHN PATTERSON WAS IN INDIA, representing his father's firm. And now Robert, a handsome young man, was going on a business trip to Europe. In love himself, Robert was more in sympathy than William or John with Betsy's marriage.

"In Paris, why don't I try to see Napoleon and his brothers," he suggested, "and find out how they feel about Jerome's marriage?"

None too happy at leaving America, Robert sailed in February, 1804. Mary Caton had scores of beaux who would make the most of his absence.

In London, Robert talked over his sister's troubles with the American minister, James Monroe, and with the envoy's daughter. Eliza Monroe had gone to school in France with Josephine's child, Hortense. She gave Robert a letter to Hortense, who had married Jerome's brother, Louis Bonaparte.

Robert, arriving in Paris on March 11, went to see the

American minister, Chancellor Livingston, who had sworn in Washington as president at Federal Hall in New York. Livingston had received a letter from Betsy's father, asking him to explain to Napoleon that he had done all he could to discourage Jerome's courtship. Since then, Robert Livingston had been trying, without success, to see the First Consul, give him Mr. Patterson's message, the letters from Jefferson and Madison, and to explain the marriage to him in the best possible light.

"I've seen Joseph, the eldest of the four brothers," he told Robert, "and all I could get out of him was that he'd see you some night, in secret. Mr. Patterson, I was shocked. I hope you won't go."

Robert agreed with Livingston that a clandestine visit would be undignified. So he was pleased, on returning to his lodgings, to find a cordial invitation from Lucien Bonaparte to call.

As he did not speak French, Robert took with him as interpreter a friend living in Paris, Paul Bentalou, who had served in Count Pulaski's cavalry during the American Revolution. Lucien lived like a prince at the Hôtel Brienne, in the Rue St. Dominique, for he had enriched himself as minister to Spain. A tall man, with a frank, self-assured manner, Lucien and his pretty wife received the two Americans cordially.

"Tell Mr. Patterson that our entire family, with the exception of Napoleon, are pleased with Jerome's marriage," Lucien said through Paul Bentalou. "Since the rest of us approve, I'm sure the Consul will become reconciled to it. I'm in the same situation as Jerome. I married without Napoleon's consent. He hasn't spoken to my wife."

Lucien thought that, since Jerome had wed an American, he should stay in the United States and become an American citizen. If he did, Lucien said, his family were discussing giving him an income of $15,000 a year. Robert agreed, it would be a sensible thing for Jerome to do.

"Will you dine with me tomorrow?" Lucien asked Betsy's brother on parting. "I shall hope to see you every few days."

Robert was greatly encouraged by his visit with Lucien. But Bentalou kept wishing they could have a talk with Joseph.

"Napoleon has less friction with his placid, older brother than with the three younger ones, who are more self-willed and obstinate. Then Napoleon has the Corsican clan respect for Joseph as the eldest brother, the head of the family. When Joseph speaks, he speaks for Napoleon, while Lucien hates Napoleon and likes to stir up trouble."

It seemed that Lucien had made a second marriage that, after years of quarrels with Napoleon, finally led to an open break. Lucien's first marriage to Christine Boyer, the daughter of an innkeeper, hadn't pleased the ambitious Napoleon. After her death, Lucien had been married in secret by a priest, the previous May, to Alexandrine Jouberthou, the widow of a bankrupt stockbroker, who gave birth to a son by Lucien the evening before the wedding. Napoleon, knowing nothing of this marriage, suggested to Lucien that he marry the widowed Queen of Etruria. Lucien refused, but he didn't say he had a wife and baby in Paris. Napoleon was annoyed, his first attempt at kingmaking had failed. But there hadn't been a rupture between the brothers until six months ago, when Lucien, thinking himself to be strong enough to hold his own against Napoleon, went through a civil marriage with Alexandrine and recorded the birth of their son.

Napoleon was furious. Lucien had rejected a queen for a woman without family or wealth, when he wished his brothers to marry princesses and help him climb in the world. But because of the help Lucien had been to him in the *coup d'état* when Napoleon seized power, he decided to forgive Lucien's second foolish marriage. Napoleon told him that, if he kept his marriage secret, and Alexandrine promised not to use the Bonaparte name, he would act as if nothing had happened, and Lucien could go on living quietly with her. Lucien indignantly refused. There was an angry scene. Napoleon banished him from France. The March of 1804, when Robert Patterson came to see Lucien, he was packing to go to Italy to live.

Robert presented Eliza Monroe's letter to Mme. Louis Bonaparte. Hortense ignored it. And when he finally was able to make an appointment with Joseph, Robert found himself up against a more timid person than the independent Lucien.

Joseph was a rich and pompous man. Before Napoleon's rise to greatness, he had married Julie Clary, the daughter of a wealthy Marseilles soap maker. Since then, the diplomatic services Joseph had rendered France added to his sense of his own importance as the head of the Bonaparte family.

He had hesitated to see Robert while Napoleon was upset, first over Lucien's marriage, then over Jerome's. Joseph finally invited Mr. Patterson to dine at the Hôtel Marbeuf, his home in the Faubourg St. Honoré, due only to Lucien's urging. But Joseph was so quiet during the meal that Robert returned to his lodgings hardly knowing what to make of the evening. Before leaving for Amsterdam on March 29, he wrote his father:

> On Saturday I had the honor of dining with Mr. Joseph Bonaparte. None of the family were present but his lady. It is a little singular he did not throughout the evening speak a word of his brother's marriage, and only mentioned

his name when I was departing . . . As he possesses the confidence of the First Consul, he probably declined saying anything on that subject, lest I might imagine he gave the
sentiments of his brother. My being admitted to his table
cannot but argue more favoribly to our wishes than otherwise, though it had been infinitely more satisfactory and
pleasing had he been less reserved.

The Consular recognition or disavowal of the marriage
will be determined by future occurances. Much will depend
on Jerome. If he acts the part of an honorable man everything must go right. It is the duty of my sister, as a wife, to
retain and increase the affections of her husband; and her
exertions ought, if possible, to be doubled, from the peculi-
arity of her situation.

Mr. Patterson forwarded Robert's letter to Washington,
where the Jerome Bonapartes were enjoying the giddy social
whirl of which they never tired. Robert had written that the
Bonaparte family were anxious to have a picture of Betsy.
If she would send him one, he would give it to them.

"When Napoleon sees your lovely face, Elise," Jerome
said, "he can't help but love you. He's very susceptible to
pretty women."

It so happened that they were having their portraits
painted by Gilbert Stuart. The artist had started Jerome's
picture, also three different positions of Betsy's head on one
canvas from which Stuart intended to do a portrait of her,
when he could decide which was the loveliest angle. Betsy
liked to have Jerome hold her hand while Stuart painted her.
She said it gave her a sweeter expression.

Their portraits were progressing slowly, for Gilbert Stuart
was busy with other commissions. Now Jerome became so
impatient to get his wife's portrait to his family, so Napoleon
could see Betsy's beauty, that at every sitting he pleaded with
Stuart to hurry until the touchy painter grew angry. He was

painting Dolly and James Madison and refused to finish Mme. Bonaparte's picture out of turn.

Jerome's incessant pestering got on the overworked artist's nerves. The breaking point came when Bonaparte found fault with the way Gilbert Stuart had painted Betsy's gown. "Oh, you want an exact copy? That you can buy at any dressmaker's," snapped the artist, who resented criticism of any kind. He threw down his brush. After that, Stuart refused to work any longer on Mme. Bonaparte's portrait or to part with it at any price.

"Bonaparte, if you bother me any more about it," he threatened, "I'll put rings through your wife's nose and give her picture to any tavern-keeper who will hang it up."

The canvas remained rolled up for years in Gilbert Stuart's Boston studio, where his daughter Jane, who thought the unfinished painting beautiful, loved to look at it.

Betsy shrugged. "Let Stuart keep the portrait, Jerome. When we get to France, I can plead our cause better than any picture can. Oh, I'll make Napoleon listen, I can persuade him to forgive us, I know I can!"

"I know you will, Elise. But we should wait to sail until we hear from Mama. I'm counting on her to win Napoleon over. She's the only person in the world he's afraid of. Napoleon is like a little boy with Mama."

Finally, a letter came from Jerome's mother. Madame Mère wrote that she and her daughters were looking forward to welcoming Jerome's bride. "Napoleon is very angry, but I'm doing my best to intercede for you. Perhaps, after the Coronation—" And Letizia Bonaparte went on to tell her son amazing news. Napoleon, no longer content with being First Consul, was to proclaim France an empire, with himself and Josephine as emperor and empress. The Pope would crown them at Paris in December.

Betsy listened, starry-eyed, flushed, incredulous. Could it be that her dreams were coming true! "Oh, Jerome, we must get to France for the Coronation!" She saw herself, wearing a diamond coronet and velvet robes, making her entrance into the Cathedral of Nôtre Dame like a queen. "Darling, if Napoleon becomes emperor, what will be the title of his brothers and sisters?"

"Prince and princess."

"And mine, as your wife?"

"You'll be a princess too, an Imperial Highness."

Overcome with joy, Betsy threw her arms about her husband's neck. "Your Imperial Highness," she whispered, remembering Mammy July's prophecy. She had never believed anything so ridiculously farfetched could happen. But, good heavens, there might be something in it! She wouldn't be a queen, but to be a princess, the first American princess, how jealous Mary Chase and the Catons would be!

Madame Lacombe had told her about the endless corridors and the magnificent painted ceilings of the Tuileries. But to actually live there, as Jerome said they would! Betsy's thoughts raced ahead. She heard the cheers of the crowd as she drove through Paris in her carriage with postillions and outriders, as glittering with diamonds she entered her box at the theater.

Friendly letters came from Jerome's sisters. Pauline, who had remarried, her husband being Prince Camillo Borghese, head of an aristocratic Roman family, wrote of the gorgeous robes and jewelry they were having made for the Coronation. Her younger sister, Caroline, complained bitterly that Napoleon was humbling his sisters by forcing them to carry the train of Josephine's ermine mantle. Caroline vowed the sisters would do all in their power to make the Empress appear ridiculous, for, jealous of Josephine, they hated her as only Corsicans can hate. And did Jerome know that Mama refused to attend the Coronation? In protest against Napoleon's harsh treatment of Lucien, Signora Letizia had gone to Italy to join the son who had been cast out of the family circle.

"That's just like Mama, she's always on the side of the child who is in trouble!" Jerome exclaimed. "You'll love her, Elise. She's still a beautiful woman, but dresses plainly in black, for she is very frugal. Napoleon scolds her for not spending more money and looking like the mother of a great ruler. To which Mama replies that, since his good fortune cannot last, she's saving the allowance Napoleon gives her for when her children need it."

His father, Jerome said, had been an Italian who settled in Corsica. Carlo Bonaparte died when Jerome was three, and his mother had courageously brought up eight children in poverty. Corsica's war for independence forced Signora Letizia to flee to France. Caroline and Jerome, thought too young to risk the dangers of flight, were left with their grandmother. With Elisa, Pauline and Louis, Letizia crossed to Toulon, in the south of France, where she was met by her eldest sons, Joseph and Napoleon. Joseph, shortly afterwards, married Julie Clary, daughter of a Marseilles soap maker. Napoleon was with the French army, stationed at Nice. Lucien, a clerk in the army military stores. Napoleon took charge of his brothers and sisters, and from then on ruled them, although he was not the eldest. They all loved and respected him, but when he gave an order, it had to be obeyed.

On being appointed general-in-chief of the Army of the Interior, Napoleon's first thought was for his family. For Joseph, the post of French consul at Genoa. For Lucien, a better job in the army commissary department. He took

Louis as his aide and sent Jerome to school at his expense. As for the girls, Napoleon was determined they should marry well. He married Pauline to Victor Leclerc and Caroline to another of his generals, Joachim Murat.

Due to the generosity of a governor of Corsica, his eldest sister, Elisa, had been educated at St. Cyr, a school in Paris for the children of poor noblemen. Elisa, domineering and mannish, fancied herself as an intellectual. She had married an insignificant Corsican, Felix Bacciochi, against Napoleon's wishes. He was never very fond of her. But that didn't prevent him from doing his full duty by Elisa. There was never a more devoted son and brother.

As he climbed from general, to consul, to emperor, Napoleon carried his family up with him. Now they were all to be Imperial Highnesses! What girl of nineteen wouldn't have been beside herself with excitement? Not even Napoleon's continued ominous silence could keep Betsy from wanting to sail for France at the first opportunity.

It came in June, 1804. Betsy's father, Jerome and Betsy set out for New York. Jerome had remained so long in America that the seas were dangerous. The British were boasting how they would capture Napoleon's brother. But through his shipping connections, Mr. Patterson had heard of two French frigates, the *Cybele* and the *Didon,* that had anchored in the Hudson to take on provisions. Jerome hoped he and Betsy could slip away on the *Didon,* the fastest ship in the French navy.

On the 14th of June it was published in a New York newspaper that—

"M. Jerome Bonaparte, his lady and Mr. Patterson of Baltimore, her father, arrived in this city on Tuesday. Report says that the young couple are about to depart for

France, but the correctness of the rumor is considered questionable. They attended the theatre last evening, accompanied by the captains of the *Cybele* and *Didon* frigates, and several gentlemen. That these vessels may leave the Hook without apprehension, a pilot boat was yesterday chartered to cruise in the offing, in order to discover whether there are any British ships of war in the way. Bonaparte's baggage was put on board the *Didon* yesterday; and if so, it is possible the French frigates will sail in the morning."

Would Bonaparte and his bride sail on the *Didon?* If so, would they be captured by a British warship? For weeks the New York papers had speculated at such length on the subject that reports reached Halifax. Two British frigates rushed to New York. The *Didon* found her passage to the Atlantic barred by enemy ships. On the 19th of June, the New York newspapers reported that "Jerome Bonaparte and lady were rowed up yesterday from on board the *Didon,* and safely landed opposite their lodgings in Washington Street at 12 o'clock."

Betsy had been thrilled to hear the French officers of the *Didon* call her "Your Imperial Highness." But when she implored them to sail out of New York harbor and take their chances against the enemy, they refused. "The British warships on the coast would make our capture certain, Your Highness." So Betsy was back in New York, tapping her dainty foot in vexation.

> *Rumor:* Jerome and his lady have taken their departure in the *Silenus,* which sailed a few days ago for Amsterdam. *Fact:* We are informed they are still in the city. It is expected they have abandoned their contemplated departure for the present. *Rumor:* The Bonapartes have taken a summer residence near this city. *Fact:* This may be true. It is certain, however, that General Ray, the French Commissary, has taken the cabin of the brig *Rolla,* which vessel is about

to sail for Bordeaux; it is believed that Bonaparte and his lady are going home in this vessel.

While conflicting reports circulated about them in the press, Betsy and Jerome went about in New York society. Gouverneur Morris' diary mentions his dinner guests at Morrisania, his country estate that is now the Bronx, as: "M. and Mme. Bonaparte and a young Englishman of genius named Moore, a young man who has translated well several odes of Anacreon."

The Irish poet, on leave from a government job in Bermuda, was visiting the United States. He wasn't impressed by what he saw. The little man from Dublin, spoiled by English society, looked down patronizingly on Americans. But when he laid eyes on gorgeous Betsy Bonaparte, Moore saw someone in our country he could admire.

Next day at breakfast, Betsy smiled, remembering how the foppish Irishman had chirped, "How can so small a head contain so much wit!" She wore a new pink negligee and felt very gay and lovely this morning.

"Jerome, dear!" Betsy said to him across the table. "Mr. Moore accused me of marrying you just to escape from America—Why, darling, what's the matter?"

Her husband looked up from a letter he was reading, his face drained of color. "Bad news. Admiral Decrès, our minister of marine, wrote this last April. His letter was seized by a British frigate off New York. They have just sent me a copy. Decrès writes he has talked with Napoleon, who says to tell me that my allowance is stopped. Pichon isn't to give me any more money—"

"How terrible!" Betsy was stunned. "How can we live here without money? Jerome, demand of the captain of the *Didon* that he take us to France at once!"

"He wouldn't let you on board, my love. Do you want me

to read to you what Decrès writes? He says the captains of all French ships are forbidden to receive on board 'the young person to whom you have attached yourself—' "

Two spots of red burned in Betsy's cheeks. "Why, the insulting beast, he doesn't even call me your wife!"

After six months of silence, the First Consul had spoken. And when Napoleon struck, he struck hard.

Admiral Decrès reminded Lieutenant Bonaparte that he was a deserter from the navy. Was it honorable, he asked, for a naval officer to remain idle, thousands of miles away, while France was at war? Jerome was ordered to return at once to his naval duties. On one condition only would Napoleon forgive him, that Jerome come home *alone*. If he brought his wife, she wouldn't be allowed to set foot in France.

Betsy flung herself on the couch in a passion of weeping. Her husband bent over her tenderly. "Jerome, tell me that nothing can ever come between us," she begged, her arms so tight about his neck that she nearly strangled him.

"Don't cry, dear little one," he begged. "I'll never leave you, I swear."

Betsy believed Jerome meant it. Wasn't she wearing the garnet necklace he had given her, with his solemn promise of *Fidélite* engraved on its clasp? But could Betsy trust Jerome's detestable French entourage? She was aware that Alexander Le Camus, behind her back, was slyly urging her husband to sail on the *Didon* without her. Jerome was easily led, his wife had discovered. At all cost, he must be removed from Le Camus' influence.

"Darling, let's you and I go off alone on a real honeymoon," Betsy suggested. "Why don't we go and see Niagara Falls?"

Jerome took to the idea at once. Since 1795, when the Duc

de Rochefoucauld-Liancourt had written about his travels in the United States, a book widely read in Paris, a journey to the falls of the Niagara was a trip that all Frenchmen visiting America wished to make. So on the 9th of July, 1804, the New York papers reported:

> Jerome Bonaparte has abandoned all intentions of immediately returning to France, and contemplates commencing in a few days a pretty extensive tour; in the course of which he will visit the Springs of Lebanon and Ballston, and view the grand Falls of Niagara. His lady will be of the party.

After the Erie Canal was opened in 1825, Niagara Falls became the fashionable honeymoon spot. Twenty years later, Barnum's Museum in New York featured an artificial cascade for brides and grooms unable to afford a trip out to view the real falls. But western New York State in 1804 was still the frontier; a journey west of Albany not one on which to take a lady.

Betsy, however, had plenty of her father's toughness in her. In July, she left with Jerome on the sloop *Sally* for Albany, amused to find herself the only woman on board. As they sailed through Tappan Bay, a clergyman, going to Claremount as tutor to the Livingston children, came to her as spokesman for the other passengers.

"You'll observe, lovely lady, that we all must sleep in the same cabin. At bedtime, so you can undress, the men plan to walk the deck for half hour. Time enough surely for you to put on your nightcap! A half hour in the morning, we'll also leave you the cabin."

Betsy smiled. "Thank you, kind sir. You've removed my only objection to Hudson River sloops."

As they sailed through the Highlands and out into Newburgh Bay, the gentlemen voted Mme. Bonaparte precisely what they wished ladies in a ship's cabin to be, not too free and easy, nor so starchy as to make travel on a sloop difficult.

By Poughkeepsie, they sailed. The Catskills loomed to the left, the Livingston Manor lands on the right. The sloop raced along at ten miles an hour, when the wind blew. If the breeze slackened, the captain cast anchor, the passengers went ashore to pick berries. At Kinderhook, taking with them a deckhand and his fiddle, they danced until midnight in a tavern. The *Sally* was becalmed only seven times. And the 160-mile trip to Albany, that might have taken as long as a month, was over in four days.

Uncomfortable and slow as were the Hudson River sloops, land travel was worse. At Albany, Betsy and Jerome crowded with other passengers into the weekly stage that would take them as far west as Geneva, 200 miles in six days. Only five years before, the road beyond Utica was hardly more than an Indian trail. But New York State was having a real estate boom since the Indian lands had been opened to white settlers. There were new log huts along the road, spaced a mile to five miles apart. But food was hard to obtain, taverns few and far between. The beds were so full of fleas that the Bonapartes slept with their clothes and shoes on, even their gloves. A strange experience for Jerome, used to the Tuileries!

At the frontier town of Geneva, the road ended. The Bonapartes bought horses and food for a four-day ride to the falls. The next seventy miles to the tiny settlement of "Buffaloe" was wilderness, where lodgings were under the stars. But as Betsy rode through the woods, looking like a boy in shirt and breeches, her spirits rebounded. They met pioneer families on horseback, going out to turn western New York into fertile farm lands and flourishing towns. The settlers were happy and unafraid. She absorbed their courage.

"Papa wasn't able to lock me up in Springfield and keep us

apart, Jerome," Betsy said. "And Napoleon isn't going to bottle me up in America!"

The Bonapartes camped one night on Lake Erie. Next morning, they followed the Niagara River, trying to keep pace with some driftwood, carried on faster by the rushing water than their horses could trot. "Look, Jerome, smoke!" Betsy pointed. It wasn't smoke, but a white cloud of spray from the falls. They reined-in, and when the noise of their horses' hoofs stopped, they could hear a roar like thunder, as the river rushed over a precipice ahead.

Dismounting, they tied their horses to a tree. Taking the roar of the falls as a guide, they pushed through a tangled thicket to find themselves out on an overhanging slab of rock. A precipice yawned beneath them. Betsy's heart leaped at the sight of an immense curved sheet of green-blue water plunging into the gulf below. But one look was enough for Jerome. He dragged his wife back from the wet, slippery rock, where a false step meant death down in that boiling caldron below.

That night, Betsy and Jerome, possibly the first honeymooners to visit Niagara Falls, lay in each other's arms by the campfire, happy and in love, like thousands of young couples who have visited the falls since. Would he ever be so happy again, Jerome wondered. He was an easygoing young man, who hated friction. Here was peace. He wished he didn't have to go back to Europe. How wonderful it would be to live in Washington as French minister, forget Napoleon and just be happy!

Their idyl, unfortunately, couldn't last forever. The end of August found the Bonapartes at Ballston Spa, a New York State resort made famous in 1767, when Sir William Johnson came there for his gout. Such a fashionable mineral spring naturally looked down its elegant nose at a little upstart neighbor, Saratoga.

There was plenty to do at Ballston besides sip the waters—dancing, card-playing and the flirtations with which people in resorts fill their idle hours. One evening, as Betsy and Jerome danced, one of a hundred couples dipping and whirling in the candle-lit ballroom of the Sans Souci Hotel, Jerome marveled at his tiny wife. Could this lovely feminine creature in silver-embroidered percale, her hair in a tiara of braids interwoven with pearls, be his boyish companion on that rough journey into the wilderness of western New York?

General John Armstrong, twirling his moustache, stood admiring the Bonapartes. What a handsome couple! When the music stopped, he walked over to them.

"Congratulations, sir, I hear you're to replace Mr. Livingston as American minister to France," Jerome said.

"Yes, my brother-in-law is old and deaf. I'm sailing the first of September to take over Robert's job."

In a flash Betsy saw a way out of her difficulties.

"Please take me with you, General. Napoleon has forbidden me to step foot in France, as you've probably heard. But he couldn't keep me out, if I entered France under the protection of the American minister, say as a member of your staff."

It was a most daring request. General Armstrong hesitated. He didn't want to get into trouble with Napoleon at the very start of his mission to France. "As my secretary, eh? Dear lady, you'd make such a pretty one you'd disrupt the staff." The General tried to pass off Mme. Bonaparte's remark as a joke.

It was no joking matter. Betsy's mind was made up. She was going abroad with General Armstrong; and as Jerome had found, when his little wife made up her mind about anything, there was no talking her out of it. John Armstrong would discover it, too, for in the days that followed, wherever he was, there was Betsy Bonaparte. She danced and played cards with him. She flirted with him; she laughed at his jokes. Whenever the General wanted her, and often when he didn't want her, Betsy left her husband and friends to take walks with him.

"Would you let me go to France with you? *Really?* Now, don't think you must, just to be kind. But, oh, my dear General, if you would only take me—*please!*"

Stars shone in her eyes. General Armstrong, poor man, never knew just when or why he had agreed to do what Mme. Bonaparte wanted, only that it seemed to be all arranged. Jerome was to follow a few days later, on the *Didon*.

Betsy burned once more with energy and hope. She and Jerome were as good as on their way to France. Now everything would be all right.

7. The Course of True Love
Is Never Smooth

THE DAY CAME. Betsy had hardly believed it would. She and Jerome were driving through the lovely Jersey countryside, with the trees turning golden in September, on their way from Baltimore to New York, to sail for France. Betsy, leaning back in the public stagecoach, felt herself entitled to a smile of triumph.

"Jerome, the rest is going to be easy. When I get to Paris, I shall insist that General Armstrong take me to meet Napoleon at once. Robert failed to see him, but I will. Trust a determined woman! By the time you join me, your brother and I will be friends. Wait and see!"

Her infatuated husband agreed. Napoleon had only to meet Betsy. No man, exposed to her charm, could resist her.

As the stagecoach creaked up and down the hills on the Jersey Pike, Betsy rode along thinking what she would say to the Emperor. No tears, no undue emotion. She would be sweet, persuasive, tactful—Good heavens, what was that? The wild rocking of the stage woke Betsy from her pleasant daydreams. "Jerome, what's going on?" She clutched his arm.

One frightened glance out of the window told her. Stage drivers couldn't be kept from racing. Going down a steep grade, their coachman was whipping his horses into a gallop to pass a rival stage ahead.

When part way down the hill, the carriage jolted to an abrupt stop and turned half over in the ditch, it was Mme. Bonaparte who leaped out first. "What's happened?" she demanded.

"A wheel's broken." With a sheepish look, the driver climbed down from the box. "You folks will have to wait while I fix it."

"Jerome, we can't wait," Betsy cried, close to tears. "We must be in New York by six, or we'll miss the boat. For pity sakes, hire another carriage!"

He persuaded her to wait. The driver wasted a long time trying to mend the wheel himself. Finally, one of the passengers had to walk back to the last relay post, several miles distant, for help. It was an hour before it came. Pacing up and down, biting her lip with impatience, Betsy watched the slow-moving men fix the wheel and the axle that had cracked as well.

Two hours later, the coach lumbered on again. Betsy was never to forget that nightmare ride. At Jerome's pleading, the driver whipped his horses to their utmost. But one of them went lame. After that, the coach crawled along. Betsy, biting her nails, felt as if she were going mad. If General Armstrong hadn't waited for her, she had missed the boat.

Lights, New York at last. The dusty post road changed to the city's cobbled streets. But the horses were tired, the carriage wheels turned slower as they neared the wharves of

Lower Manhattan. It was eight o'clock, the docks dimly lighted. Betsy's fears grew by leaps and bounds as she peered ahead. Had the boat gone?

It had. As the carriage drew up in front of the empty wharf, Betsy wept, her head pressed against Jerome's shoulder. "Don't upset yourself so, my love." He tried to calm her. "If you'd gone with General Armstrong, Elise, we'd have been separated. Now, somehow—" and he was vague about it "—we can sail together."

If they had taken an earlier stage? If the wheel hadn't broken? If she had slipped into France with the American minister, might her life have been different? Betsy would often wonder. She knew that by cutting connections too close, she and Jerome were partly to blame for missing the boat. And writing to her father from New York, September 5, 1804, she omitted telling him about the accident to the stage. Instead, Betsy blamed her disappointment on General Armstrong. She always suspected he lost courage and sailed early, to escape her. Perhaps he did.

> We have made a journey here for nothing, as General Armstrong, after writing to Mr. Bonaparte that he would be delighted at taking me to France with him, changed his mind, and went off without me. Tomorrow we are to leave this place for Philadelphia and from thence we go to Springfield immediately; so that, as I shall see you soon, it is unnecessary to say any more.

While New York buzzed with rumors "that M. Jerome Bonaparte and his little Baltimore beauty have taken French leave, and slipped off in the vessel which carries General Armstrong, our lately-appointed Minister to Nantz," the Bonapartes sadly took the stage back to Maryland. They arrived at Springfield the day Robert sent them an editorial printed in Paris on October 12th. In a business letter to his father, he enclosed a clipping from the *Moniteur,* to the effect that there could be no truth to the report of Jerome's marriage:

> The American journals speak often of the wife of Mr. Jerome Bonaparte. It is possible Mr. Bonaparte, a young man who is only nineteen years of age, may have a *mistress.* It is not possible he can have a *wife,* since the laws of France are such that a minor of nineteen cannot marry without the consent of his parents.

"How dare they use that—that—insulting word!" Betsy, shocked to be called Jerome's mistress, sank sobbing onto a chair. She had never been so humiliated.

"I'll sue the rascal, Elise. I'll make him apologize, tell all France you're my legal wife!"

Jerome, sick at heart, paced the floor. He knew that in France the press was censored. This scurrilous article could never have been printed in the *Moniteur,* except by authority of the government. Napoleon was making his attitude known all too plainly.

Betsy felt somewhat better when a letter from Robert in Holland arrived. Writing to his father on business matters, her brother referred, casually, to the "absurd" editorial in the *Moniteur.* Robert thought it had been "inserted by way of retaliation to the many abusive ones which appeared in our (American) prints." As to their hope of winning Napoleon over, he didn't "think the prospect so gloomy." At present, the Emperor, still furious over Lucien's marriage, refused to discuss the matter. But Robert heard that Madame Mère was doing her utmost for Jerome. Robert still thought Jerome would be happier in America. But if he returned home, he mustn't fail to bring his wife with him, no matter what the consequences. Personally, Robert didn't think Napoleon's threat to keep Betsy out of France would be enforced.

> I understand it was the intention of my sister to have come out on the same ship with General Armstrong, which some misunderstanding prevented. Presuming she will persevere in her intention, I shall go on in a week or two to Paris to meet her. Mr. Monroe and his family are in Paris. He will do everything in his power, I am persuaded, to procure her a cordial reception.

With two American ministers to help her, Betsy felt her cause was far from hopeless. She was further encouraged when, in October, Joseph Bonaparte wrote a warm, brotherly letter to Jerome concerning his return to France.

> I cannot give you advice respecting that journey. It would be excellent, if taking your passage on a man-of-war, you might have a glorious engagement which could enable you to soften the dissatisfaction of those who love you . . . I do not know your resources in the country where you are. Don't forget that everything I have is yours.
>
> Tell Mrs. Jerome from me, that as soon as she has been acknowledged by the head of the family, she will not have a more affectionate brother than me. I have reason to believe, after what I have heard of her, that her character will promote your happiness, and inspire us with esteem and friendship that I will be very much pleased to express to her.

Betsy was elated. "Jerome, we've won Joseph over! You've always said, as the eldest son, he spoke for the family. Doesn't that mean that Napoleon has relented?"

"I wish I thought so, Elise. You'd better read Joseph's cautious letter again. He merely promises to be your affectionate brother, *if and when* you're received by Napoleon. Meanwhile, Joseph tells me to return on a French warship. Can't you see, my dear one, that means without you?"

Betsy saw and sighed. Although Le Camus and Dr. Garnier urged him to do so, Jerome still loyally refused to sail on a French frigate without his wife. For weeks the Bonapartes had been trying to find an American merchant ship to take them both to France. Cargo boats were slow. Napoleon's brother would run a greater risk of being captured by the British on a freighter than on a warship.

> "Interesting and pleasing intelligence is received from a gentleman in France respecting Jerome Bonaparte and his lovely bride," a New York paper reported. "It is confidently reported in the first circles of Paris, that the Emperor has forgiven his brother, and taken the young couple into favor. The circumstance is said to have been aided by a portrait of the lady which had been transmitted to the mother of Bonaparte; and being much celebrated for her beauty, it was sent for by the Empress Josephine."

Le Camus wrote this release and others, and sent them to the newspapers, to pave the way for the Bonapartes' secret departure. To throw off their guard the British cruisers patrolling the coast, Jerome told friends, "Betsy and I intend to remain in America, at least until the war is over."

They went to live at Coldstream, where the Bonapartes had spent their honeymoon. One Thursday night in late October, they were seen in Baltimore at the theater. For several days after that, their absence wasn't noticed. Then a rumor started, "Jerome is off!" It was said that the Bonapartes, with a relative of Betsy's, had left Baltimore on the fast-sailing schooner *Cordelia*. But there had been so many false reports about their previous departures that not even the *Maryland Gazette and Baltimore Daily Advertiser* that published the rumor as a fact, believed its own headlines.

The report was true as far as the departure was concerned, only the Bonapartes sailed from Port Penn on the *Philadelphia* bound for Cadiz, Spain. Cabin space on a merchantman was limited. Jerome's retinue would follow on another ship. With the Bonapartes were but Louis Pichon, ceding his post to a new French minister, Turreau, and, of all people, Nancy Spear.

"Do you think in Cadiz, Betsy, you'll go to a bullfight?" Nancy had hung over her niece as she packed. "They're sickening, but I've always longed to see one. In Spain, there are flowers everywhere, and you can pick oranges right off the trees."

Gracious, she wants to go with us! Betsy was astonished. She had never imagined her aunt as wanting to travel, beyond going each winter to Washington to visit her sister Margaret. But here Nancy Spear was saying, trying not to sound too eager, "Betsy, do you think I'd be in the way if I came along? I wouldn't be a bit of trouble, and I'd be company for you."

"Why, Auntie, we'd love to have you!" Betsy replied, torn between thinking what a nuisance she would be and wanting something exciting to happen to her aunt. Imagine going to a bullfight after years of cheerfully, patiently sharing your sisters' lives!

"Oh, no, I'm too old for such a trip! I'd have to come back on the ship alone." Nancy raised a flock of objections, but her eyes shone. "Besides, Dorcas needs me."

"Rubbish! I won't even miss you, Nancy. You've thought of other people all your life, now have some fun for a change."

"No, Dorcas, I can't." But presently Nancy was saying, "Betsy, do you think my brown wool pelisse will be warm enough on the boat?" And at night she couldn't sleep for thinking of handsome Captain Kennedy, of being captured by the British, or meeting pirates—what if they made her walk the plank?

Nancy trembled whenever she realized that, after all these monotonous years, adventure was coming into her life. But she still hardly believed it on the dark, stormy night when she drove with Betsy and Jerome to Port Penn, on the Delaware, to board the ship. The wind was howling, the rain falling in sheets. They must sail at once, Captain Kennedy said, perhaps they could run out of the gale. He didn't know it, but he was going right into the worst hurricane on the Delaware in anyone's memory.

The *Philadelphia,* overloaded with grain, was no boat for a heavy sea. Two days out of Port Penn, at the entrance to the Atlantic, it was beyond the power of the helmsman, lashed to the wheel, to keep the ship on her course. She began to lurch and roll. Huge waves swept her fore and aft, carrying away one mast, then the other.

With masts and sails gone, the *Philadelphia* became unmanageable. There was nothing to do but ride out the storm, provided her bow could be held into the weather, and the ship withstand the buffeting of the waves that grew more frightful as the hours passed. Each time she rolled over, the water poured in avalanches through the smashed portholes, spilled in torrents down the staircases and ladders into the hold. Nancy Spear, who had already had her fill of adventure, crouched in the water-soaked cabin, praying.

On deck, the Bonapartes, Pichon and the crew were desperately trying to man the pumps. Jerome, seasick as he always was in rough weather, had begged Betsy to remain below with her aunt. But Betsy refused. "I'm not afraid," she replied. Jerome admired his wife's courage more than anything else about her. "My wife, my dear little wife," he said proudly and, taking Betsy in his arms, kissed her before everyone.

The *Philadelphia* withstood six hours of the hurricane. Until afternoon, she managed to face into the wind. The end was just a matter of time now, as her bow swung about, presenting the ship's broadsides to the full impact of the waves.

At the mercy of the sea, the helpless vessel slipped into the trough of the waves that drove her relentlessly toward Cape Henlopen, at the mouth of Delaware Bay. The remaining life of passengers and crew was measured in hours or minutes, unless they abandoned ship.

Only one lifeboat hadn't been swept away. Captain Kennedy, who had fractured an arm, hesitated to launch that frail bark. "It'll be dashed to pieces against the ship's side."

"Come, take a chance!" Betsy cried.

Fired by the girl's courage, the sailors managed to lower the boat into the angry sea. The rough men had disliked having women aboard, but they cheered as the little lady was the first to jump down into the tossing craft. When everyone on board had been crowded into the lifeboat, the sailors rowed toward shore.

At nightfall, the lighthouse keeper of Lewes, at the entrance to the Atlantic, fought his way along the beach in the teeth of the wind. To his amazement, he saw a rowboat loaded with people coming out of the storm. He waited between breakers, then ran into the water to help them land.

That evening, the lighthouse keeper's unexpected guests sat down to a meal of roast goose and applesauce. They laughed and sang, so great was their relief at being alive. Betsy was the merriest of all, though she kept bewailing her lost gowns and jewels.

"Shame on you!" her aunt scolded. "You should be on your knees, young lady, thanking God for saving your life, and all you think about are your clothes."

"Oh, I love my Paris finery, Auntie!" Betsy replied. She refused to return to Baltimore until the *Philadelphia* was washed ashore and her trousseau rescued. The lighthouse keeper's daughter long remembered how the young bride ran back and forth from the house to the yard, anxiously watching her soaked dresses as they dried on the line.

Again the Bonapartes had been prevented from sailing. But on the first of November, when they returned home, Betsy was confronted with a worry that made her forget everything else. Her mother was to have her thirteenth child. Betsy knew it was dangerous for Mama to have a baby so late in life. But to everyone's relief, Dorcas came safely through the ordeal. She gave birth to her twelfth living child.

Now Peggy had a new baby to mother. Betsy, looking at the wrinkled, round face, red from crying, in Dorcas' arms, wished with all her heart that the little girl was hers. And she had always said she loathed squalling, soggy babies!

"What are you going to call her, Mama?" Betsy asked. To her surprise, her mother replied, "Jeromia, for my son-in-law. I've grown very fond of your husband, Betsy."

Jerome was pleased. He needed cheering, for the christening of Mary Ann Jeromia was hardly over before he received news from France that greatly alarmed him.

Bonaparte had sent Ensign Meyronnet abroad to size up the situation. His aide wrote him that an Imperial Court had been created. Joseph and Louis were made princes, and if Napoleon failed to have a son, the crown was to pass to their heirs. They were to receive still higher honors, for Napoleon was preparing thrones for his brothers—Joseph was to be King of Naples and Louis, King of Holland. Nor had Napoleon forgotten other subservient relatives. Elisa, Pauline and Caroline were created princesses. Murat, Caroline's husband, had become an admiral and prince; Eugene Beauharnais, Josephine's son, was raised to the rank of Serene Highness. Only Lucien and Jerome, the brothers who had dared to show some independence, were ignored.

First intimidated when Napoleon stopped his allowance,

now denied all titles and honors, Jerome was humiliated. Betsy had never seen him so upset. Not even to be a prince!

Strangely enough, it was Betsy who remained optimistic. "It's an outrage, Jerome. But if that's going to be Napoleon's policy, to place his brothers on the thrones of the countries he conquers, he'll give you a crown in time." Her eyes shone with excitement. "You'll make a splendid king, dear," Betsy said. That is, with me to guide him, was in the back of her mind.

"And you'll make a beautiful queen, Elise."

Like two children, they excitedly discussed what kingdom Napoleon might offer them. Jerome preferred warm countries. "If the Emperor makes us King and Queen of Egypt, will that please you, Elise?"

Not discouraged by shipwreck or bad news from France, the Bonapartes continued their efforts to sail, although Betsy's father urged his son-in-law to do as Lucien advised, remain in America.

"Napoleon's still popular, but with English gold stirring up trouble, the Bourbons may well get back. Then you'd be safe here and could make a home for your family in exile. That may have been in Lucien's mind when he suggested you stay in the United States. I'd be glad to take you into our business, Jerome. With your West Indian experience, you'd be useful to me."

"No, Papa, I must return to France. I've heard no more about my family settling money on me, if I remained in America. That was only some wild talk of Lucien's, while Joseph, who speaks for Napoleon, has told me to come home."

The truth was, Napoleon, by stopping Jerome's allowance, had found the surest way to bring the prodigal back. As his money dwindled, the free-spending young man, too decent to be willing to live off his rich father-in-law, grew as anxious as Betsy to get to France. Jerome was hurt at being shut out of the honors his brothers were receiving—fearful, too, of what might happen to him. If Napoleon banished Lucien, the brother who had helped him to power, what would he do to him, who had done nothing for the glory of the family?

Betsy watched her husband anxiously. She noted a new restlessness in Jerome. He no longer reproved Le Camus when Alexander urged him to sail alone. Would Jerome return home without her? That fear was constantly in Betsy's mind. "If I could only have a child," she wept.

There came another chance for the Bonapartes to sail when they heard that the 44-gun French frigate, *Le President*, was at Annapolis. Jerome, using the charm of which he had an abundance, persuaded the captain to disregard Napoleon's orders and take Mme. Bonaparte aboard. They sailed on November 24, 1804, down the Chesapeake. But the 44-gun British frigate, *Revolutionnaire*, was waiting at Hampton Roads. The French commander refused to pit his 44 French guns against the 44 English guns, so, on December 5th, Betsy and Jerome were back in Washington.

That same month, Robert wrote his father from Paris about purchasing land in Florida on speculation. Now it could be bought at four cents an acre. They must buy before Florida was ceded by Spain to the United States or America took it by force. He mentioned that the *Cycle* and the *Didon* had reached France safely.

His brother (Napoleon) is extremely angry at his (Jerome) not coming with them. After speaking the other day of him in very harsh terms, he observed that, as to his marriage, he could view it in no other light than a *camp one*, the laws of France acknowledging no contract of this nature valid when entered into by a person under 25 years of age.

Jerome read Robert's letter with anger. What did Napoleon think Betsy was, an adventuress? The temporary sweetheart of a young man on his travels? Who in the Bonaparte family could compare with her in beauty, in intellect, or in birth? Even Josephine. Julie, Joseph's wife, was the homely daughter of a soap boiler. Lucien's first wife Christine, a tavern waitress so ignorant she couldn't read or write; Murat, the son of an innkeeper. Yet Napoleon had accepted them in the family. Since then, success had turned his head.

Jerome liked to watch his wife while she dressed for a ball. He considered himself to be an authority on ladies' fashions. He selected Betsy's jewels; he fastened the flowers in her hair; he made her parade in front of him, while he complimented her on her gowns. Betsy's manners were exquisite. It amused him to see how his bride of nineteen had assumed the airs of a *grande dame*.

One evening the Bonapartes were in Washington, going to a ball at the French legation. Jerome, in a military cape, wearing his sword and carrying under his arm a plumed hat, came into his wife's room. He found Betsy in a chiffon negligee, reclining on the pillows of her couch.

"Elise, you're not dressed, are you ill?" he asked in alarm. Betsy wasn't like most women, she never kept him waiting.

"I'm just not going tonight. I don't think I should dance any more—" She smiled happily, the words came with a rush. "Darling, I'm going to have a baby."

Jerome's face lighted up with joy and love as he dropped to his knees beside the sofa and took his wife tenderly in his arms. "I didn't want to tell you until I was sure," Betsy

whispered. And they talked for hours of the wonderful thing
that had happened to her. Betsy had never seen her husband
so happy. How badly, all along, he must have wanted a
baby!

"We'll call him Napoleon," Jerome said. "That's sure to
please him."

"Suppose it's a girl?"

"Elise, don't mention such a calamity!"

Betsy knew the family situation. To keep in power, Napoleon needed an heir, yet he was married to a middle-aged
woman with grown up children, not likely to have another
child. Joseph had only daughters. Lucien's son was illegitimate. Napoleon was fond of Louis' and Hortense's son,
whom he called his heir. But Napoleon had dearly loved
Jerome as a boy. He might prefer his son to Louis' boy. If
they could give Napoleon the heir he wanted so badly, surely
he would forgive them.

Their son would be a link to the throne. Jerome was more
eager than ever to get to France. Their cause would be
strengthened if Betsy's baby, due in July, was born on French
soil.

"Elise, can you stand a rough ocean voyage?" he asked anxiously, remembering the shipwreck. "Nothing must happen
to you."

"Of course I can. I never felt better. A sea trip will do
me good." She loved Jerome for his tender solicitude. Was
there ever a sweeter husband!

They returned to Baltimore in February, 1805, shortly before a letter came that Robert had written in Paris on the
16th. He had heard rumors as he was about to mail off a
business report to his father and opened his letter to add two
paragraphs.

"They're in cipher," William warned the assembled Patterson family. "Why, Robert is afraid to sign his letter! It looks like bad news."

"Well, let's hear it." Betsy went to a drawer in her father's desk to fetch the key to the cipher Robert had said he would use, if he had secret information. The paper Robert left with his family read: *A n, B r, C p, D b, E o, F s, G c, H u, I d, J c, K x, L a, M f, N k, O i, P w, Q j, R e, S y, T g, U h, V m, W z, X t, Y 1, Z q.*

"A stands for N, B for R, and so on," Betsy explained to Joseph and Edward, excitedly looking over her shoulder. Using the cipher, she read the letter to them:

> *T. L b v f x b e a t* (General Armstrong) informs me he saw a person yesterday who mentioned to him that *x u r R v c-b* (the Emperor) says it is his determination to *x u b e p Q-r o a-x e c b o f e a* (throw Jerome into prison) the moment of his arrival, where he will remain till he *b r c h i o l x r i* (repudiates) his *p o m r* (wife) and *v l b b o r i* (marries) another which he designates.
>
> The gentleman thinks from the decided manner in which Napoleon spoke he will certainly put his threats into execution. *L.* (General Armstrong) and myself are now of the opinion *Q.* (Jerome) will only be safe by remaining where he is. Be on your guard when you receive advices different from other quarters.

"Repudiates his wife . . . marries another . . ." Betsy dropped Robert's letter with a cry. She staggered back against Jerome, who, with his arm protectively about her, faced her father. "Why did you show Elise that letter, Papa? I knew of my brother's threats. Mama wrote me about them, weeks ago."

"She did? I didn't know you'd heard from your mother, Jerome. Why didn't you tell me?"

"I didn't want to upset you, Elise. Mama warned me that

the Emperor had sent orders to every French port to have me arrested, if we came to France together."

"Robert says Napoleon wants you to marry—" There was a dull hurt inside Betsy, as if a hand were squeezing her heart. Relief and joy swept through her when Jerome shrugged, "Just threats! My brother likes to shout at people and intimidate them. But he can't frighten me!"

The Patterson family looked at Bonaparte with new respect. Betsy smiled at him proudly. Jerome loved her. It would take more than the all-powerful Napoleon to separate them.

"Papa, you'll have to send us abroad on one of your ships," Betsy said, not for the first time.

He had always refused heretofore. His merchantmen, William said, weren't fast enough to outsail a British cruiser. The English were boasting they'd never let that rich prize, Napoleon's brother, slip through their fingers. But it so happened that Mr. Patterson had chartered a speedy clipper he was sending on a trading trip to Europe and the East Indies.

"I'd take a chance on the *Erin*," he replied. "I believe she's fast enough to run away from the swiftest brig in the English navy."

In the greatest secrecy, for fear the British warships blocking the coast would get wind of it, the three-masted *Erin* was made ready for the voyage. A cow was put aboard to give the passengers fresh milk; live chickens, pigs and sheep to provide fresh meat. At dawn on Sunday, March 10, 1805, Betsy and Jerome went down to the Patterson wharf at the foot of Gay Street to board the ship, bound for Lisbon. With them were Betsy's brother William; Mrs. Eliza Anderson, a family friend; Bonaparte's staff and servants. But not Jocco. Betsy had persuaded Jerome to give the monkey to George, who loved pets. Nor was Aunt Spear along.

"Nothing would induce me to go to sea again," Nancy said. "One shipwreck is enough."

Jerome wept on saying good-bye. Dorcas had been like a mother to him. She had given him the first real home he'd known since a child in Corsica.

"Children! Come kiss me . . ." Betsy embraced them: stolid Joseph, gay Edward, quiet George; Peggy, fat and freckled; frail Henry; Caroline, a reserved child; and chubby Octavius. "When I see you again, you'll have grown so I won't know you," she told her brothers and sisters.

Magnolia rushed up. "Good-bye, honey, rub dis wishin' bag when ye wants a wish to come true . . ." She pressed a little bag into Betsy's hand in which were thirteen pennies, nine cotton seeds and the hair of a black hog. Betsy laughed and hugged her. How she wished the flighty Magnolia were going along as a companion instead of sour, efficient Mrs. Anderson!

Betsy's flower-painted trunk was hoisted aboard. Her father spoke gruffly, "Cut short the good-byes, time to go." Betsy kissed her parents. How many years would pass before she saw them again? She clung to her weeping mother. "Don't cry," she begged her family. "I'm going to a wonderful new life. I'm going to be very happy."

The boat started off. Betsy and Jerome stood by the rail, waving to the receding shore as Baltimore faded from sight.

Though the *Erin* sailed at dawn, and arrangements for their departure had been made in the greatest secrecy, as the ship moved out into Chesapeake Bay, eyes were watching. The next day, a fast British sloop sailed from New York, ostensibly bound for Bermuda, but really to capture Jerome. The English vowed that Napoleon's brother, who had eluded them at Martinique, should not escape them a second time.

In Paris, on March 9, 1805, Robert sat down to write his father a note in cipher so dangerous he dared not sign it:

D—s e h t u x as ae vrlap xe geve M—r. Om fur pe hyi de mebxh alvx v a eays drot frax dlgn. Brcebx flsf xulx Y—. p lf lbbr fxri lxvoyla laiur of aip geamoar i v a xurvueyr xurbr.

Greatly worried, Mr. Patterson, using the key, translated the code to read, "Betsy ought by no means to come to France. I think she would be fortunate in only being sent back. Report says that Lucien was arrested at Milan."

Robert's warning came too late. His letter passed Betsy in mid-ocean.

8. The Prodigal's Return

THE *Erin*, slim and built for speed, like all Baltimore clippers, was a roller, and roll she did, as she ploughed through the March seas. But the American merchantman slipped through the British blockade, Jerome escaped capture; and when, on April 2, 1805, after twenty-one days of rocking like a cork, the ship cast anchor in the Tagus, below Lisbon, Bonaparte informed his father-in-law that the worst enemy they had encountered during an uneventful crossing was seasickness.

Betsy, Jerome and Mrs. Anderson hardly left their berths during the entire voyage. "But you know as well as anybody," Bonaparte wrote in his imperfect English, "that seasick never has killed nobody."

As soon as the *Erin* anchored, French gunboats surrounded her. Napoleon's consul at Lisbon, Serrurier, came aboard. Heels clicked as he bowed head to knees before the Emperor's brother. Then, with a glance at the lady, the consul asked, less respectfully, "And your traveling companion, Lieutenant? What can I do for *Miss Patterson?*"

Betsy, scarlet at the insult, replied with spirit, "You can tell Napoleon for me that *Mme. Bonaparte* is ambitious and demands her rights as a member of the Imperial family."

Serrurier shrugged. He was sorry, he said, but Napoleon had sent orders that Lieutenant Bonaparte's "traveling companion" was not to land, but to be sent back to America, while Jerome was to go alone to Milan, where the Emperor was, by way of Perpignan, Toulouse, Grenoble and Turin. If he went elsewhere, he would be arrested.

Betsy, who had counted upon charming even Napoleon, realized he wasn't going to run the risk of seeing her. She burst into tears. Serrurier, a susceptible Frenchman, wrung his hands. He declared himself ready to do anything he could for the pretty lady, except what Madame wanted, issue her a passport.

Jerome pleaded that his wife was six months pregnant, she must be allowed off the ship for fresh food and exercise. The consul grudgingly agreed that "Miss Patterson" might enter Portugal for a few days, provided her visit was kept secret. So *incognito,* as Monsieur and Madame d'Albert, Betsy and Jerome landed at Lisbon and took lodgings in St. Paulle Street, near the river front.

They went shopping; they did some sightseeing; they took walks in the evening. The Spanish ambassador, the Pope's nuncio and others of the diplomatic corps friendly to France came to call. Their visitors all told Jerome the same thing— it would be folly for him to provoke Napoleon further. He had better report to Milan alone and try to make peace with his brother, or he would be arrested. Napoleon had written his mother:

> I shall treat this young man severely, if in the only inter-
> view I shall grant him, he shows himself unworthy of the
> name he bears, and persists in wishing to continue his in-

trigue. If he is not prepared to wash out the dishonor he has brought on my name by abandoning his country's flag on sea and land for the sake of a wretched woman, I shall cast him off forever.

Serrurier made it plain that neither as Mme. Bonaparte nor as Miss Patterson would he dare to issue Betsy a passport. Since the prohibition against entering France did not extend to her husband, however, their only hope of being forgiven and having Napoleon acknowledge their baby seemed to be for Jerome to go alone to Milan and have a heart-to-heart talk with his brother.

Meanwhile, William Patterson urged his sister to await her husband in Holland. At a family conference, the night before the *Erin* left Baltimore, their father had said, "I think it would be more dignified for Betsy to go to Amsterdam, where her brother Robert is, and our firm has business connections, and remain there until Jerome arranges with the Bonaparte family to receive his wife. If they refuse, Betsy, you're to return to America immediately. Do you hear me?"

So the young Bonapartes made plans for a reunion in Holland in June; and on April 9th, Jerome set out for Italy, taking Le Camus with him. His physician, Dr. Garnier, he left to look after his pregnant wife, also a topaz necklace Jerome had bought in Lisbon to console Betsy during his absence.

At the moment of parting, the lovers clung together. Jerome would be away only two months, but it was the first time they had been separated since their marriage. Two months is an eternity at twenty. Betsy's tears wet his cheek.

"Come, come, my Elise, you must dry those tears and be brave." Her young husband kissed them away. "I shall rejoin you in Amsterdam, and be with you in July, when our child is born. Why are you crying? You've nothing to fear.

I love you, I will always love you. I promise you, nothing Napoleon can say will persuade me to give you up."

Jerome's voice rang with sincerity. He was so sure of being able to overcome his brother's objections to their marriage and of joining Betsy in Holland by June 1st, or the 15th at the latest, that when he rode away, she waved good-bye to him with a smile and a dry handkerchief.

A week later, the *Erin,* all sails set, left for Holland. The sail north was slow. Bucking the wind all the way up the French coast, the ship took twenty-six days to reach the mouth of the Zuider Zee. On their arrival there, May 10th, Betsy's troubles were not over. Warnings against her had been posted in Amsterdam three weeks earlier. Holland, under the Batavian Republic, was practically French territory. Napoleon had sent orders forbidding Mme. Jerome Bonaparte, "or any person assuming that name," from landing in Amsterdam or at any Dutch port.

When the *Erin* reached Helder, where ships stopped in the Texel Roads to take on pilots for Amsterdam, orders came from R. J. Schimmelpenninck, Napoleon's agent, forbidding Captain Stephenson to approach the shore or anyone to go aboard his vessel. The unarmed American merchantman lay at anchor, guarded by two French warships, for eight days.

Fresh food aboard the *Erin* was exhausted, the ship having been two months out of Baltimore without taking on provisions. Salt beef and tough ship's biscuits were hardly the best diet for Betsy in her condition. William managed to get a protest ashore to Sylvanus Bourne, the American consul at Amsterdam, who in turn appealed to Schimmelpenninck to be allowed to supply the ship with provisions. He asked that, if Mme. Bonaparte wasn't to be permitted to enter Holland, she be allowed to go and find refuge elsewhere.

Food and wine was sent aboard the *Erin.* But with it came

a curt order for Captain Stephenson to leave the Texel. Not on any excuse was he to return to Amsterdam or try to enter any other port of the Batavian Republic.

Betsy heard the sentence in despair. "But I can't leave Europe—" She mastered a sob. "It's important. My baby must be born on French soil."

That was now impossible. Nor could Mme. Bonaparte face another voyage across the Atlantic, with her child due in two months. Dr. Garnier feared that seasickness might bring on a miscarriage. He insisted that Betsy get ashore at once. William argued that the nearest haven was England, where the Patterson firm had influential business agents, and James Monroe, the American minister, was his father's friend.

No obstacle was put in the way of Mme. Bonaparte's landing in England. Lord Hawksbury, the Home Secretary, was not only willing that the American clipper should dock at Dover, he was delighted. To have the sister-in-law of Britain's arch enemy, Napoleon, seek refuge in England was ironic. A London paper, the *Morning Chronicle* of May 20, 1805, recorded the event with glee:

> It was reported yesterday that Mrs. Jerome Bonaparte had arrived in the Downs, and had applied to Lord Hawksbury for passports to land, she having been refused leave to land in Holland. Passports were immediately sent down to Deal to permit her to come ashore.

The twenty-year-old girl had become a celebrity. When the Baltimore clipper docked, the inhabitants of Dover flocked to the pier to see her land. Napoleon's army was poised across the Channel at Boulogne for an invasion of Britain, every able-bodied Englishman drilling to resist the French, but Pitt, England's prime minister, with more urgent matters on his mind, had to send soldiers to Dover to hold back the sympathetic crowds that nearly mobbed the pretty American whom that ogre Bony had treated so badly. With William beside her, Betsy drove through the streets, bowing right and left with regal dignity, as though a crown was already on her lovely head.

Her drooping spirits soared at finding herself famous. Betsy's heart went out to England. James Monroe and his family were eager to introduce her to London society. But with her baby nearly due, all the poor girl asked for at present was peace and quiet. In June, Betsy prevailed upon the Monroes to find her lodgings outside of London.

In a house in Park Lane, at Camberwell, part of teeming London today, but then a quiet Surrey village two miles from town, Dr. Garnier delivered Betsy of a son on July 7, 1805. As Mrs. Anderson and Charles Aveline, a male midwife, hovered over her through a difficult birth, Betsy's one thought was, if one of us has to die, let him live. Him? The baby mustn't be a girl.

Eliza Anderson placed a squalling bundle in her arms. The young mother stared down at it drowsily. "Is it a boy?" she asked anxiously.

"A fine, healthy boy," Mrs. Anderson assured her. "Why didn't anyone think to tell you?"

Happiness flooded Betsy's heart. She closed her eyes for a moment of triumph. She had scored a point against the Bonaparte family, produced a son. If Napoleon once held this baby in his arms, he might make Jerome's son his heir. Her child would inherit the throne of France.

A pink hand pushed out of the blanket. Betsy kissed the tiny fingers.

"Jerome wants his son named for Napoleon," Betsy replied, when William asked her what was she going to call his nephew. But before Napoleon's name, Betsy put the name of the man she loved with her whole heart, and from whom she thought she was only parted for a short time.

"My little Jerome Napoleon Bonaparte," she murmured and, gazing down lovingly at the rosy, round face, drew the baby closer.

On their way to Italy, Lieutenant Bonaparte and Alexander Le Camus stopped one day at an inn near Truxillo, Spain. There Jerome met the Andoche Junots, going to Lisbon, where General Junot was to take up his duties as French ambassador.

Laure Junot was pleased to see Jerome again. Panoria Permon, her mother, had befriended the Bonaparte family in their days of poverty, when they first arrived in France. Mme. Junot had known Jerome as a child in Corsica. She tells in her *Memoires* how, when the Junots lunched with the two young men, she was pleased to find how much the irresponsible Jerome had improved. He was sedate, almost serious, as he opened his anxious heart to them.

He had just heard that, the previous February, Napoleon had obtained his mother's signature to a formal protest against her son Jerome's "pretended marriage," performed in America without her consent. Jerome being a minor, that made his marriage illegal according to French law. Nor did a marriage in France become legal until it was registered, and Napoleon had issued an order forbidding every notary in France to register Jerome's marriage. Therefore, Napoleon declared, the marriage had never occurred, and any child born of the union was illegitimate.

"I'm Mama's favorite, next to Napoleon. I can't believe she signed that paper published in her name," Jerome said, in a hurt tone. "In her letters, Mama seemed pleased with my marriage. So did Joseph. Legally, it's their consent I need, not that of Napoleon, the second son."

The Junots were impressed by Jerome's sincerity. He was obviously deeply in love with his American bride. But they knew better than he how angry Napoleon was. After lunch, in the garden, the General gave the young man some fatherly advice, to be sensible and not to oppose the Emperor's wishes.

"Sir, would you have me dishonor my given word?" Jerome asked indignantly. "I'm sure Napoleon will withdraw his objections when he has listened to me. He has always been kind and just. Perhaps I did wrong in marrying without his consent, but any punishment will only hurt my poor, innocent wife. Surely, Napoleon doesn't want to insult the daughter of one of America's most distinguished citizens!"

Jerome proudly showed the Junots Betsy's lovely face framed in a miniature he wore on his breast. They were struck by her resemblance to his sister Pauline.

"Do you imagine I could desert such a girl?" he asked, tenderly replacing his wife's portrait next to his heart. "I only wish my brother would consent to see Betsy, for but a moment. I'm certain she'd win him over."

The sentimental Laure was thrilled to hear Jerome declare, "I've made up my mind, nothing Napoleon can say will induce me to give Elise up!" Her husband tried to influence the young man no further. Bonaparte's visit to America seemed to have made a man of him, Junot thought. Let him stick by his wife, then, and take the consequences. The General only hoped that, under the tongue-lashing his brother would give him, Jerome would show some of Lucien's firmness.

Bonaparte's blithe assurance that he could calm Napoleon's wrath and rejoin his wife by June remained with him while he and Le Camus hurried across Spain and France to Italy. As the baby of the family, Jerome's mother had spoiled him. Even Napoleon had always been to him like an indulgent father. Jerome did not think his brother's anger would last long. He had transgressed so many times before, only to be forgiven, thanks to his mother's pleas, that Jerome was sure his disgrace would only be temporary. Napoleon would give in again. He wrote Betsy that she mustn't worry about the future, but have confidence in her husband. ". . . the worst that can happen to us, is that we may have to go to some foreign country and live simply. But as long as we're together, aren't we sure to be happy?"

Eager to be back in Betsy's arms, Bonaparte rode to Italy at a gallop. The two young men reached Turin on April 24, and Jerome wrote to the Emperor, who was at Alessandria, near Milan, asking for an interview. Indulgence has its limits, as he was soon to learn. Lucien had disobeyed Napoleon, now Jerome. This time, the Emperor was thoroughly angry. He refused to see Jerome, until the prodigal declared himself repentant.

Eleven days were passed by an unhappy young man in a quandary. Should he rejoin Betsy in Holland and submit to whatever disgrace the Emperor chose to inflict upon him? Or to gain his ends, wouldn't it be wiser to pretend to yield, and in that way get a chance to talk with his brother? So Jerome went to Alessandria and, on May 6, wrote to Napoleon again, a more humble letter, begging for forgiveness. The Emperor replied the same day.

> My brother, there are no faults you have committed which may not be effaced in my eyes by a sincere repentance. Your marriage is null and void, both from a religious and a legal point of view. I will never acknowledge it. Write Miss Patterson to go back to the United States. I will give her a

pension of 60,000 francs a year, on condition that she return to America, and does not take the name of my family to which she has no right, her marriage having no existence. Your marriage being thus annulled, I will . . . resume the feeling which I have had toward you since childhood, hoping that you will show yourself worthy . . . by your anxiety . . . to distinguish yourself in my armies.

The Emperor was leaving on an inspection trip. But with his letter came a summons for Jerome to come to his headquarters on a day in mid-June. Jerome having sufficiently bent the knee, Napoleon would see him when he returned.

9. *He Loves Me; He Loves Me Not*

In MILAN, before the Empress Josephine and the Imperial Court, Napoleon was crowned King of Italy, May 5, 1805. On a June day, six weeks later, as the clock struck nine in his headquarters at Alessandria, the Emperor, wearing a plain gray uniform and the Legion of Honor, strode into the room where he held his morning receptions. His secretary, Baron Meneval, was glancing through the mail. A buzz of voices came from the antechamber beyond, crowded with people waiting to ask some favor of Napoleon.

"Lieutenant Jerome Bonaparte," Meneval announced.

The Emperor was standing like a statue by his desk when his brother entered the room. Three years had passed since Jerome had seen Napoleon. He was stouter and he looked tired. Jerome stepped forward to embrace him, but the Emperor's face, as expressionless as a mask, stopped him. After an exchange of salutes, Napoleon looked straight at Jerome, his cold, hard eyes boring into him.

"So, sir," he said severely, "you're the first of our family to shamefully desert his post. It will take many splendid actions to wipe that stain from your reputation. As to your love affair with your little girl, let's forget it!"

The blood rushed to Jerome's face. To have Napoleon dismiss his marriage so lightly was insulting! Jerome falteringly tried to plead his cause and, as he did so, he felt himself shrinking. Why did his elder brother always have this belittling effect on him? His union with Betsy was no sordid intrigue, no passing fancy, but true love, he declared. The Patterson family was one of the best in America. His marriage was legal, according to French law, both civil and religious. It had been performed by the leading Catholic bishop of Baltimore; and following French custom, he had obtained the consent of his mother and eldest brother, if somewhat after the event—

Napoleon silenced his brother with a black look. "You, young hothead, you've made a fool of yourself with your mad infatuation!" He strode about the room, beside himself with anger. "Send that girl you've been living with back to America!"

Jerome lifted his clenched fist, then let his hand fall. Even had he dared to strike his brother, you couldn't hit the Emperor. He tried stammeringly to speak. Napoleon must listen. It meant his life, his happiness. "My wife's in Holland, expecting our child in July. I couldn't desert her. You can't try to part us. You've no reason, no right—!" His voice rose hysterically.

That his bumptious young brother should dare defy him, the master of Europe! Napoleon glanced frowning at the closed door to the anteroom. "Silence! Do you want the whole palace to hear us quarrel?"

"Let them!" Jerome shouted. Let the whole world hear him! He asked nothing shameful, merely the right to keep his wife and child. Had Betsy been with Jerome to encourage his resistance, the sight of her beauty might have melted Napoleon, her tears touched his heart. But Jerome stood alone, facing the man, who, in spite of his affection for his youngest brother, had always bullied him.

"Your wife? Bah! That girl's no more than your mistress. Your American marriage, as far as I'm concerned, never took place. And if I won't recognize it," thundered the French dictator, "no law in France can make it legal, for I am the law."

Rounding on Jerome, Napoleon hurled at him a broadside of stinging accusations. He reminded his brother of the many follies he had committed: he was a deserter from the navy; there were the sums, running into the thousands, Jerome had drawn without any authority on the French officials in every port he had visited; to cap the list of his crimes was his unfortunate marriage, without notifying his family.

"We learned of it first from a Paris newspaper," the Emperor flung at his brother bitterly. To a Corsican, such a marriage broke the ancient clan law. It was an offense Napoleon refused to forgive.

Jerome listened in mounting anger to his brother's harsh words. "Did you ask Mama's permission, when you married? Or Joseph's? Or indicate that your affairs were any business of ours—" he blurted out. But the Emperor stopped his pacing up and down, his hand thrust into his coat, to silence his young brother with an ugly scowl. Napoleon would not stand any criticism of his acts. He ignored Jerome's remark.

"Lucien's disgrace should be a warning to you. Do you want to be like your brother, living in exile, cut off from the honors I can give my family, because of some wretched woman? Do you think Lucien is happy? Or his wife either?"

"Lucien may be happier than your Majesty thinks," Jerome replied through gritted teeth. "He has no honors, but he has his wife."

"So you prefer your little girl to a career and riches? If I cast you off, where do you intend to meet her? In Holland, you said?" Napoleon, with a harsh laugh, played his ace. "What would you say if I told you that Miss Patterson isn't in Holland? Or at any port where you could join her. But in *England*."

That broke him. Jerome turned pale. Napoleon smiled for the first time, enjoying his brother's consternation. Not a word about the orders he had sent to Holland, forbidding poor Betsy to land. Instead Napoleon said, "My agent in Holland has informed me the *Erin* arrived in Amsterdam on May 10, then for some reason went on to Dover. By now Miss Patterson is in England. She has put herself under the protection of our enemies, who naturally are delighted to welcome her."

Jerome remained stunned. Why hadn't Betsy gone to Bremen? Or some other neutral port? Why had she been foolish enough to place herself beyond his reach, on enemy soil? Step foot in England, he would be captured, Betsy knew that. The English were saying how they'd like nothing better than to parade Napoleon's brother in chains through the streets of London.

"Miss Patterson is sensible enough to realize that you two must part," Jerome, with the blood hammering in his temples, heard the Emperor say. "From England, she no doubt will return to America. Don't worry about her, Jerome. I'll take care of your little girl financially, quickly make her forget her troubles."

Napoleon, pacing the room his hands behind his back, had been watching his brother's face. He saw Jerome was losing courage. No more threats. It was time to try another approach. Coming over to him, he placed his hand on his shoulder affectionately.

"I'm sorry I lost my temper. Let's talk this matter over calmly. You deserted your ship, Lieutenant. I ought to have you court-martialed. Instead, I'll give you another chance, provided you don't disobey me again. Don't be a fool and ruin your life for a girl whose beauty will fade. I've great plans for you, Jerome. When the interests of the world are at stake, one must learn to make sacrifices, as I am doing. Look at Josephine. We've lived together for years. I love her, but I'm thinking of divorcing my wife and marrying a younger woman who can give me an heir. I owe it to France. I think only of the happiness of my people."

"Your case doesn't apply to me, Sire. I've no dynasty to found."

"But you're part of my policy. Don't imperil my future plans. We five Bonaparte brothers must stand together. Each one needs the other. And I need you, Jerome."

Napoleon reminded his brother how, rising in the world, he had carried his family up with him. This, of course, was only what he should have done. One's first duty was to one's clan. But it was also the duty of each one of the family to bow before the authority in power. In return for what he had done for them, Napoleon expected his brothers' help. They must not let private emotions interfere, but think only of making useful alliances for him.

"I cannot understand anyone letting family ties or personal inclinations come before your love for your country," the Emperor said. "Together, we Bonapartes can do great things for France—" He began to speak of his troubles. He had an army poised on the cliffs of Boulogne, ready to invade England. But Napoleon dared not move, for fear that Prussia, Austria and Russia would attack him from the rear. He

mı st first surround France with a protective ring of satellite
nations. "That's where you, Joseph and Louis can help me
make France the most powerful country in the world.
Lucien, too, if he divorces his wife. I intend to place Joseph
on the throne of Italy, and you—"

Striding over to a map stuck full of red pins hanging on
the wall, the Emperor pointed out the large sections of
Europe he had conquered.

"Do you want a throne? I'll give you one, Jerome, and
everything else your heart desires, once you get rid of that
American girl. But if you prefer her to the great projects I
have in mind, then you're no longer my brother. Go back
to America. I never want to hear your name mentioned
again. But you'll be sensible, won't you, my dear fellow?
Now get out of here, get back to the navy and try to clear
your reputation—" Napoleon began to threaten again.
"Show up at our Genoa naval base in two days, or I'll have
you arrested for desertion and thrown into jail!"

Jerome always shrank from contention. Telling himself
that he surrendered for the moment only, with the firm determination to conquer in the end, he went to Genoa, bitter
and sullen. But he went. Napoleon had brought his unruly
young brother to heel and taught him his place. That was
to obey.

When the door slammed behind Jerome, Napoleon, fling-
ing himself in a chair, mopped his brow. To win his brother
over, he had threatened; he had appealed to Jerome's sense
of clan loyalty and to his patriotism; he had tempted him
with honors—and convinced the obstinate fellow, he hoped.

"Well, that's over, Meneval." The Emperor sighed. "I
don't think I'll have any more trouble with Jerome. He
isn't another Lucien. If he's a good boy, I'll be generous with
him. Pay his debts; see he's given an allowance of 150,000

francs a year and a naval command. Now take a letter to the Pope—"

Napoleon began to dictate to his secretary a letter to His Holiness in regard to an event that in June, 1805, was the talk of Europe—a balloon sent up in Paris had reached Rome! Napoleon advised the Pope to preserve it, so that future generations might marvel at this first achievement in aerial navigation. In closing, he referred casually to Jerome's marriage. He asked Pius VII for a bull to annul it. The Emperor explained that his brother, a minor, had married a Protestant young woman in the United States; "an ignorant Spanish priest" had been so lax as to perform the ceremony. He could easily have it annulled in Paris, but, for appearances sake, he preferred to have it done in Rome.

With Napoleon's letter went a jeweled crown that his uncle, Cardinal Fesch, was sent to Rome to present, by way of inducement, to the Pope. But William Patterson had forestalled him. Betsy could thank her shrewd father, who had not only seen to it that her marriage was binding in the sight of the Church, but had the Reverend John Carroll write a detailed account of the ceremony to His Holiness.

So when the Pontiff, unmoved by costly gifts, replied, he stated that the Catholic Church held the marriage tie inviolate. He could not find any reason for annulling a marriage performed with all the formalities required according to Catholic laws by the Archbishop of Baltimore, the leading Catholic churchman in America—certainly, no "ignorant Spanish priest." As for the Protestant bride, the Church, while disapproving of mixed marriages, considered them legal.

Napoleon, who had expected a favorable answer, was furious, especially as he wanted a divorce himself. He threatened to demote the Holy Father to Bishop of Rome for his defiance and never forgave him. Their quarrel over an American girl had far-reaching effects. It culminated in the confiscation of the Papal States, the imprisonment of Pope Pius VII at Fontainebleau and the ex-communication of Napoleon.

The frown from the Vatican failed to discourage the Emperor in his determination to repair the mischief Jerome had done in America, however. In order to destroy any possible ground for future claims by Jerome's son, Napoleon wanted an annulment of the marriage. He turned to the ecclesiastical court in his own archdiocese of Paris, more pliable than the Pope.

Someone besides the Emperor was thinking of the future of a boy who might one day sit on the throne of France. All the ceremonies attending the birth of a royal prince were observed in Camberwell, England. When Jerome Napoleon Bonaparte was two weeks old, Betsy had the certificate of his birth signed by the doctor, nurses and servants present. Then their signatures were certified as genuine by the Prussian and Austrian ambassadors at London and registered by a notary. This practice harks back to the days when a royal birth had to have enough witnesses so that a foundling wouldn't be introduced at the last moment.

The battle of wills was on. Napoleon was out to prove that Elizabeth Patterson was but Jerome's mistress, her son illegitimate, while the plucky American girl was equally set on establishing her claim to being Jerome's lawful wife and the mother of his legitimate child, who would some day demand the rights of an Imperial prince.

Bo—short for Bonaparte—as they called the baby, was a "fine large fellow." Robert, who had come from Holland to stay with Betsy, William having returned to America, wrote his father July 27:

> I have now the pleasure to inform you that my sister is well recovered from her confinement. She has been downstairs two days. The child was vaccinated five days since, and is doing well. We are still without any news from the Continent. The vigilance of Jerome's friends will, I am afraid, completely prevent his hearing from us and we from him.

Jerome was in Genoa, promoted to the rank of captain and in command of a squadron, but surrounded by Napoleon's spies and, they suspected, virtually a prisoner. Betsy had written to him three times in care of Lucien and had no reply. She doubted that Jerome received her letters.

In Amsterdam, Robert had seen Alexander Le Camus, sent by Jerome to Holland to tell him of Napoleon's offer to pension Betsy off with an income of $12,000 a year, provided she returned to America and dropped the name of Bonaparte. But Jerome also sent a message by Le Camus, assuring his wife he would be true to her. Things weren't as hopeless as they seemed. He was certain that, before long, the Emperor would acknowledge their marriage, and he and Betsy would be allowed to live happily together. Meanwhile, she must be patient.

"Mr. Patterson, Captain Bonaparte wishes to know why your sister didn't go to Bremen, where he could join her?" Le Camus asked. "Any other place than England would have been all right. But that she should choose the country that was fighting his brother hurt Jerome to the quick. A member of the hated Bonaparte family, he cannot enter England or even write to his wife there, without his letters being seized. And her being with the enemy has further irritated the Emperor."

From Genoa, Jerome had made another appeal to Napoleon, Le Camus said. The Emperor replied that nothing his brother could say or do would make him reconsider his decision and had ended a cold note by saying, "Miss Patterson has been in London, and caused great excitement among the English, which only increases her guilt."

Betsy was indignant. Why should she have gone to Bremen? The Pattersons had no business agent there. She couldn't even speak German. As for flaunting herself among the English, much as she longed for the gaiety of London, for fear of hurting her chances with Napoleon, Betsy had hardly left quiet little Camberwell.

The pension Napoleon offered her, she knew to be a bribe for her to leave Europe. Betsy intended to ignore it. She was determined to remain abroad, at least until spring, even after she received a letter from Dr. Garnier, who had gone to Genoa, saying that Jerome wished her to return to America. Due to the war, her husband would be on duty with the fleet for at least a year. He strongly objected to her waiting for him in England.

Return to America? Betsy shrank from the thought. She had left home in a blaze of glory, for a glamorous life at Napoleon's Court. She wasn't going back to Baltimore as a disappointed, deserted woman.

"This is only that villain Garnier trying to get rid of me, Robert," Betsy said. "I'm sure Jerome knows nothing about his letter."

It worried her, however, and she was relieved to hear, although indirectly, from Italy. Some friends of the Marchioness of Donegal, an English friend of Betsy's, had seen Captain Bonaparte in Genoa. Jerome sent his wife a message by them that he still loved her and was overjoyed at the news of the birth of their son, about which Dr. Garnier had told him.

In August, Betsy also received through the Marchioness her

first letter from her husband since he had seen Napoleon. To her consternation, it confirmed his wishes, sent through Dr. Garnier, that Betsy must go back to America.

"God who sees my heart," Jerome wrote, "knows that I only love and live for my good wife." When he could take Betsy in his arms again, he would tell her about his talk with the Emperor. "My brother," he went on, as if fearing his letter would be read by Napoleon's spies, "is as good and generous as he is great, and if for the present political reasons compel him to act as he is doing, in time things will be different." He begged her to be patient and not refuse the pension the Emperor offered her. It would only irritate him, and to provoke an open quarrel would ruin everything. Instead, it would be wiser for Betsy to seem to accept the inevitable. His earnest wish was that, if he could not send for her in two months, she should return to Baltimore and wait there, where it was possible he might be able to join her. Jerome hinted he was being constantly watched. He would write to her, but she wasn't to let anyone, except her mother, know she heard from him. He warned her to be careful to say nothing against Napoleon. Anything she said would be reported to the Emperor. But she mustn't despair. All would turn out well in the end. Jerome begged his wife to trust him and to believe that she and their son were all he loved in the world. He sent her a hundred kisses, and ended by assuring her he loved her more than ever.

Betsy felt sick as she contrasted this evasive letter with those Jerome had written her on the way to Italy, full of courage and confidence he could win over Napoleon. She was frightened to see how he had changed.

The Marchioness of Donegal heard rumors from Italy of a woman named Bianca Carrega being seen about with Jerome, "who, reported reconciled to Napoleon, is to be made Archduke of Genoa." More upset than she would admit, Betsy was considering running the risk of arrest and slipping into Italy as Madame d'Albert, the name Jerome used in writing to her, when she heard that his squadron was being sent off on a mission.

"If I'm successful," Captain Bonaparte had confided to friends, "I shall ask Napoleon as a reward for my wife and child."

He was sailing to Algiers to demand the return of the French and Italian prisoners the Dey had captured. It was a task involving little risk, yet one that, Napoleon hoped, would restore his brother's prestige. He had instructed the French consul at Algiers to pay the Dey a large ransom for the galley slaves. All Jerome had to do was load them aboard his ships and, on August 31, return to Genoa, to the roar of saluting cannon, a hero. Escorted by his sailors and the freed captives, the handsome naval captain walked under floral arches to the cathedral, where a *Te Deum* was sung. That night, there was a banquet at the Governor's palace in his honor.

He felt himself entitled to make another appeal to the Emperor. Napoleon replied that nothing would alter the stand he had taken concerning Jerome's marriage, but his brother could have a furlough in Paris.

In September, Paul Bentalou, who had acted as interpreter for Robert Patterson with Lucien Bonaparte, received a letter from Betsy and one from his friend Robert. Bentalou was asked to try to deliver them to Jerome.

Captain Bentalou was just out of jail, having been arrested a month ago by Napoleon's secret police while carrying a letter from William Patterson to Jerome. But the loyal Paul, hearing in October that Bonaparte was in Paris, ran the risk of another imprisonment in the Temple, to deliver the two letters from England to Jerome's house in person. Bentalou handed them himself to the servant who opened the door, so he was sure that Jerome received them.

A friend of Bentalou's told him how sad and pensive Captain Bonaparte had looked the next evening, at a ball given by his sister Caroline. As she danced with him, he had spoken tenderly of his wife.

"I'll always remember that shipwreck on the Delaware, how brave Betsy was, the first to leap into the lifeboat. My dear little wife! I was so proud of her courage, I took Betsy in my arms before everybody and kissed her."

For fear of Napoleon, Jerome was afraid to do anything openly. But in October, 1805, he arranged with the wife of an English diplomat to take to England for Betsy two boxes containing jewelry, a thousand Louis d'or and some Paris clothes. He also managed to send off two letters without having them seized by Napoleon's agents. He wrote Betsy on October 4, 1805:

> My dear and well-beloved wife, life is nothing to me without you and my son. We will be separated a little longer, my Elise, but finally our troubles will end. Don't worry, your husband will never abandon you. We'll not be able to live like princes, my darling, but we will live decently.

On the 16th he wrote her again: "My Elise, after the war, you'll see your good husband. I'm surprised you haven't sent me your portrait and that of my son. You know how I love Octavius and other children. Imagine how I adore my own, whom I cannot even kiss! Teach him to love and respect his father, say to him, 'Your father will always prefer you to high rank.'" He loved his wife dearly, Jerome said; he longed to see Betsy and their son, but he reminded her that France was at war. For the present, she must wait patiently while he served his country. "After I've done my duty as the brother of the Emperor, I'll fulfill those of a father and a husband . . . I love my country, I love glory, but I love them as a man who never forgets he is the father of Jerome Napoleon and the husband of Elise. I kiss you, and I love you as my life."

Betsy read Jerome's love letters months later in America, having sailed for home on September 27.

James Monroe, never optimistic of a reconciliation with Napoleon, had been urging Betsy for some time to go back to Baltimore. Mrs. Anderson, unhappy in England, threatened to sail on the *Robert*. Betsy induced her to stay. But the maid Prudence, "of no earthly use," was sent home on another Patterson ship, the *Baltimore*. Robert, anxious to get back to Mary Caton, wrote his father, "I don't think it's any use to wait longer than spring." By then, Betsy agreed, the matter would be decided, one way or another.

If he didn't send for her in two months, Jerome had written his wife on July 29, she must return to America, where he hoped to join her. Through August, Betsy waited. She grew thin and haggard. By September, when no summons came, Betsy bowed to the inevitable, in outward submission and inward despair, and asked herself, what could be gained by staying through a long, dreary English winter and listening to Mrs. Anderson's complaints?

It was a good time to sail. Napoleon, afraid to attack England with a coalition of enemies at his back, had abandoned the invasion. He had wheeled about and was driving his army across Europe, to fall on the Austrians. The French navy, that had long threatened England, was down in the Mediterranean, where Nelson in his *Victory* and the British fleet were closing in on them off Cape Trafalgar. American ships were venturing out into the Atlantic with more confidence than in years.

James McElhinny, the Pattersons' London agent, informed Robert that an old 180-ton brig, the *Mars,* was sailing September 27 for Baltimore. Captain Murphy had a cabin suitable for a lady. Not very luxurious, he feared, for by September 16, 1805, when Mr. McElhinny wrote to Mr. Patterson that his family had decided to sail, he was worried about the accommodations.

> Mme. Bonaparte and her child, her brother Robert, and Mrs. Anderson will embark in a few days on board the brig *Mars,* Captain Murphy, which will soon be ready to sail for Baltimore. I could have wished it had not been so late in the season, but still I am in hopes from the vessel being a fast sailer, that she will be safe with you before the northwest winds become severe on your coast. The child as well as its mother are in a good state of health, which is fortunate, as I fear they will not find themselves as comfortably accommodated as they were on board the *Erin,* the cabin of this vessel being very small. However, they are determined to go.

Betsy was in full retreat before Napoleon. To leave Europe was a sign of weakness. And it was dangerous to put the wide Atlantic between herself and Jerome. But what could she do but obey his wishes?

When she returned home, her spirit crushed, her complacency shattered, her welcome from her father would be, "I told you so . . . I warned you . . . if you'd done as I said in the first place, and now look at you!" And the neighbors, secretly pleased over the downfall of one who had been so proud, would ask, was Napoleon going to defy the Pope and annul her marriage? If Jerome hadn't deserted her, when was he coming to Baltimore? But Betsy must face it.

There was the possibility that Jerome meant what he wrote
that he might be able to join her in America.

The day Betsy and her child, Robert Patterson and Mrs
Anderson sailed, James Monroe came to see them off. "I'm
sorry I wasn't more helpful," he said.

The courage in Betsy came out and shone as it always did
in the face of adversity. She was enraged and humiliated
but no one would guess it.

"Oh, I'm delighted to be going home, Mr. Monroe. I've
good reason to believe my husband is coming to America!"

As prestige fell, pride rose. Jerome's discarded wife held
her lovely head high, when the American minister kissed her
hand in farewell.

10. Chin Up and Smiling

IN THE PATTERSON HOME in Baltimore, Betsy sat writing to her husband. From the window, she could see the harbor, where her father's ships lay at anchor, and the masts of the *John & Peter,* arrived that morning from Havre. Dare she hope the clipper had brought her a letter from Jerome. No, better not to hope. Dropping her eyes to the paper, she wrote the date, September 30, 1807, and then, *My dearest.*

No matter what fears and doubts tormented her, Jerome was still her dearest. Betsy wrote the salutation; like a cry from her heart, the words called to him across the two years since she had last seen her husband in Lisbon. She hadn't had a letter from him for fourteen months. Compressing her lips, Betsy drove the quill over the paper.

> My dearest: I am writing to beseech you to tell me the truth, shall I ever see you again? It is over a year since I have heard from you . . .

She laid down her pen. What should she say next? Should she tell him how, a year and a half ago, when Jerome was in the Caribbean with the French fleet, she had wakened each morning to think, will he come today? He had written her on the way to Brest, to take command of the battleship *Veteran,* that his going to the West Indies was "to see again my Elise, my dear little wife, without whom I couldn't live." All that spring of 1806 she had watched daily for him to arrive in the Patapsco. Hundreds of times she rehearsed her greetings, felt herself rushing into his arms.

He hadn't come. Instead, in May, Bonaparte wrote from French Guiana, delighted because he had met a Baltimore sea captain, who could tell him of seeing Betsy and his boy a few days before sailing. It was the first happy moment he'd had since he left her in Lisbon, Jerome said. He begged her not to believe any disquieting rumors she might hear about him. "You know me, Elise, you can feel certain that nothing can ever separate us." Had he been willing to forsake her, he would be more by now than a mere captain in the navy. But he preferred his wife to a crown. "I would refuse to inherit the Empire if I must choose between it and my wife." After the war, if Napoleon continued obstinate, they would live in America, and he'd gladly give up all thought of being a prince for her sake. Meanwhile, Betsy wasn't to worry. She must ignore what envious people in Baltimore said, keep well and write to him often. He begged her to bring up their son to be a real Frenchman. "Teach him at an early age that the great Napoleon is his uncle, and he is an Imperial prince."

To Betsy's dismay, her husband's next letter from Martinique, dated June 20, brought up his old grievance. Why had she gone to England? He told her that, about the time she left Holland, Napoleon had decided to accept her as his wife. If she had remained at Amsterdam three days longer, she would have been allowed to land. He insisted her going to England was all that had separated them. Could Betsy believe that?

Jerome had written her last, at sea, on July 17, 1806, over a year ago, a short note, signed formally, J. Bonaparte.

I do not write you but a few words, my dear and beloved Elise. I am well and regret being but fifty leagues (150 miles) of you without having the joy of seeing you. I kiss you with all my heart; a caress to Napoleon and my compliments to your family.

But eager to think the best of her husband, Betsy was sure that he had been on his way to Baltimore, when off the Virginia coast, the *Veteran* came upon an English convoy. Was a chance to be a hero too much for Jerome to resist? He started in pursuit; captured the sixteen enemy ships north of the Azores; and headed with them for France, where he arrived safely, chased into a Brittany port by British warships. The papers were full of it.

Captain Bonaparte had deserted the fleet again, run off with the Admiral's best battleship. The British press declared, this time, he would surely be court-martialed. Instead, to everyone's surprise, Napoleon made Jerome an admiral; a prince, with hereditary rights after Joseph and Louis; and decorated him with the Legion of Honor. People concluded the Emperor must be building up his only unmarried brother to make him an acceptable match for royalty. For last October Jerome's marriage to Betsy had been annulled, on grounds that his mother had not been previously notified, by the Archbishop's Court of Paris, under orders from Napoleon. Normally, this court took orders only from Rome. But they did not dare refuse the French dictator.

"So he admits there *was* a marriage, otherwise it couldn't be annulled!" Betsy, in her humiliation, felt that she had won a small victory over Napoleon.

Since then, Jerome had been fighting with the French army in Silesia, where he had behaved well enough to be made a general, as well as an admiral. But night after night Betsy still dreamed that her husband came to her and she lay in his arms until morning recalled her to reality.

Lost in memory of those dreams, Betsy jumped at the sound of the door opening. She looked up to see her father, a newspaper in his hand. "Writing?" He frowned.

"Yes, to Jerome," she replied defiantly.

William Patterson looked searchingly at his daughter. Childishly small, and thinner than on her return from England two years ago, Betsy, with her short brown curls, didn't look twenty-two, he thought. Not too late for her to make a new life for herself, she would have to now. Not too late for her to marry again, some fine American.

"The skipper of the *John & Peter* brought me news from France. Daughter, it's going to upset you."

"I'm past being upset. Who's Napoleon going to force Jerome to marry now?"

Betsy managed to keep her voice steady, although she dreaded what her father might say. Even before Napoleon annulled Jerome's marriage, he was matchmaking all over Europe for a royal bride for his youngest brother, for the Emperor was strengthening his hold on the Continent by setting his relatives on every available throne. Several princesses had turned Prince Jerome down. The widowed Queen of Etruria, though ugly and deformed, declared she would rather lose her kingdom than become the consort of a man whom the Pope considered married.

William Patterson cleared his throat. He hated to hurt Betsy, but this would end the mess that had brought unhappiness to all the family, so he was blunt.

"Jerome was married last month to a German princess. Want to read about it?"

With trembling fingers, Betsy took the newspaper he handed her. She read how the French Emperor, having conquered Prussia, had grouped several little German states into a kingdom, to be called Westphalia, over which the twenty-two-year-old Jerome would rule as king. He then presented his brother with a royal wife, sight unseen, the daughter of a king Napoleon had made, Frederick II of Wurtemberg. Prince Jerome and Princess Catherine were married on August 12, 1807, at the Tuileries in Paris, before the Bonaparte family, whom the Emperor had made kings and queens and princes and princesses (all but Lucien), and the nobles of the Empire.

So Jerome preferred a crown! Mammy July's words had come true. Elizabeth Patterson of Baltimore, the first American girl to do so, had married a king. But Betsy wasn't to be his queen; and she remembered, the old Negro woman had never said she would be. Catherine was to be Jerome's queen.

Betsy, tearing up her letter, burst into tears. Jerome had abandoned the woman whom he had sworn before God and man to love, honor and cherish until death. She would never see him again.

Her father put his hand on her shoulder. "I'm sorry, Betsy. I told you how it would be." She looked up, and he turned away from the hurt in her eyes. "I replied then, Papa, that if things didn't work out, I wouldn't whine, and I won't."

Betsy kept her promise. But no one knew what it cost her. During the months that followed, the sweet, trusting girl in her died. Her soft heart took refuge in a protective shell; and the first plate was forged in that proud, smiling armor of cynical self-sufficiency that for the rest of Betsy's life shielded

her true self from the world. At first, on her return from
England, she had been able to face Baltimore, her head high.

"I'm only visiting Mama and Papa while Jerome is at war,"
Betsy told the Caton sisters. "You think he has left me?
Listen to this—" And she read to Mary and Louisa one of his
tender love letters:

> . . . and believe, my Elise, that my first thought on waking
> like my last before going to sleep, is always of you, and if I
> wasn't sure of one day rejoining my dear wife, I couldn't go
> on living. . . .

Had Jerome written those loving words only sixteen
months ago? Now, with the papers full of his second wedding, all Baltimore knew that Betsy, who gave herself such
grand airs and boasted she'd made the most brilliant marriage ever made by an American, had been jilted.

"I don't wish her any hard luck," Mrs. Caton said, "but
the way Betsy ran after Bonaparte, no wonder he tired of
her!"

Polly Caton's disappointment over Jerome still rankled.
Educated abroad, she had served as hostess for her father,
when Charles Carroll of Carrollton was in Congress. In
Philadelphia, Polly grew to admire foreigners. She had married Richard Caton, an Englishman whose ancestors fought
at Agincourt, but who was engaged in the cotton business in
Baltimore. Mrs. Caton longed to find distinguished European husbands for her four daughters and, charmed with
Jerome's born-to-rule air, had done her utmost to capture
him for her eldest, Mary. He fell for Betsy's brown eyes
instead.

What a pleasure now it was for Polly Caton to say, "Bonaparte was wild about my Mary, but Frenchmen are so fickle,
I wouldn't let her encourage him." Baltimore was given to

understand that Betsy Patterson had only caught Napoleon's brother on the rebound.

Secretly, Mrs. Caton came to the conclusion, after Betsy's unfortunate experience, that Americans made the best husbands. On his return from Europe, Mary Ann Caton was allowed to announce her engagement to Robert Patterson. They had been married in Annapolis on May 7, 1806, at a lavish wedding that for months was the talk of Baltimore.

Now, over a year later, Baltimoreans were excitedly discussing another wedding. Her many friends had been privileged to read the letter that Madame Pascault had received from her daughter, Henriette. Jean-Jacques Reubell, promoted to general, was in Europe as Prince Jerome Bonaparte's aide. His wife Henriette, who would be Princess Catherine's lady in waiting, was sent by Napoleon to General Junot's estate at Raincy, to welcome Jerome's bride to French soil.

"Mama, did you ever see such roses? Smell! Aren't they delicious?" Betsy exclaimed one day. "I'm going to slip over to Madame Pascault's with a bunch."

Betsy lifted the knocker a half hour later. Madame Pascault, fat and smiling, held out a plump hand. "Betsy, what lovely flowers! Thank you, dear." She moved to the tea table by the fireplace. The candles were lit. "You're just in time for a cup of hot chocolate. One lump or two?"

"One lump, please." Betsy sipped the rich drink. She took a sandwich and a piece of cake. Her heart raced. Sick with longing to see Henriette's letter, but too proud to mention it, except casually, Betsy chattered on about her garden, the weather, the jacket she was knitting for Bo. Suddenly, she exclaimed, "But listen to me, going on about myself. What I want to know is, any news from Henriette?"

Madame Pascault had her daughter's letter. She carried it

with her, to read to everyone she met. But she hesitated now. It seemed cruel. She said in pity, "It wasn't much like your lovely wedding, dear. So gaudy and artificial. Would you like to hear what Henriette wrote, such nice things about you?"

When the bridegroom first saw the stout, unbecomingly-dressed German *fraulein* they'd chosen for him, Henriette said, Jerome's expression was so glum, his suite felt sorry for him. They knew he liked svelte, smartly-dressed women and must be regretting another bride, who, Jerome had told them, "created a paradise for me in a strange land."

The ceremony at the Tuileries that followed was the first royal wedding in the Bonaparte family. The bride was a Protestant, but the Emperor overlooked that. Through the Wurtembergs, Jerome would be related to the Czar of Russia. Napoleon, delighted, spared no expense. Henriette's account of the lavish ceremony in the Gallery of Diana, with Prince Jerome in a gold-embroidered white satin suit and the dowdy bride wearing a magnificent pearl necklace, the gift of the Emperor, caused Betsy some pangs of envy as she listened, remembering her own simple wedding.

During the service, Jerome hung his head. "He looked like a man obeying orders," Henriette wrote. Betsy felt faint. Trembling, she spilled her chocolate. She had to put down the cup.

"Poor Catherine! Already she is haunted by the thought of her predecessor—" Henriette went on to say how Jerome and his German bride, pronounced man and wife, were stepping into the coach that would take them to Westphalia, when Catherine looked intently at her new lady in waiting. "Mme. Reubell, are all American women as beautiful as you?" she asked.

"And that night—" Madame Pascault continued reading. But Betsy jumped to her feet. "Thank you, it was most

interesting," she murmured and fled, unable to hold back
the tears any longer. The kindly Frenchwoman looked after
her. "Poor child!" she sighed.

Jerome couldn't forget Betsy, any more than she could
forget him. He wrote her from Paris after his wedding and
begged his Elise to forgive him. He was a victim of his
brother's ambition, he pleaded, more to be pitied than
blamed.

The May following, Jerome wrote her again from Cassel,
the capitol of his new kingdom, that he was sending Auguste,
Alexander Le Camus' brother, to America to fetch his son.
"I wish our child with me in Westphalia, to console me for
being separated from my beloved Elise, whom I've never
ceased to love." He knew it would hurt her to lose Jerome
Napoleon. But Betsy must sacrifice herself, as he had done
when he renounced her for political reasons, and let him give
their son the advantages to which the boy's rank and name
entitled him.

Betsy was sweet, but firm. Le Camus was sent back to
Westphalia with a miniature of the three-year-old child from
whom his mother refused to part. Nor would Betsy consent
to the suggestion of the French minister at Washington, that
Napoleon might adopt the boy, if she sent him to France
alone. But Mme. Bonaparte informed Turreau that, since
there was no longer any reason for not doing so, she would
gladly accept the pension of $12,000 a year that Napoleon
had offered her.

When he heard of it, Jerome wrote on November 22, 1808,
to demand indignantly, why was she appealing to the Emperor for support? Wasn't he a king now, able to look after
his child and the boy's mother, and give them all the titles
and riches they wished. His Elise and his Jerome had a place

in his heart no power on earth could take from them. If they came to Westphalia, he would make her the Princess of Smalkalden, give her a castle and an annual income of 200,000 francs. The letter was signed, "Your devotedly for life, Jerome Napoleon."

The first American princess! Betsy's heart leaped for joy. Wouldn't that silence the gossips in Baltimore, gloating over her misfortunes! Nor did she think Jerome was merely offering her a title so she would hand over her son to him, for he wrote his feelings for her hadn't changed, she was still the woman he had vowed to love his whole life long—and always would. There was no reason why they couldn't be happy, if she came to Cassel.

To be with Jerome again, in her heart still so dear! Betsy was tempted. Never would she admit that her marriage was any less legal than Jerome's second marriage, so wouldn't she be the rightful Queen of Westphalia, even if another sat on the throne? Then Betsy forced herself to stop being a fool. Was she willing to share Jerome with his German wife? And if Henriette Reubell was to be believed, with several other women besides? Betsy's pride rebelled. "Westphalia isn't a large enough kingdom for two queens," she replied, declining the King's offer with scorn.

All Baltimore was informed, however, that Mme. Bonaparte had turned down a title. When her friends expressed astonishment that she should prefer Napoleon's pension of 60,000 francs to the 200,000 francs from King Jerome, Betsy retorted, "I prefer to be sheltered under the wing of an eagle to hanging from the bill of a goose."

Her witty remark was repeated all over Baltimore and Washington. Betsy's tongue was becoming increasingly sharp. She never missed a chance to speak scornfully of

Jerome. Let nobody think she still loved him and dare to feel sorry for her. She didn't want anyone's sympathy.

The Reubells, bitter and disgruntled, returned to Baltimore in 1809, the General having been dismissed by King Jerome for incompetence. Henriette regaled Betsy with the goings-on in Westphalia. The King was popular at first, she said. But he found the treasury empty, the people taxed to the limit. Since Napoleon insisted on taking half the revenues of his puppet nations, Westphalia's budget could only be balanced by the strictest economy. Being a king hadn't changed Jerome in the least. Having no money, he began spending it. He raised money by loans and spent it, not to balance the budget and reduce taxes, but in maintaining in his miniature kingdom, fifty miles square, a court on so grand a scale as to be the laughingstock of Europe.

"He's well-meaning," Henriette insisted, "but Jerome's weak. He can't say no to the worthless hangers-on who surround him."

He was scattering titles and pensions, chiefly on the cronies of his old navy days. Louis Pichon was in Westphalia, in charge of the treasury; Meyronnet was grand marshal of the palace; Le Camus, as Count of Furstenstein, minister of foreign affairs—for the only kind of cabinet ministers Jerome wanted were those who would tell him that everything was going splendidly, when actually there was chaos. Westphalia was on the verge of bankruptcy.

Betsy, listening to what the Reubells said, decided she had done well to rely on Napoleon. He had given her a $12,000 annuity. Turreau hinted the Emperor might do even more.

"Tell him, I wish to be a duchess," Betsy replied. Nothing came of it, although she long continued to hope.

She saw Napoleon divorce Josephine, whom he loved, and marry the eighteen-year-old daughter of the Emperor of Austria, who could give him an heir. Marie Louise had been brought up to hate the stout, middle-aged conqueror of her country. But she meekly married Napoleon, obedient to her father's wishes, just as Jerome had renounced his American wife and married Catherine of Wurtemberg for political reasons.

"In Europe, it's the good of the family or one's country that matters in a marriage, not as in America, the happiness of the individual," Betsy explained to her disapproving family. "Sentiment doesn't come into it."

Looking at the way the Emperor had treated her through the eyes of a European, he didn't seem so reprehensible; and grateful to Napoleon for her annuity, Betsy always spoke well of him. She was immensely proud of being a Bonaparte. Napoleon had forbidden her to use his name. She obediently signed her pension receipts "Elisa Patterson," but otherwise she risked the Emperor's wrath by refusing to give up the name he had made famous. Except for her child, all Betsy had gotten out of her marriage was the right to the Bonaparte name. She clung to that.

These were bad days for her, a deserted married daughter flung back on her parents. It would have been hard on any girl. For proud, ambitious Betsy, living in a tiny back room with her child in her father's crowded house, it was torture.

The only thing that made life bearable was her son. Betsy loved him, passionately. Now that she had a child of her own, a little being who called her Mama, who demanded all her time, all her attention, Betsy understood why Peggy had enjoyed looking after the Patterson babies. She spent happy hours, knitting, sewing, caring for little Jerome. Even her shame and humiliation could not rob them of their joy.

Perhaps it was well that Betsy had so much to do she didn't

have time to brood over her troubles. In 1807, Mary Ann
Jeromia died. Her mother was ailing, so was the once-healthy
Peggy, and the housekeeping duties she detested again fell
upon Betsy. She was back leading the humdrum existence
from which her glamorous marriage had rescued her—going
to market with Moses, keeping Mammy Lu in a good humor,
scolding lazy Homer and flighty Magnolia, nursing the old
and sick Negroes. To make matters worse, Betsy's father was
forever reminding her of how he had opposed her marriage.
Hadn't it turned out just as he said?

"You mustn't judge Jerome harshly, Papa," she retorted.
"He wasn't free to act as he wished, or he'd never have left
me. He still loves me. I've got to believe that or go mad."

Betsy's pretended contempt for Jerome had never fooled
her father. "And you love him, too, after the way he's treated
you?"

"Don't you realize, Papa, that you can't live with someone
you love for sixteen heavenly months, then learn to hate him
over night."

With an exclamation of disgust, Mr. Patterson left the
room and Betsy weeping. Why couldn't she forget Jerome?
It would be much better for everyone if she could. Betsy
found the answer in the copy of Le Rochefoucauld that
Madame Lacombe had given her. The French cynic wrote,
"Absence diminishes moderate passions and increases great
ones, as the wind extinguishes candles and fans a fire."

Betsy wanted to die so badly that in May, 1809, she got
some poison from Mammy July. The old woman said it was
tasteless, but sure. All you had to do was put the liquid in a
drink, take a sip and all your troubles were over. But, before peace came, how did you know it wouldn't hurt? Betsy,
with a shudder, hid the vial in her bureau drawer. Then she

re-read Sam Graves' letter, and with flushed cheeks, the poem he had enclosed, entitled: *Thoughts in Bed, the Same She had Once Occupied.*

> In bed, dejected and oppressed,
> I wearied turn from side to side;
> Impatient to obtain that rest
> Which to my troubles is denied:
> But I alas! no rest can find,
> Although my aching brows recline,
> For where her head hath once inclin'd,
> I now lie upon the pillow mine—

Samuel Colleton Graves was coming to see her again. He was civilian secretary to Admiral Coffin, the commander of his ship, and had come to Baltimore from New York several times before, when his squadron of the British Royal Navy was in port. But this time would be different, for his heart, Sam wrote, would no longer allow him to keep silent.

What would she say to him? Perhaps yes, Betsy thought, if he pleaded hard enough. Samuel Graves was the son of Admiral Thomas Graves of the British Royal Navy; his mother was Dame Proprietress of the Bahamas, with plantations in the Bahamas and South Carolina. Sam would do a great deal for his stepson. Betsy sighed. Jerome, dear little boy, needed a father. He had been hard to manage lately, refusing to eat his spinach, hiding from Old Belle when it was time to go to bed and bringing field mice and caterpillars into the house. As for her, it would be pleasant to have a husband again. Betsy was desperately lonely for a man's love. And Sam would be good to her. Not exciting, with his round, pink face, his bald head and small, woman's hands, but certainly kind and considerate. He always noticed what she wore; he never forgot to bring her flowers.

Betsy emptied the vial of poison out of the window. If

she didn't have courage enough to kill herself, she might as well make Sam Graves happy.

"Peggy, do you think Betsy's going to marry that funny little Englishman?" Caroline asked excitedly, on the day that Samuel Graves was due in Baltimore.

The family suspected, by the way Betsy was acting, that she was going to say yes to her British suitor. She was smiling and gay again, like a young girl. At noon, when Sam was expected, Mme. Bonaparte, lovely in white, a Cashmere shawl about her shoulders, sat in the parlor waiting. Hearing the sound of his carriage wheels at the door, Betsy, suddenly panic-stricken, wanted to run upstairs and hide from him. But it was too late, Moses was ushering her British suitor into the room.

He was shorter and prissier-looking than Betsy remembered him, with his scented sideburns and chirpy voice. But Sam kept the conversation going at dinner, talking brightly with Mr. Patterson about foreign trade, and with the ladies on lighter subjects, the theater in London and the Paris fashions.

The meal over, Betsy clung to her family. She nervously suggested they play cards with Edward and George. But Sam had other plans. His carriage was at the door, he said. Why didn't they drive out to Coldstream and see the estate that Betsy had told him about?

It was after dark when they returned. The Pattersons heard the carriage roll up. Then, to their surprise, it drove away; Betsy came into the house alone.

"Sam had to go back to his ship," she explained hurriedly. "Has Mammy Belle put Jerome to bed? I'll run up and see if he's all right."

Her son was bathed and in bed, when Betsy rushed into the

room and sat down beside him. "Bo, darling, you don't need a father! I'll be both Papa and Mama to you," she cried hysterically.

Jerome didn't know what Mama meant. But he liked it when she took him in her arms and rocked him to sleep.

Next morning, Betsy, white and tense, sat at her desk composing a letter to Samuel Graves. How could she have gone to Coldstream, where she had spent her honeymoon with Jerome, with that sap! She might have known that Sam would want to kiss her. And Betsy longed passionately to be kissed again, as Jerome had kissed her by the same brook beside which she and Sam had strolled yesterday. Betsy remembered Jerome's kisses, how he used to press his beautiful mouth to hers hard, as trembling she lay almost swooning with ecstasy in his arms. Jerome's kisses hurt; but Sam's prim pecks, were those kisses? Betsy had pushed him away and fled to the carriage. On the drive home, by inventing engagements for days ahead, she had persuaded Sam to return to the British fleet and his duties as secretary to the Admiral.

Several drafts went into the wastepaper basket that morning, but a letter finally went off to Samuel Graves, explaining that Mme. Bonaparte felt that, for her son's sake, she must remain a Bonaparte and not remarry.

Sam, brokenhearted, replied from Boston in verse, quoting Dryden: *Death ends our Woes.* Mrs. Graves added her pleas to his, writing Mme. Bonaparte to take pity on the "unhappiness of a beloved son," and suggesting that Betsy might be making a mistake, sacrificing herself for her child. But although Samuel Graves continued to write her ardent letters, even after his return to England, Betsy had made up her mind. She put his love poems in her Bible and kept them, but she never saw him again.

11. The Twig Is Bent

WILLIAM AND ROBERT, Betsy's brothers, had gone meekly into Patterson & Sons. John, trying to escape, once talked of becoming a doctor. He was eager to make something of himself, not be just his father's son in his father's business. But, even more, John wanted to marry Mary Nichols, daughter of Wilson Cary Nichols of Warrentown, Virginia. His father, Mary's father and Mary wouldn't hear of John being a doctor. "Do you know how long it takes a young man to get established in medicine?" Mr. Nichols asked. Years, John knew, and that he had better enter his father's firm. So he did, and had married Mary Nichols in May, 1806.

Edward talked of being a musician. John advised him against it. "You'd better get over your aversion to business and make some money, if you want to get married," he told him, for Edward was in love with his cousin Sydney, daughter of the Samuel Smiths. So Edward, like all his brothers, when the time came, went into the shipping business with his father.

By the summer of 1811, John Patterson had long ago sub-merged his real self. He sometimes regretted giving up med-icine, but most of the time his thoughts were on ship sailings and cargoes. He was happily married to Mary, fond of his children and safe in the family concern.

It was only on Sunday mornings that William Patterson didn't rush off early to work. He read the newspapers, then drove behind Zeke to the First Presbyterian Church, where his children and grandchildren filled several pews. Then all the Patterson clan, except Robert, who lived at the Catons' Brooklandwood, and Edward, who on Sundays rode over to Montebello to see Sydney Smith, came back to the South Street mansion for a roast beef dinner.

After a long, droning grace, William Patterson opened his eyes to glance about the table, well content. A fine family, he thought. He had much this Sunday for which to thank the Lord: Robert's marriage to Mary Caton, unlike Betsy's mistake, had been a wedding of which Mr. Patterson heartily approved; Edward had outgrown his silly musical notions; and Betsy, the black sheep of the family, was home again, under his thumb.

She sat across from him, in Mama's place, her teeth on edge, murmuring responses to John's wife, who was boasting about her children. Mary knew that Betsy wasn't listening. Moses passed around steaming dishes, shuffled back to the kitchen, to return with more. The Patterson young men, dutiful echoes of their father, talked business. Their wives of servants and food.

The seemingly endless meal over, they sat in the dark, stuffy parlor through the long Sunday afternoon. The ladies could not sew or knit on the Sabbath. Logy from the heavy mid-day meal, they sat gossiping, talking about their clothes, the weather. Then they were back on the all-absorbing topic of food. Betsy yawned with boredom until her jaw nearly cracked.

Her only escape was to Washington, where Dolly Madison, a loyal friend, frequently invited Mme. Bonaparte to visit at the White House. James Madison had succeeded Jefferson as president. And Betsy, who had expected to pity poor Dolly, having to go back to obscurity in rural Virginia when Jefferson's term as president was over, sighed enviously. Dolly Madison was First Lady, while Mme. Bonaparte's prestige was sadly dimmed since her honeymoon days when she had dazzled Washington society as the bride of Napoleon's brother. Robert Smith was Madison's Secretary of State; his brother Samuel, still in the Senate. But Betsy preferred to stay at the White House. General Smith blamed her loss of Jerome for his not being minister to France.

Grateful to Dolly Madison for her hospitality, Betsy tried to make life pleasant in Baltimore for Mrs. Madison's son, Payne Todd. He was at St. Mary's College, Emmitsburg, Maryland, the school run by the Seminary of the same name, a branch of the Society of St. Sulpice in Paris, founded in America by refugee priests. Dolly Madison wrote her sister:

> Payne is in Baltimore yet, and as much admired and respected as you could wish. He writes me that Mrs. Bonaparte is very kind to him, and he is invited out all the time.

At twenty-six, Mme. Bonaparte's sensational figure and her exquisite clothes still fascinated Washington. Letters of the period comment upon the "extreme liberality" with which Betsy displayed her beautiful back and shoulders. Another White House guest, Phoebe Morris, wrote her father:

> How I wish you could see Mme. Bonaparte, I think I never beheld a human form so faultless! At a ball her sylphic body was so thinly veiled as to display all the graces of a

> Venus de Medicis. She appears particularly lovely in a crepe robe of a beautiful azure color interwoven with silver . . . It is impossible to look on anyone else when she is present.

Mme. Bonaparte's wit was as scintillating as her beauty. At the squeezes, as Dolly Madison's crowded receptions were called, the gallants crowded around her. And Betsy, who had always accepted her attraction for men with cool indifference, became feverish about romance, as if to restore her ego and prove that it was through no fault of hers that she had been rejected on her honeymoon.

The most elegant of Betsy's Washington beaux was Sir Charles Oakley, a secretary in the British legation. A plump, supercilious man, so tightly poured into his gaudy uniforms, they looked like the skin on the grape, Sir Charles taught Mme. Bonaparte to play billiards. He escorted her to balls and to the races. Betsy, hungry for admiration and affection, let it be known that she might become Lady Oakley. But when Sir Charles proposed, Betsy put him off with the same excuse she gave her other suitors—her first duty was to her child, and Bo's future prevented her from remarrying.

Yet Betsy, proud of her conquest of Sir Charles, hoped Bo's father would hear of it. She knew how the rumor that she might marry an Englishman would displease him. If only she could be sure that rascal of a French minister would report on her romance to France! But Turreau had been replaced by Serrurier, who at Lisbon had separated her from Jerome. When Betsy met the wretch at parties, she refused to speak to him.

In Washington, Betsy felt young again. She could forget Jerome and be gay. Dreading the time when she must return to Baltimore, to her domestic chores, Mama's sick room and Papa's bad humor, Betsy stayed on at the White House until she outstayed her welcome.

"Darling, it's been such fun having you here, I wish you could remain longer," Dolly said. "But we're having a tiresome old dinner tomorrow for the French minister. Feeling as you do about Serrurier, I realize how awkward it would be for you to meet him."

Dolly can't wait to get rid of me, Betsy thought. She started to say, she could eat in her room. Instead, she said, "Oh, it's time I went home. I was just going to tell you."

"I'll be so lonely without you, dear," Dolly sighed, next morning, as they kissed good-bye. "Promise to come again soon. Remember, James and I love having you, any time."

Betsy climbed dejectedly into the carriage with her bandboxes, without any help from the White House coachman, sulky at being sent on the long drive to Baltimore. She rode home through the depressing rain, remembering drives through these woods with Jerome, on their way to Washington, a town eager in those days to entertain for Napoleon's brother and his bride. Betsy was wanted then. She wasn't a discarded wife and a political liability whom you couldn't invite to dinner for fear of offending the French minister.

Her head ached by the time she reached home. She found her family at supper. Betsy sat down to corned-beef and cabbage, thinking of the terrapin and canvasback duck she was missing. She should have been at the White House, fascinating President Madison's guests with her beauty and bright repartee. Now all she could think of to say was, "More pudding, Papa?" or "Of course Mrs. Madison rouges, Caroline. Her high color can't be natural!" or "Bo, don't talk with your mouth full of food!" In Washington, she'd have been gay and witty.

Papa, pushing back his chair, went off to his study. Now what? An evening of chess with George. At the White House, there would be music and dancing. Betsy heard her mother's plaintive voice from upstairs. "I'll go and sit with her, Peggy," she said, with a worried glance at her sister's face. Peggy looked ill. But as Betsy climbed the stairs, she thought, this for the rest of my life, I might as well be dead!

Quarrels with Papa were a relief. At least, they broke the monotony. By 1812, Betsy and her father had something new to disagree about, should Jerome be a French boy or an American boy?

Bo, at seven, was short and plump. A shy, gentle child, he could hardly be called handsome or especially clever. But his doting grandfather thought him the most brilliant, the best-looking boy ever born—sentiments with which Jerome's mother heartily concurred.

Otherwise, they seldom agreed about him. Betsy, already in a private war with Napoleon, found herself involved in another with her father over her son's education. To Mr. Patterson's indignation, she was bringing up Jerome to be what his father wished, a French boy. As a Bonaparte, and a possible heir to the French throne, Jerome Napoleon must be a Catholic. Over the angry objections of her Scotch-Irish father, a Presbyterian, Betsy had Archbishop John Carroll, who married her, baptize the boy.

Now Jerome was sent to St. Mary's, a Catholic college that his Presbyterian uncles, Henry, George and Octavius were attending, and where Edward had been a student, to learn French from the Sulpician priests. Soon he was able to write:

My dear Grandfather: I have never written to you a letter in French because you do not understand it; but to give you proof of my good will to learn it, I take my pen for this purpose. I want to give you a proof of my love for you, in writing you a letter in French. How do you do? For me, I am very well, and I have a great desire to see you!

Farewell, my dear grandfather, it is all I write to you for the present; but I want you to answer my letter soon. I am your very obedient and loving son, Jerome Bonaparte.

Bo's father said, "Teach him at an early age that the great Napoleon is his uncle, and he is an Imperial prince." As soon as the boy was old enough to understand, Betsy told him about his uncle's victories at Austerlitz, Wagram and Jena. Her arm about him, she tried to fire Jerome's imagination by telling him of the famous battles. Feeling the boy's body against her, his dark head touching her cheek, Betsy was hardly strong enough to bear her love for him. Her son was all she had left of her exalted dreams.

"Baltimore isn't our permanent home, darling,—at least, I hope it isn't," she told him. "Soon your Uncle Napoleon is going to allow us to live in Paris, where exciting things are going to happen to you, Bo, because you're a prince, the nephew of the man who is conquering Europe, whom you may succeed on the throne of France."

William Patterson did what he could to counteract such nonsense. By gad, it was enough to turn the boy's head! To Betsy's annoyance, he frequently took his grandson to the waterfront, to inspect the schooner *Rossie,* Joshua Barney's privateer. Mr. Patterson had helped to build the ship, to prey on British commerce, for by 1812 England and America were on the verge of war again.

The white-wigged gentleman in a cocked hat and his plump grandson stood hand in hand, looking at the famous boat. "Just think, Jerome," William Patterson said, "in one short cruise with the *Rossie,* Barney captured British ships and cargo to the value of a million and a half dollars, the biggest prize money in history!"

Jerome danced with excitement; he could hardly wait to go to sea and become a privateer like Commodore Barney.

Mr. Patterson won that skirmish. The gay old seadog who had brought Betsy Patterson and Jerome Bonaparte together became their son's hero, not Napoleon.

When Bo asked about his father, Betsy told him that he was the son of a king. "Your Papa can't come to America to see you, darling, because he has to stay in Europe and rule his kingdom. But he loves you, dearly. He writes to us whenever he can."

In March, 1812, they heard from Cassel after a six-years' silence. King Jerome and Queen Catherine had no children; and about to go with Napoleon on his Russian campaign, where he might be killed like the humblest of his soldiers, Jerome's thoughts turned to his only child. He wrote a tender, fatherly letter and begged his son not to forget him; and to the woman once so passionately loved, for whom he still retained a deep affection:

> My dear Elise: What a long time it is since I have had news of you and of my son! In all the world you'll never find a better or more loving friend than I am. I have much to write to you, but as I fear this letter may be opened, I'll merely tell you I'm well, and ask news of you and my son. Be assured that all will be arranged sooner or later. For the best, as well as the greatest man in the world, is certainly the Emperor.
>
> Your affectionate and good friend, Jerome Napoleon.

Betsy's spirited reply to this new assurance of her "loving friend" that "all would be arranged" was to get a divorce from him.

Divorce in those days was secured through the state legislatures. Considerable lobbying was done. A delegate, Benjamin Le Compte, wrote that Mrs. Barney and Mrs. Caton were "industriously electioneering"; the bill wouldn't come to a vote until after the Colts' ball in Annapolis, at which the

"Duchess" (as Betsy was called in Baltimore) would appear and "exert the blandishments of her beauty" on the susceptible solons.

On December 15, 1812, the House of Delegates took up the Patterson-Bonaparte divorce bill. A Democrat member voted to strip Jerome of his title of King of Westphalia in the third paragraph. This was carried, and the bill passed with 42 yeas, 29 nays. That sent it across the hall of the State House to the Senate. On the afternoon of January 2, 1813, it passed the Upper House. That night, Governor Levin Winder signed 195 bills—to open a road to Buckey's Town, Bridge the Choptank, found the University of Maryland, authorize a lottery to build a Lutheran church, prevent gambling booths within two miles of any Methodist camp meeting and annul the marriage of Jerome and Elizabeth Bonaparte.

Betsy wasn't securing a divorce in order to marry again, but because, disillusioned, she had ceased to expect anything of Jerome. Betsy subscribed to the *Moniteur Westphalian* that kept her informed of the corruption in ruined Westphalia and of the unpopularity of the King as the court gaieties continued at Jerome's sumptuous palace of Napoleonshohe, while the people were sunk in poverty. She also knew of his infidelities, to which, Henriette Reubell insisted, Queen Catherine pretended to be blind.

The knowledge that she had rivals for Jerome's heart no longer upset Betsy. It stood to reason that, with a wife as dull as Catherine, Jerome would seek consolation elsewhere. "I'm the only woman who could have held him," Betsy told her beautiful face in the mirror. And the gossip that the King of Westphalia bathed in red wine only amused her. Didn't his sister Pauline take milk baths? But Jerome's conduct of public affairs, so incompetent and wasteful that he seemed deliberately to be trying to ruin Westphalia, concerned Betsy greatly. She had long hesitated over the divorce. Could she break the legal bond that, in America, still linked her to the man she loved?

Betsy clung sentimentally to that last tie, but finally severed it. If she should die, she didn't want her spendthrift husband to be able to claim any of her fortune. She was saving every cent of her pension from Napoleon with one object in view—as soon as her son was old enough, she was going to take him abroad. As an Imperial prince, in the line of succession to the French throne, Jerome must have the best education possible. Betsy firmly believed this could only be had in Europe.

"What's wrong with Harvard?" her father demanded. "It's a big school now, with two hundred students; and good enough for Bo, even if he is royalty, or so you tell me. I want my grandson educated to be a good American."

"Jerome is a prince. He must go to school where he can meet boys of his rank."

His daughter's snobbish remarks always sent Mr. Patterson into a temper. "When will you stop being such a fool over royalty, Betsy? After what happened to you, I should think you'd never want to see Europe again. America is God's country, the golden land of opportunity. Where else could a poor Irish immigrant boy, such as I was, have become a millionaire? I want my grandson to stay home, be educated in America and be proud of being an American. Now I warn you, my girl—" he shook his fist at her "—that I'll disown you, if you take Bo to Europe and turn him into another Jerome—"

"How dare you, Papa! You never understood Jerome. Europeans are different."

Her father snorted. Betsy never failed to speak ill of Bonaparte; but, he noticed, let others say a word against him, and she flew at them.

Such arguments always ended in a draw, with neither side convinced. William Patterson was headstrong, and his daughter had inherited his will of iron. Betsy refused to listen to her father. He opposed her going to Europe, as he had opposed her marriage, and was always saying that true happiness could only be found at home. Ridiculous!

The death of his daughter Peggy in June, 1811, at eighteen, and his wife's long illness, left William Patterson more dependent than ever on his eldest daughter. It was not a happy household. Caroline was always sick these days, and Mr. Patterson's domineering ways had reduced his wife to such utter subjection that she had long ago faded into the background. Dorcas was gentle and loving to her children, but she played little part now in their lives or their upbringing. Too ill to knit or read, she would sit, smiling sadly, staring by the hour out of the window or into the fire, withdrawn into a world of her own, away from her family.

George, Henry and Octavius were at school at St. Mary's, William, Joseph and Edward seldom at home, and the house seemed a prison to Betsy, shut up there with her dour father. She couldn't help contrasting what she was with what she might have been. It's not fair, Betsy thought resentfully. "I'm young, only twenty-six," she cried to herself. And her mirror told her that she was still beautiful. Was she to spend the rest of her life cooped up here on South Street? It looked so, and Betsy, feeling pent-up and thwarted, grew increasingly rebellious.

12. Signal of No Surrender

AMERICA WENT TO WAR with England the same fatal summer of 1812 that Napoleon invaded Russia, took Moscow, then lingered in Russia until the snow came, before starting a disastrous retreat. England, short of men from her long struggle with Napoleon, was stopping American ships at sea to take seamen from them. Britain's excuse was that they were deserters from the British navy. But she often took by force men who were Americans and made them fight for her. Since England refused to give up this kidnapping, as the Americans called it, in June of 1812, war was declared.

But England was preoccupied with a much vaster struggle against Napoleon. Wellington was busy fighting the French in Spain. It was eight months before Betsy looked out of her window, one February day in 1813, to see ten British men-of-war anchored down the Patapsco.

"It's the enemy!" Magnolia ran into the house screaming. "Oh, save me! We're goin' to be killed."

To the Pattersons' consternation, the fleet of Admiral Sir

George Cockburn had come to blockade Chesapeake Bay. The British hated Baltimore. It was the home port of most of the privateers, those small, fast boats built and owned by private persons like William Patterson, but allowed by the government to carry arms, so they could slip past the blockading fleet and out to sea to attack enemy ships.

In the War of 1812, more privateers sailed from Baltimore than from any other port in America. So the English selected that "nest of pirates" for special revenge. But Napoleon, after his disastrous retreat from Russia, raised a new army in the spring of 1813. He set out against the Prussians and the Russians, coming at him through Germany. And the English were kept too busy by the French in Spain to fight in America.

Cockburn's fleet lay in the Chesapeake all summer, with an occasional marauding raid ashore. Joshua Barney was put in command of a flotilla of gunboats to oppose him. It was over thirty years since the Commodore had fought in the Revolution, but the British still feared him.

One June day, Betsy entered her father's study to find it filled with grim-faced men discussing how to make Baltimore strong. Barney was saying, "As soon as the English are able, Baltimore will be the first town attacked."

Patterson took a puff on his pipe. "Secretary of War Armstrong must think so. He's doing nothing to defend Washington."

The men decided, let the nation's capital remain open to the enemy if it wished, but Baltimore would be prepared. Betsy heard Colonel George Armistead, in command of Fort McHenry out on Whetstone Point, tell how he was getting the star-shaped fort guarding the entrance to the harbor ready to resist attack. Betsy listened with interest. She had a special affection for Fort McHenry, because at the racetrack nearby, she had first seen Jerome with Joshua Barney, nine years ago.

"Colonel Armistead," Betsy said, "your flag on the fort is so dirty, I can't see it any longer from my window. You need a bright, new flag."

"We do, Miss Betsy, one so large the enemy will have no trouble seeing it from their ships."

"A signal of no surrender, Colonel!"

Who would make the flag? Patterson suggested a widow, Mary Pickersgill, who made flags for his ships. Rebecca Young, Mrs. Pickersgill's mother, lived with her and could help. She was a professional flagmaker, who had made the Grand Union flag of 1775 that Washington unfurled at Cambridge.

Mary Pickersgill was Commodore Barney's sister-in-law. He agreed to go with General John Stricker to Mrs. Pickersgill's small brick house on the waterfront and ask her to make Fort McHenry a new flag.

Colonel Armistead wanted a flag for the fort so big the British could see it from far down the bay and know that Baltimore was going to fight. So it was decided to have it thirty feet wide by forty-two feet long, with fifteen stars and fifteen stripes. This was too large a flag to be made in Mrs. Pickersgill's tiny house. Mrs. Young, Mrs. Pickersgill and her fourteen-year-old daughter Caroline moved into a brewery, where they sewed every day on the huge banner spread out in the malt room. Betsy liked to drop in to watch them at work.

By the time the flag was finished, however, the world was shaken by such startling events, few persons noticed that Fort McHenry had a new flag. All of Europe was in arms against Napoleon. He was beaten at Leipsic. The French were compelled to evacuate Germany. The Austrians and

Prussians marched on Paris. Wellington, crushing Joseph Bonaparte in Spain, invaded France.

Betsy, anxiously scanning the *Moniteur,* learned that the Russians had entered Westphalia; Jerome had fled, his faithful Trinette with him. Catherine, who preferred to risk imprisonment with her "Fifi," whom she loved in spite of his faults, had indignantly refused to desert her husband and seek the protection of her father, the King of Wurtemberg.

King Jerome joined other fugitive monarchs in Paris—King Joseph of Spain, King Louis of Holland; his sisters, Elisa, Grand Duchess of Tuscany, and Caroline, Queen of Naples. "Jerome preferred a crown to me," Betsy said to herself. "Now he has lost it, he has only his fat little Trinette."

In June, 1814, America heard that the Allies had forced Napoleon to abdicate. They were sending him off to exile on the Island of Elba, in the Mediterranean.

"Well, Betsy," William Patterson said with a satisfied chuckle, "I guess, now, you won't be so proud of being a Bonaparte."

Still, Napoleon's downfall had its compensations. If the Emperor was to end his days on Elba, as people were saying, wasn't Betsy free to go abroad? Europe was open to her for the first time since her marriage. Napoleon could no longer keep her from landing. Then, looking out of her window, she saw those ten enemy ships down the Patapsco, blocking Chesapeake Bay. Nelson's sailors prevented her from sailing as effectively as Napoleon had.

In August, 1814, the war began in earnest in America. Cockburn's fleet was joined by another British fleet. Fifty ships under Vice-Admiral Sir Alexander Cochrane brought three thousand soldiers, who had fought with Wellington and been released after sharing actively in Napoleon's defeat. General Ross landed his troops and, to everyone's surprise, marched them, not to Baltimore, but toward America's young capital, with its new government buildings not yet finished.

There was little to stop the enemy's advance, except Barney's gunboats, that, after a skirmish, fled up the Patuxent River. Bottled up by the British fleet, the Commodore burned his ships to avoid capture and marched his sailors overland to join General Winder's hastily gathered militia at Bladensburg.

When a messenger galloped to Baltimore with news of the Bladensburg Races, as the battle to defend Washington was called, so many of Winder's untrained soldiers having dropped their guns and run away from the invaders, there was consternation in the Patterson household.

John and Joseph hurried to the Fountain Inn to hear what the messenger had to say. They returned, shamefaced, to tell their family how Winder's green militia took to their heels.

"The militia wanted to fight," John declared, "but orders came to fall back. In fact, the only Americans to put up any kind of a scrap at Bladensburg were Barney and his sailors. They say that Joshua was taken prisoner. President Madison and his Cabinet, caught on horseback between the lines, were almost captured—"

Joseph broke in excitedly. "The British marched on Washington. They burned our Capitol and the President's House—"

"Oh, what happened to poor Dolly?" Betsy cried.

"She saved Washington's portrait and other valuables from the White House, then fled to Virginia to join the President."

The Pattersons were horrified. How shocking to think of

America's new government buildings in ashes! But Baltimore had no time to weep over the fate of Washington. Their turn was next. Spies reported that General Ross, elated over his success, was loading his troops aboard transports to sail up the Chesapeake and annihilate Baltimore, after Cochrane's fleet destroyed Fort McHenry.

Baltimore, however, was better prepared than Washington. Bridges had been destroyed; old ships sunk to block the entrance to the inner harbor. Betsy's uncle, General Samuel Smith, was in charge of the defense of the town. He set every available man to work, digging breastworks at Hampstead Hill, on Patterson land, to stop any attack from the east. But how much could be done in three weeks?

On Sunday, September 11, Betsy ran to the window. The bells of St. Paul's were ringing, not for church services, but to warn of a cloud of sails down the harbor. Cochrane's fleet had returned to give Baltimore the same punishment as Washington. Seven battleships lay off North Point. Sixteen smaller boats had crept up to within two and a half miles of Fort McHenry.

Drums were beating, calling all men to the defense of their homes. A British army had landed only twelve miles down the Patapsco and was marching on Baltimore. Four of Betsy's brothers were in the Maryland militia. Robert was an inspector in the 3rd Division; John and George, privates in Captain Dobbin's company, 39th regiment; Edward, aide-de-camp to his uncle, General Smith. They hurried into their uniforms; blue coats faced with scarlet, gold sashes and epaulets, tight white breeches and high boots. They seized their muskets and fastened on their leather helmets with tall cockades.

Betsy kissed them good-bye. Caroline, Henry, Octavius and Jerome Bonaparte had been sent inland to safety at

Springfield. But she refused to leave the town from which most of the women and children had been evacuated.

The streets were lined with cheering, waving people, flags flew and fifes tooted *Yankee Doodle* as the Maryland militia, under General Stricker, marched out to face Wellington's Invincibles who had helped to crush Napoleon. It was the same army that had easily captured Washington three weeks before, while Baltimore had for defense only an army of volunteers, composed of ministers, lawyers, clerks, merchants, sailors, teamsters and farmers. Some wore uniforms, but most of the men were in frock coats and tall beaver hats. Many were but boys, carrying a gun for the first time.

An anxious night followed. At dusk on the following day, Edward, his uniform mud-coated, his cockade shot off, galloped up to the Patterson house. He had been sent back to town by General Smith to report that Stricker's force, ten miles out on the Philadelphia road, had met Wellington's veterans advancing from North Point, after landing from their transports. For two hours the militia held its ground against the British regulars. Then outnumbered, they were forced back to Hampstead Hill.

"General Ross boasted he'd eat his supper in Baltimore, even if the heavens rained militia," Edward told his family. "Well, he won't. Ross was shot by two Baltimore boys, hidden in a tree. His death left the British disorganized. They may not attack."

"Perhaps not by land, but they will by sea," replied his father grimly. "Ross' death will make the English hate us more than ever."

He was right. At dawn, the British proceeded with their double assault. Colonel Brooke, who had replaced Ross, planned to capture Baltimore by land, Admiral Cochrane by water. All day, Brooke strained his ears for the sound of the ships' guns. Late at night, word came to him that the harbor was blocked by sunken hulks, Cochrane's ships couldn't get within gun's range of the town. Colonel Brooke, afraid to continue without the help of the fleet, ordered a retreat. The land attack had failed. But next morning the enemy ships, stopped two miles below Fort McHenry, opened fire. The British were confident that a few hours' bombardment would reduce the little fort to ashes.

From the Captain's Walk on the roof of her house, Betsy watched the shells whistle across the water, her eyes on Mrs. Pickersgill's flag. Baltimore's safety depended upon Fort McHenry. The enemy must slip past its guns to get close enough to bomb the town. Her father, beside her, exclaimed, "If the flag keeps flying, and the fort holds out, we're saved!"

The roofs of most of the houses were crowded with people, their anxious eyes, like Betsy's, fixed upon that starry "Signal of No Surrender." All that day and into the next night, Baltimore shook under the thuds of bursting bombs. The scream and roar of shells was deafening, the air thick with smoke, as the British poured a shower of rockets into the fort from their ships. The enemy was too far away for McHenry's guns to be able to fire a shot in return. The fort's shells fell short of the British boats. The only way Betsy and the watching town had of knowing that Colonel Armistead's forces hadn't surrendered was that Mrs. Pickersgill's banner continued to fly from the flagpole.

Occasionally, the British ventured nearer, to be met by such a burst of flame from Fort McHenry's guns they dropped back out of range. Twilight came. Betsy remained on the Captain's Walk. As darkness fell, she saw the Stars and Stripes still floating in the fading light.

"Armistead apparently intends to keep the flag flying all

night," her father said, "as a sign to Baltimore that the fort hasn't surrendered."

Each time the blackness of the harbor was shattered by the light of a bursting shell, Betsy looked to see if the Stars and Stripes still waved. Her hopes soared when she saw the flag. When she couldn't catch sight of it through the smoke, her spirits sank.

Toward morning, the scream of shells ceased. After that, the silence and darkness was more frightening than the din of battle. What had happened out at Fort McHenry? Had the garrison fled? Unable to see, Betsy went to bed, but not to sleep. Tossing restlessly, she dragged out the hours until morning in agonizing suspense.

By the "dawn's early light" Betsy climbed anxiously to the roof. Would she see the Stars and Stripes waving on the fort? Or the British Union Jack? Her pulses leaped, for "our flag was still there." From the flagpole on the fort fluttered the Star-Spangled Banner. Although more than a thousand bombs had been dropped on Fort McHenry during a twenty-four-hour bombardment, the fort hadn't surrendered. Baltimore was saved.

Betsy wasn't the only one who watched Mrs. Pickersgill's flag that night. A young Maryland lawyer, Francis Scott Key, had gone out to the British fleet to obtain the release of a friend taken prisoner. The British granted Key's request, but told the two Americans they must remain on board until the attack on Fort McHenry was over. From the deck of the enemy ship, Key watched the bombardment all night, like Betsy, anxious and afraid, unable to tell whether or not the fort had surrendered.

When at dawn he saw the Stars and Stripes still flying, and the British sailing away, Key put his surge of emotion in words, scribbling down the patriotic poem that came to him on an envelope he found in his pocket. He revised the verses as he was rowed ashore and finished our national anthem, *The Star-Spangled Banner,* on the breakfast table at the Fountain Inn.

The poem, set to the tune of *Anacreon in Heaven,* was first sung by Ferdinand Durang at the Holliday Street Theater, in Baltimore. Soon it was on everyone's lips. People sang it in the taverns; they hummed it in the streets. Young ladies warbled it at the pianoforte. *The Star-Spangled Banner* exactly expressed the patriotic feelings of the Americans, and their relief that the war was over.

Baltimore went wild with joy. On February 14, 1815, with the peace treaty in President Madison's hands, a brick mansion on South Street was a blaze of candlelight. Betsy smilingly welcomed the relatives and friends who came to shake Mr. Patterson's hand. They sat down forty to dinner; bottles of William's best Madeira were brought up from the cellar.

Because dawn had found Mary Pickersgill's shot-torn banner flying, and not the English Union Jack, there was cause for rejoicing. Patterson & Sons had almost been ruined by the British blockade. Their warehouses were piled high with cargoes for Europe and the Far East. Now Negro stevedores would again load Patterson's fleet of clipper ships; Patterson sails would once more dot the seven seas.

After the Peace of Ghent, the shipping business swept forward on America's high wave of prosperity. Each night, William Patterson came home from his counting-house, half-dead with weariness, but happy, as he always was when making money.

One evening, he sank down at his desk with a grunt, to check over the bill of lading of the first Patterson ship to sail since the blockade was lifted, the *Intrepid,* bound for

Liverpool. Betsy, yawning on the sofa, suddenly announced, "Papa, I'm off to Europe on the *Intrepid*."

"By gad, you're not, in any ship of mine!" Seeing his daughter so defiant, still bent on going to Europe, made Mr. Patterson so angry the words choked in his throat. "What will people say of a girl who deserts her father? As my only daughter left, it's your duty to stay here and take care of me."

Was it? Since Betsy's return from England ten years ago, a succession of deaths in the family—Peggy, four years ago, her mother last May, Octavius in October, Caroline in December—seemed to chain her at home. Was this to be the drab end to a life, once full of glamor and excitement?

If she fled to Europe, Betsy could imagine what Polly Caton would say! "My dear, she's gone abroad, left her father with no one to look after him. How like Betsy, so heartless!" Yet Mrs. Caton was forever talking about taking Louisa, Elizabeth and Emily to London, so they could meet titled Englishmen.

"Who's been filling your ears with nonsense, Papa? Old Mr. Gilmor? Polly Caton? Let them talk! Baltimore has always hated me. I don't conform. I'm sick of paying any attention to what people say! I'm sick of everything!"

He continued to work. Looking at his head bent over his writing, Betsy wanted to scream.

"Why shouldn't I live abroad? You'll be all right. Aunt Nancy will gladly come and take care of you. I'm only thirty. I don't want my life to be all over. It isn't fair to keep me here, caged up, as your housekeeper."

"Baltimore's the finest place in the world. Betsy, you've just made up your mind not to like it."

William Patterson was immensely proud of the town he had helped to develop into a great seaport. He seldom left it, except for an occasional business trip to Philadelphia or

Washington. Looking out of the window, he saw his warehouses and his docks and the Bank of Maryland of which he was president. He also saw the humble cottage at 18 South Street in which Dorcas and he had first lived, where Betsy was born. He saw South Street, down which he had walked to work in those days, while other men rode. He had often stopped on this spot, near Water Street, where he now lived and thought, when I'm rich, I'll build a fine house here.

Well, his dreams had come true—he was rich, he had one of the finest mansions in Baltimore, and the only richer man in Maryland, Mr. Carroll, was related to him by marriage. That Betsy should scorn all that her father had struggled so hard to attain and want to go gadding off to Europe and live among strangers was outrageous.

Betsy looked resentfully at her father, as, apparently ignoring her, he went on with his work. Papa doesn't love me, he has never understood or sympathized with anything I want to do, she thought hotly. And he thought, why doesn't Betsy marry again, some nice American who would anchor her down? The girl's driving me crazy! Father and daughter were like strangers, and far apart, as they said good-night.

Betsy didn't sail on the *Intrepid* or—her father saw to that —aboard any of his ships. But by every method known to her, and they were many, she continued to try to find excuses to get away. Over the years, the bickerings at home and the humiliation of being pitied in Baltimore, where she had once been admired and envied, got on Betsy's nerves. Her nerves affected her digestion. She began having stomach trouble and ate nothing for days, not being able to keep down even bouillon.

Ill health would prove to be a blessing, though, if it helped her to escape. The climate of Baltimore was ruining her health, Betsy declared. She implored her father to let her take the cure at some health resort, preferably in Europe.

"Doctor Cradock says I should try Cheltenham, in England, for my liver, Papa. Those pains in my back—"

"—are pure imagination!" William, hiding behind his newspaper, refused to listen to a recital of his daughter's ailments. His indifference stung Betsy to the quick.

"Let me go to England! Do you wish to kill me, Papa? You couldn't act differently, if you did. If I'm kept here, Doctor Cradock says I'll be in my grave in two months. I'm ill, very ill, more so than you realize."

Betsy rushed upstairs and began packing. Let Papa rave! Living at home with her father, with few expenses, she had been able to save most of her pension from Napoleon. The money she had accumulated was sufficient for her to do anything she wished. For the first time in her life, she was financially independent of her father. It was only her fear of him that kept her home.

"Papa can't stop me from doing anything I want to do," Betsy asserted, trying to give herself courage. But world conditions could.

That March of 1815, when the Peace of Ghent opened the seas again to American shipping, the world was rocked by Napoleon's dramatic escape from Elba. He slipped past the English ships guarding the island; landed at Cannes, in southern France, with a handful of men, and, three weeks later, was in Paris, at the head of an army rallied to Napoleon Bonaparte by the magic of his name. The Bourbons fled. His old capital welcomed the Emperor with an outburst of wild enthusiasm.

Napoleon was back in power. Betsy mournfully unpacked her trunk. There was no sailing for Europe, now. The Continent was closed to her.

The world held its breath as Wellington's army massed in

Belgium to invade France. Betsy was concerned to learn that Jerome, in Trieste when Napoleon landed from Elba, had hurried to Paris to join his brother. He had gone to Brussels with him and all the military forces that could be drained from the Empire, to fight the British.

Then came Waterloo. Napoleon gave the ex-King of Westphalia the honor of opening that last battle, by leading his infantry division in an assault on Wellington's right. Jerome was no physical coward. He fought bravely at the head of his troops. After the bloody fight that followed, Betsy was pleased to have something creditable to tell Bo about his father.

"Just think, darling, he led six thousand men right into the face of a murderous fire from the Coldstream Guards. Half of his division was wiped out, your papa slightly wounded. Afterwards, your Uncle Napoleon seized his hand and exclaimed, 'My brother, no one could have fought better!' And when the flight from the battlefield began, your father rallied what remained of the French army and fought in the rear-guard, giving your Uncle Napoleon and his marshals time to escape."

But Napoleon's star had set. With his second abdication, the Hundred Days were over. The Little Corporal's spectacular career ended when the Allies sent him to exile again, this time to a place from where he couldn't escape—St. Helena, an isolated island off the West African coast.

In the same month of August, 1815, that the British warship *Northumberland* took Napoleon to St. Helena, Betsy, after ten years in America, landed in England.

13. Escape

F REE AT LAST to go where she pleased, Betsy was at Cheltenham, an English spa that rivalled Bath, since George III came to drink its waters. At the spring each morning, she could chat with people of wealth and fashion. But in her ears still rang the quarrels with her father that preceded her escape from Baltimore. He had angrily refused to help toward his daughter's expenses or let her cross the ocean on a Patterson ship. Betsy was forced to pay for her passage, on another line, and had to leave Jerome with his grandfather in order to get away.

Now, to her further irritation, Betsy discovered Papa had written to James McElhinny, his London agent, that her illness was imaginary, nothing more than a desire to get to Paris.

"The Cheltenham doctors assure me," she wrote him indignantly, "if I hadn't had sea air and a change of climate, the accumulation of bile on my liver would have killed me in three months." She implored her father to keep his thoughts to himself in the future, no matter how bitterly he felt toward her.

To impress him, Betsy filled her letters with the names of her new titled friends. She had taken a house adjoining that of Sir Arthur and Lady Brooke Falkener. She was going to a ball at Lady Condague's. The Portuguese ambassador, Count Tonsall, had sent her, through Viscount Lord Strangford, an invitation to a dance for the nobility of Cheltenham. Then, for fear Papa would think the gay life was corrupting her morals, Betsy assured him that "there is no danger of my committing a single imprudent action . . . Let people think you are proud of me, which indeed you have good reason to be, as I am very prudent and wise."

> "God grant it may be so," Mr. Patterson replied. "I must, however, say that your ideas of wisdom do not accord with mine. People must look at home for real happiness. It is impossible to find it for any length of time elsewhere. I hope you will soon be tired and dissatisfied with Europe, so as to induce you to return, convinced like myself that it is the proper place for you to reside. I shall be uneasy and unhappy until you return."

But Betsy was free at last. Papa could only scold her from across the Atlantic. The part of an invalid was too wearisome a role to play long. With her liver ailment cured by the gaieties of Cheltenham, nothing would satisfy Betsy but to be in Paris, the city Napoleon had for years kept her from entering. It was too expensive at present, crowded as Paris was with the Allied Army of Occupation. She went to Geneva, until Albert Gallatin, Madison's Secretary of the Treasury, whom Betsy had known in Washington, was appointed minister to France.

"My dear, there'll always be a *couvert* for you at my table," Mr. Gallatin had said. Betsy started for Paris, to accept his hospitality. The Gallatin son, nineteen-year-old James, tells in his diary on August 11, 1816, how Mme. Bonaparte arrived at the American legation— "Her baggage nearly filled the antechamber"—the first Bonaparte to enter the city where no other member of the family dared be seen for fear of arrest.

The Corsican clan had toppled from the dizzy heights to which Napoleon raised them. The Emperor was in his island prison of St. Helena; Joseph, in flight to America; Caroline, in Austria; Elisa, at Trieste; Madame Mère, Cardinal Fesch, Lucien, Louis and Pauline, living in exile in Italy. But the Bonaparte most hounded by the Allies had been Jerome. Louis XVIII, the new King of France, had given orders that he was to be arrested and shot.

Afraid for his life, the King of Westphalia had wandered about France in disguise, behind a false beard, until he found refuge in Austria. As the Count of Montfort, Jerome was living, virtually a prisoner, in Trieste. Catherine, who remained devoted to her husband in the midst of his misfortunes, after seven years of marriage, had given birth in 1814 to her first child, a son.

It was ironic that, with the Bonapartes banished, the American girl whom Napoleon hadn't considered good enough to reign as Jerome's queen should have all Paris at her feet. The old families of the Faubourg St. Germain, the diplomatic corps, statesmen and titled foreigners, all were enthusiastic in praise of the lovely Mme. Patterson, as Betsy called herself in Europe. Never had an American created such a social sensation in Paris. Her romantic love story made Betsy a heroine. Everyone wanted to meet her, including the man who had humbled Napoleon, the Duke of Wellington. She had beauty and wit; she was thought to be fabulously wealthy.

At last, Betsy was able to play the role for which she had always felt her talents fitted her. In the elegant drawing rooms to which the Gallatins took her, she could talk literature with Chateaubriand, history with Sismondi, science with Humboldt, art with Canova, politics with Mme. de Staël and exchange beauty secrets with Mme. Recamier.

She could also talk over financial matters with her host, America's able ex-Secretary of the Treasury, and ask his advice about investing her savings. Albert Gallatin was impressed with Betsy's shrewdness. "My dear, you married the wrong brother," he said. "Had you met Napoleon, the fate of Europe today might be quite different."

When she wasn't discussing money matters, Betsy was sure to be talking about Jerome. Her one thought was her son. She was ambitious for him and had long talks with Mr. Gallatin about Jerome's future. To his amusement, she showed him a list of European princesses who would be the right age for her boy to marry.

Gallatin smiled. "My dear Betsy, as Bo is only eleven, aren't you a little premature?"

The American minister had an audience one day with the King. Louis XVIII, old, fat and gouty, still had an eye for a pretty face. "Mr. Gallatin," he said, "I hear that Mme. Patterson is with you. I hope you'll bring her to the Tuileries."

Betsy was flattered, but she declined the honor. "Please remind the King that I'm a Bonaparte, Albert. Since I received a pension from Napoleon, I couldn't appear at the court of his successor. I've plenty of vices, but ingratitude isn't one of them."

At a ball at the Hôtel Charost, under the Empire the home of Pauline Bonaparte, now the British embassy, Betsy noticed she was much stared at, and that some of the ladies curtsied to her. "Who do they think I am? Royalty?" she asked the Duke of Wellington, now British ambassador, when he came to offer Mme. Patterson his arm to escort her out to supper.

"People think you're Pauline Bonaparte, you look so much like her," he replied. "They're amazed that, with Napoleon banished, the Princess Borghese dares to show her pretty face in Paris."

Betsy smiled proudly, as on the arm of the British ambassador she swept through the rooms where Pauline had reigned. How flattering to be mistaken for the most beautiful woman in Europe!

It was during this first visit of Betsy's to Paris that she made a lifelong friend in the Irish-born Lady Sydney Morgan, author of an 1806 best-seller, *The Wild Irish Girl.* Lady Morgan was in Paris with her husband, Sir Charles Morgan, a retired physician, doing research for a book on France she was writing. To her salon Lady Morgan invited only women who were beautiful and accomplished, only men who were handsome and intelligent. Among them were many English writers who came over from London. One day, Betsy was pleased to find there, Tom Moore, the Irish poet whom she had met in America, at Gouverneur Morris' home, while on her honeymoon.

Moore, famous since he published his Irish ballads, was delighted to renew his acquaintance with the lovely American. She was now unattached, the little Irishman noted, and set out to charm her. Betsy failed to respond.

"Beautiful lady, you're not even listening to me," the poet complained. "If I could only get down through those layers of ice about your heart. You've got the face of an angel, but what are you like behind that face? Were you in love with that rake you married?"

"Of course not, I married for position; anybody's a fool who marries for love," was Betsy's flip reply. Moore afterwards described Mme. Patterson as beautiful, but "devoid of all sentiment," and scornful of love, of which he said, she only made fun.

The truth was, men no longer attracted Betsy. Her father needn't have worried that she was leading a dissolute life in Europe. She had given all her love in one wild burst of passion. There seemed to be none left. Betsy flirted, all her friends did, but it was largely to prove to herself that her beauty could still attract men. They soon felt the chill in the lovely American "with no heart," and turned to more responsive women. Betsy could have married easily enough, had she wished, but having been Jerome's wife, the memory of those sixteen happy months kept her from making a loveless marriage.

Instead, she let disappointed suitors think her head was so turned from having been married to a king, she couldn't stoop to being the wife of a mere commoner. And Betsy transferred her love for the man who had deserted her into a fierce, possessive love for their son. She was desperately lonely for Bo, even among the distractions of Paris.

> "I have been ill," she wrote Lady Morgan, who was in London, *"et très triste, tout m'ennui dans ce monde, et je ne sais pas pourquoi* . . . I think the best thing I can do is to return to my dear child in the spring. I love him so entirely that perhaps seeing him may render my feelings less disagreeable."

Betsy came back to America in the fall of 1816, to find her brother Joseph about to marry Charlotte Nichols, whose sister Mary, in 1806, had married John Patterson. Her brother Robert and his wife were abroad.

The Napoleonic wars being over, the Robert Pattersons had sailed in the spring, with Mary's sisters, Elizabeth and Louisa. Grandfather Carroll paid the bills, and the purpose

of the trip was to get the Caton girls married, preferably to
titled Englishmen. In England, they had met the Duke of
Wellington and his one-armed aide, Colonel Sir Felton Hervey. In June, 1816, the Duke celebrated the first anniversary
of his triumph at Waterloo by showing the Americans over
the battlefield. They visited him at Walmer Castle, and Wellington arranged to have the beautiful Mrs. Robert Patterson
presented at court. The lovely Caton sisters created a sensation in London society, where they were known as the Three
American Graces.

Their letters home (especially after Louisa married Sir
Hervey in 1817) did not make pleasant reading for Betsy. She
had always been jealous of the Catons—Mary, especially. Life
had been much easier for the granddaughters of rich, generous Mr. Carroll than for her. Now Betsy contrasted the gay
times her old school friends were having in Europe with her
own quiet days in Baltimore. The hours passed tediously
and seemed endless in duration, shut up with Papa in the big,
gloomy house on South Street.

Betsy endured it, however, for three years, because she was
determined, when she sailed again, to buy two tickets for
Europe. It cost her nothing to live at home. But her father
refused to give her money to travel, so she remained in Baltimore and saved, until she should have enough to go abroad
with her son.

Her life was centered in Cricket, as Betsy affectionately
called her boy. She became obsessed with the idea of taking
him to Europe, and forcing the Bonapartes to accept her
child as one of the family. She had been cheated of her
rights. The same thing mustn't happen to Bo. The family
that had spurned her must be made to recognize him as King
Jerome's legitimate son. Joseph Bonaparte was in America,

as the Count of Survilliers. Betsy decided to take his nephew to see him.

After Waterloo, Joseph had done all he could to persuade Napoleon to escape to America in his place, since the brothers looked very much alike. Napoleon refused the generous offer; he gave himself up to the enemy. Joseph sailed and, dodging the British cruisers, managed to reach the United States safely. He lived briefly in New York, in a house overlooking the Hudson; then took a home on Ninth Street, above Spruce, in Philadelphia. He had recently purchased a country estate at Bordentown, New Jersey, called Point Breeze, where he was living when Betsy and her son came to see him.

The Count of Survilliers, a graying man of forty-five, greeted them alone at the door of his white mansion perched on the Jersey bank of the Delaware River. His wife had remained in Switzerland with their daughters, Zenaide and Charlotte. Pleading ill-health, Julie never came to America.

Joseph was delighted to meet his brother's American wife, about whom he had always been curious, and her son. After dinner, he took them on a tour of his house. The walls were covered with paintings the Count of Survilliers had brought from Spain. In every room there were marble busts of the Bonaparte family. He stopped before a cabinet, touched a secret spring, out shot a drawer filled with jewels.

"These are the crowns and rings I wore when King of Spain," the Count told the awe-struck Jerome.

Joseph complimented Betsy on the boy's nice manners. "You should take him to Italy," he said, "and show him to Madame Mère. His grandmother often says how she longs to clasp Jerome's American son in her arms."

Betsy was touched by Joseph's kind words. She had always been grateful to him for his support of her in her first married days, cautious though it was. In Corsica, the matriarch rules the clan. Betsy returned from her visit to Joseph more determined than ever to take her son to Italy to meet his grandmother. But first, to make a good impression, the boy must be well educated. She was anxious to enter Jerome in one of the fine Geneva schools of which Swiss-born Albert Gallatin had told her.

Betsy knew how her father felt about the Bonapartes—now more so than ever. And she realized that to separate him from his beloved grandson would bring on a violent quarrel. At supper, one night, she couldn't eat. While Moses served the meal, Betsy sat in silence or made conversation: "Did you have a busy day, Papa?" "Drink your milk, Bo, otherwise no dessert."

Supper over, the three settled down in the parlor. Her father promptly vanished behind the *Maryland Gazette.* Betsy sewed, while Jerome worked on a model of the clipper *Fair American.* Nine o'clock struck. "Bedtime!" Mr. Patterson announced, as he had every night since Betsy was a child. Jerome obediently put away his tools. Betsy kissed her son good-night and, trying to get up courage, watched him climb the stairs. "Papa, I want to go away—" She broke the silence, desperation in her voice.

William Patterson looked up over his spectacles. "You want to visit Dolly Madison?"

"No, not to Virginia. I mean go away—to Europe—" At the stricken look on his face, she tried to explain. "I've a duty abroad, something important I must do—"

He listened in silence, frowning.

"I've been saving for years for this. Waiting for Jerome to grow up. He's almost fourteen. It's time he met his father's people. The Bonapartes must be made to acknowledge him as one of the family. And I think they will, if I play my cards right. Joseph was very encouraging, Papa. He said I should take Jerome to Italy and have his grandmother see him."

"You mean," he asked, incredulously, "you're going to take my grandson away from me, off on a wild goose chase to Europe?"

"Certainly."

"By gad, Betsy," her father burst out, "go to Europe alone and live your life as you please. I've ceased to expect you to listen to me. But don't ruin Jerome by filling his head full of that European nonsense. Even in their days of prosperity, the Bonapartes were a worthless bunch. Why in blazes do you want to have anything to do with them, now that they're in exile and discredited? After the way Jerome's family treated you, I should think you'd have more pride."

Betsy listened, twisting her handkerchief around her fingers. Suddenly tears were streaming down her face. "You don't understand me, Papa. You never have. Oh, I wish Mama were here!"

It was to her mother Betsy had always gone as a child with her troubles. Dorcas Patterson had loved her foreign son-in-law. She had sympathized with Betsy at having to return home a deserted wife. But William Patterson had never realized the hurt and humiliation his daughter felt.

"It's terribly important for Jerome, for myself, too," Betsy kept saying, trying to make her father understand why she must go abroad. Couldn't Papa see that, if she could only get the Bonapartes to acknowledge Jerome's kinship with the clan, they would also be admitting that her marriage was legal? Perhaps Betsy didn't state her case clearly enough. She had always found it hard to talk things over with her father. "Are you listening, Papa?" she finally asked.

"I'm listening," he snapped. "And your reasons for going to Europe are a lot of nonsense! The Bonapartes have shown plainly enough they want nothing more to do with you. You'll only get another rebuff. You're always saying you live only for your child, Betsy. Well, I love Jerome, too. And I say that your duty is not to interrupt his schooling. The boy's happy at St. Mary's. He's doing well at his studies, Father Dubois tells me. I always hoped that some day he would go to Harvard—"

Her frown was suddenly equal to his. "Oh, no Papa, I've other plans for him. This is no new idea of mine. I've been saving for years to take Jerome to Geneva. There's a school there Mr. Gallatin told me about that teaches fencing—"

That was too much for self-made Mr. Patterson. "Fencing!" he exploded. "I suppose fencing is going to help Jerome earn his living? Because that's what he's going to have to do, if you take my grandson abroad. You won't get a shilling of mine, for his education or anything else."

"I know that, Papa. You've made it plain enough. I'll have to get along on very little. But I'll manage to do it, if it kills me."

William Patterson's eyes flashed. Tossing his newspaper aside, he sprang to his feet and turned on Betsy with unrestrained fury. "Take my grandson to Europe, turn him into a waster like his father, and I promise you, my girl, I'll disinherit you!"

"*Ssh!* Don't shout so, Papa. Jerome will hear you. And you're not to call his father a waster. I won't have it!" Betsy glared at her angry parent, pacing the floor.

They quarreled constantly, but her father had never spoken to her in this way before. His words, his strident voice, his threatening scowl, struck through Betsy to the heart, when she had hoped he would sympathize with her and understand.

"Why don't you just love me, Papa, and let me do as I

please," she retorted, "without opposing me all the time and
tormenting me with advice which I've no intention of following? Threaten me all you want. It won't do any good.
My mind is made up. I'm taking Jerome to Europe. I've a
duty to my child, so nothing you can say will frighten me into
staying home."

She had risen by now. The two stood facing each other,
both in the grip of anger, both resentful, both extraordi-
narily alike in their determined expressions.

William was the first to speak. "All right, take my grandson to Europe. But I warn you, Betsy, as I told you when
you married, you'll live to regret it!"

It was almost as hard for Betsy to break the news that they
were sailing to Jerome. He was heartbroken at leaving his
grandfather, the kindly priests at St. Mary's, his classmates
and his pets. But Jerome was used to obeying Mama. If she
wanted to go to Europe, he supposed he would have to go,
but he raised all the objections he could think of. Grandpa
had promised to take him duck hunting this fall. He was
teaching Star, his pony, to jump. And how his dog, Frisky,
would miss him!

Frisky wasn't much to look at, with his ragged yellow coat.
The mongrel had just drifted in off South Street one day,
curled up on the hearth with a sigh and decided he had found
a good home. Since then, Frisky had more than paid for his
keep by chasing rabbits out of the flower beds. Yet Mama
said he must be left behind.

Jerome prayed he might get sick. Surely, something would
prevent their going. But each day brought him nearer the
moment when he must say good-bye to Baltimore and everything he loved.

Bo, who slept in an alcove opening off his mother's room,

was used to waking at night to hear her crying in the dark. He would lie quiet, wondering why Mama cried, and what a boy nearly fourteen could do about it? But on the night of May 1, 1819, with Nancy Spear coming to keep house for Mr. Patterson, Mme. Bonaparte and her son sailing in the morning, Betsy was too excited and happy to go to sleep, and it was Jerome who lay with his face buried in the pillow. In spite of his hands pressed over his eyes, the tears ran through his fingers. He couldn't stop them.

"Darling, are you all right?" asked an anxious voice. He answered, reassuringly. But when his mother dozed off, Jerome slipped out of bed, put on a coat and tiptoed down the stairs. He was on his way out to the woodshed, to have a good cry.

Frisky welcomed him by almost wagging his tail off. His sad, anxious eyes seemed to show he knew his young master was leaving him, as Jerome huddled there with the dog's silky body heavy and warm in his arms. A cold nose touched his wet cheek. Frisky comforted him, licking away his tears, as the boy used a big soft paw for a handkerchief.

14. The American Bonapartes

On JUNE 25, after a tedious voyage of seven weeks, Betsy and her son arrived at Amsterdam, Holland. But when she asked for a passport to cross France, the French chargé d'affaires, looking at Jerome, shook his head.

"Your son looks so much like the Emperor, it might cause a Bonapartist uprising for him to be seen in France. People would think Napoleon had escaped from St. Helena."

The official was joking. But the plump boy, a hand thrust into the front of his coat, did look like a miniature Napoleon. There was a strong family resemblance.

"Yes, except for age, my son could be mistaken for the Emperor," Betsy agreed, and proudly paid the seventy-five guineas her roundabout journey to Switzerland in a private carriage cost her.

She remembered what the French chargé d'affaires in Holland had said, and, although in Baltimore Betsy was always known as Mme. Bonaparte, she never used this title in Europe. She went by the name of Mme. Patterson, her son as Edward Patterson, for fear of being hounded by the Bourbon police, like the rest of the Bonaparte family.

In Geneva, Betsy stayed for two months in a suburban boardinghouse, until she could find less expensive lodgings in town, for she could not afford a carriage. She finally rented a four-room apartment for $60 a month, engaged a maid-of-all-work and, after some sharp bargaining, arranged with a woman to furnish meals for her at a reasonable price.

Betsy saw that, even if she lived as cheaply as possible, it was going to be hard for her to get along. Her pension had stopped with Napoleon's exile. Her income of $5,500 a year, which was the interest on the Emperor's annuity, didn't permit her any luxuries. She had determined to limit her expenses to $3,000 a year and, by sending the balance to an American broker, John White, to invest for her, build up a fortune that Jerome would need some day to establish his rights as an Imperial prince.

His schooling cost her $1,000 annually. But Betsy didn't begrudge that. She was pleased with Jerome's school, where he was not only being taught languages, mathematics, history and science, but such important accomplishments for a gentleman to acquire as drawing, riding, dancing and fencing. Not that Betsy wanted Jerome to duel, but she thought fencing developed ease and grace.

"You must study hard," she lectured him, "for you'll have to earn your own living. You're the son of a king, but poor. Your father contributes nothing toward your support, your rich grandfather refuses to make us an allowance; and all I can do for you until I die is to give you a good education."

In spite of her small apartment in a poor section of Geneva, Mme. Patterson was so attractive she was invited everywhere. The city was thronged with titled foreigners. Among them were many Russians—Princess Potempkin, Prince and Prin-

cess Alexander Galitzin and Count Nicholas Demidov, whose
ancestor, a Russian serf, had amassed an immense fortune by
furnishing arms to Peter the Great.

"Mama looks ten years younger than she is, and if she
hadn't so large a son, could pass for five and twenty," Jerome
wrote his grandfather. Betsy was taking dancing lessons three
times a week and going out nearly every night to the theater
or a ball. She loved every minute of it. Through her own
efforts, she was establishing herself in the world that Napoleon had kept her from entering. Walking into Princess
Potempkin's reception on the arm of the Grand Duke of
Mecklenburg-Schwerin, Betsy felt herself that evening every
inch a queen. She hoped her ex-husband would hear of her
social triumphs.

The Prince of Wurtemberg, Queen Catherine's uncle,
looking at Mme. Patterson, exclaimed, "How could Jerome
have left such a woman!"

Bo came from school to spend weekends with his mother.
Every Saturday night she took him to a fashionable ball,
to teach him the social graces. After her quiet years in Baltimore, it was intoxicating for Betsy to dress exquisitely and,
as she swept into concerts and balls, overhear on all sides the
murmur of admiration for her charm and beauty. But by
suppertime, she would find Jerome asleep behind the palms
or morosely watching the dancers.

"My poor darling, I wish you liked parties more," Betsy
sighed. Gracious, what ailed the boy? He looked as though
he had lost his last friend.

Jerome was enduring the gaieties of Geneva stoically for
his mother's sake. He wished he liked formal social life as
much as Le Loup did. Everyone in town seemed to know
Frisky's successor. When Jerome took his handsome black
dog for a walk, strangers called Le Loup by name and said

good-morning to him. A Miss Frabri sent Le Loup an invitation to a party, to which Jerome took his pet. That was fun; but, generally, he found European social life boring, with its curtseying and hand kissing. Jerome often thought of the informal Sunday dinners at his grandfather's home in Baltimore, with his uncles and aunts and cousins gathered around the table. Homesick for the big house on South Street, he wrote Mr. Patterson:

> Since I have been in Europe I have dined with princes and princesses and all the great people in Europe, but I haven't found a dish as much to my taste as the roast beef and beefsteak I ate in South Street . . . I never had any idea of remaining all my life on the Continent. On the contrary, as soon as my education is finished, which will not take more than two years longer, I shall hasten over to America, which I've regretted leaving ever since I left.

At the boardinghouse where Betsy stayed on first coming to Geneva, she had met the American fur-king, John Jacob Astor. He ate his ice cream and peas with a knife, but Betsy liked the shrewd Astor. The son of a butcher in Waldorf, Germany, he had landed with several musical instruments (his sole capital) at Baltimore, where he was induced to trade them for his first bundle of furs. He had gone on to make a fortune in furs and real estate. Now Mr. Astor was visiting Switzerland for the same reason as Mme. Patterson, to enter his son in school. He was also trying to find a titled husband for his daughter, Eliza, who was not at all pretty.

In the spring of 1820, John Jacob Astor was going to Rome, where Madame Mère, her half-brother Cardinal Fesch, Louis, Lucien and Pauline were living. "If you should meet my Imperial relatives," Betsy said to him, "let them know that the American Bonapartes are in Europe." In April, she was thrilled when Astor wrote her:

Last evening we had the honor of an introduction to the Princess Borghese, who immediately inquired after you and your son. When I informed her that I had left you at Geneva, she expressed much regret at your not having made the journey with us. She said: "I am happy to find an opportunity of speaking frankly to you. I wish very much to see Madame P. and her son here. My object is to make some provision for the son of my brother, who is poor and can give him nothing. I am rich and have no child, and find in myself every disposition to do everything for him." She requested me to write to you without delay in her name, to invite you to make her a visit and to bring your son.

Shortly after, there was another sign of recognition from the Bonaparte family to make Betsy happy. Joseph wrote from America to offer her the use of his Château of Prangins, on the shore of Lake Geneva. It was too far out of town for Betsy, who could not afford a carriage, to live in, so she declined the King of Spain's offer, with thanks. But she was pleased by Joseph's interest in her welfare.

As for the Princess Borghese's invitation to Rome that, at first, had delighted Betsy, what she heard from Lady Morgan made her wonder whether it was wise to accept it.

Left a widow by her husband's death in Saint-Domingue, Pauline had married Prince Camillo Borghese, head of the richest family in Italy. His titles dated from the election of a Borghese to the Papal throne as Paul V, in 1605. Prince Camillo owned vast estates and palaces in both Florence and Rome, along with the finest private art collection and family jewels in all Europe. Pauline and Camillo were separated. Prince Borghese was living in Florence; his wife in Rome, in a country house Pauline had purchased outside the Porta Pia and named the Villa Paolina. Lady Morgan, who was visiting in Geneva, had recently been entertained in Rome by the Princess. Betsy questioned her closely.

"Pauline's a different person from the frivolous beauty whose amours made her the talk of Europe," Sydney Morgan replied. "Napoleon's downfall sobered her. Borghese gives his wife 70,000 francs a year, but she no longer has the million and a half francs Napoleon gave her. Betsy, I don't know what you can expect from the Princess. She is impulsive, generous and utterly unreliable. Pauline is extravagant with herself. Toward others, often downright stingy. One day, she'll dismiss several servants and cut down her expenses with petty economies. Next day, she's as likely as not to spend 100,000 francs at the jewelers. I wouldn't count on any of Pauline's promises. She dislikes Jerome's wife and may only be showing an interest in your son to annoy Catherine."

Those Bonapartes! In exile, they were as proud and self-sufficient and held their heads as high, Lady Morgan declared, as if they still ruled the world.

Should she take Jerome out of school, where he was making splendid progress, and embark on an expensive trip to Italy that might lead to nothing, Betsy began to wonder.

In a few months, Mr. Astor returned from Italy to tell her of a conversation he had with the Princess Borghese. She asked him if Mme. Patterson's father helped her out financially. Jerome had told his family that Betsy's father was one of the wealthiest men in America, so the Princess hoped that he did.

"I replied that your father was very rich," Astor reported to Betsy, "but his fortune was in houses and land, which at present didn't produce much. He had a large family, many children besides yourself, so you must economize to educate your son."

"Doesn't Jerome give them anything?" Pauline had asked.

"I said you never received a dollar from him."

"Then, with Napoleon's pension stopped, poor Mme. Pat-

terson must be in want! Write to her, Mr. Astor, to bring
her son to Rome. Tell her that my mother and I will be
generous."

Still John Jacob Astor, like Lady Morgan, advised Betsy
not to rely on any promises the Princess Borghese might
make. "She's a fickle woman, I'm told, fond of promising
her nephews and nieces lavish gifts, then quarreling with
them and forgetting her promises."

Instead, Betsy decided to pocket her pride and to appeal to
Bo's father to help her support their son. Jerome's reply to
her letter brought back bittersweet memories as Betsy tore
it open—and the realization she could hope for nothing from
him. Jerome wrote he was too poor now to provide for his
two children by Catherine. They were living on pensions
from the King of Wurtemberg and from Catherine's cousin,
the Czar of Russia. And he added, with a touch of humor,
"Surely, my dear Elise, you know me well enough to know
I never saved anything, when I had money."

It was Jerome's usual letter, full of excuses, but, after quoting it to her father, Betsy wrote, "I believe he is not as bad-
hearted as many people think." She knew all of Jerome's
faults and still remembered him tenderly. His letter upset
her for days.

The Count of Montfort was ruined, Betsy heard, his capital
spent, his debts enormous, for even in exile, Jerome tried to
live like a king. And Astor had warned her to keep away
from Pauline. But the death of Jerome's eldest sister, the
Princess Bacciochi, followed by that of Napoleon at St. Helena
in May, 1821, caused Betsy to change her mind about taking
her son to Rome.

Madame Mère and her brother, Cardinal Fesch, were getting old. If she waited for two years, until Cricket graduated
from school, it might be too late. His grandmother was the

one Jerome should meet. The old lady was said to have saved two-thirds of the one million francs a year Napoleon gave her. She had it invested secretly all over Europe. She would leave a large fortune. But it wasn't of the money Betsy was thinking, welcome as that would be. What she wanted most of all was kinship with the clan. If her son was mentioned in Madame Mère's will with the other grandchildren, it would show the world that Jerome's first-born had been accepted in the family.

So in November, 1821, the American Bonapartes left Geneva for Italy in a public coach—Betsy worrying all the way about the expense, fifteen Louis d'or each for their meals and a seat in the six-seated carriage, seven Louis for her maid who sat outside with the coachmen, tips for the servants at the inns and the three Louis the driver would expect at the end of the trip.

She caught a cold crossing the Alps at two o'clock in the morning and, on reaching Rome, was in bed for a week. The Princess Borghese heard of Mme. Patterson's arrival. Pauline wrote her a cordial invitation to call, sent it to all the hotels in Rome, but never dreamed she would find her sister-in-law staying in the cheap rooming house where she was finally located.

The next afternoon, the Princess sent her carriage with four horses and postillions to bring Betsy and her son out to the Villa Paolina. She was eager to meet the woman whom everyone said resembled her. However, when the two ladies met, both dark, petite and in their thirties, Betsy found it hard to believe that this thin, faded invalid had once been the most beautiful woman in Europe. Of Pauline's famous beauty, little remained, only her lovely, dark eyes.

Yet the Princess, who had lost her health, her looks and most of her wealth, was never so popular in Rome, for

Pauline had won everyone's admiration by her loyalty to Napoleon after his downfall. None of the family, with the exception of his mother, had loved the Emperor as unselfishly as his younger sister. With Madame Mère, the Princess shared Napoleon's exile at Elba. She gave him her jewels to finance his escape to France. After Waterloo, Napoleon, crushed forever, ill and in exile, was dearer to Pauline than ever. In spite of her own bad health, she was doing all she could to persuade the British government to allow her to go to St. Helena and join her sick brother, when she heard of his death on that barren rock in the South Atlantic, on May 5, 1821.

"The cruel English even refuse to let me bring his body back to France," Pauline told Betsy. "Napoleon asked to be buried on the banks of the Seine, among the French people whom he loved. It breaks my heart not to be able to grant his last wish."

The Princess Borghese found the American Bonapartes charming. Being in one of her generous moods, Pauline gave her sister-in-law a pink satin ball gown one day, a fur-lined spenser on another, then a plumed bonnet. She dressed Jerome in a new outfit, from head to foot; promised him a clothes allowance of $400 a year; and took Betsy and her son to call on the matriarch of the clan.

On coming to Rome after Waterloo, Madame Mère had shared a house with her brother, the Palazzo Falconieri on the Via Julia. She lived on the first floor; the Cardinal occupied the second. But three years ago, having sold her Paris property, Signora Letizia was able to buy a home of her own, the Palazzo Rinucci on the Via Condotti.

"You may have trouble talking with Mama. She speaks Italian, very little French," Pauline warned. But Betsy forgot the language barrier between them, when Jerome's

mother, a stern-faced Corsican woman, greeted her affectionately.

"How pretty you are, *cara mia!*" Signora Letizia, taking
Betsy's hand, said in a mixture of Italian and deplorable
French. "And this is my Jerome's son? Dark like his father,
but not so handsome, and I hope not so fond of the girls!
Come sit beside me—" She drew her daughter-in-law down
on a sofa. "Did you have a pleasant journey from Geneva?"

As they chatted, Betsy studied this dark-haired woman who
had been through so many vicissitudes. His mother was, as
Jerome said, still beautiful, and with her dignified manners,
a most impressive figure. In repose, she seemed cold and
reserved. But like all the Bonapartes, Signora Letizia had
fine teeth and a charming smile that lighted up her severe
features when she talked.

"Do you hate us?" she asked. "You should. My son Napoleon ruined your life."

"I feel no resentment toward any of your family," Betsy
replied. "I realize I was sacrificed for political reasons."

"You're very forgiving. And that naughty Jerome of mine,
why did you marry him?"

"Because I loved him," his discarded wife said softly.

"And still do and always will? Don't hang your head, *cara
mia.* I can see the love in your eyes when I speak his name.
His present wife loves him, too. After Waterloo, Catherine
refused to go back to her father. She followed Jerome into
exile and insists she is happy, though he's anything but a
faithful husband. What is Jerome's charm? I often ask myself, for I can't resist him either. When he writes me for
money, Pauline is annoyed when I send him what she tells
me I deny to my other children."

Betsy liked Madame Mère the best of the family. Signora
Letizia lived economically because her tastes had remained

simple, and she hoarded her money, not from avarice, but
so she could help the clan. She loved best the son that needed
her most. Madame Mère was shocked by her children's
extravagance. She scolded them for it. But she always re-
sponded generously to an appeal from any of them.

Signora Letizia was as pleased as Pauline with the American Bonapartes. She gave Jerome forty guineas to buy a
horse, but as she neglected to pay for its stabling, Betsy declared they couldn't afford such a luxury and insisted Jerome
hire a horse by the month. On his hired hack, he rode by his
Aunt Pauline's carriage afternoons; he dined with his grandmother and played *reversi* with Letizia and Cardinal Fesch in
the evenings. Since Napoleon's death, Madame Mère lived as
a recluse. She refused even to attend the theater, once her
greatest pleasure.

His grandmother took Jerome and his mother to call on
Louis, the ex-King of Holland, an invalid, separated from his
wife Hortense; and on Lucien, whom Pius VII had created
Prince of Canino. Bo wrote his grandfather in Baltimore:

> I have been received in the kindest manner possible by
> my grandmother, my uncles and aunts and cousins, and all
> my nearest and most distant relations, who are in Rome.
> We mean to stay here during the winter . . . I have been so
> much occupied in looking for apartments for Mama, making
> tight bargains, and seeing my relations, that I have not had
> time to see anything of Rome, except St. Peter's celebrated
> church, which I have seen but superficially.

The American Bonapartes did not know it, but their Imperial relatives were looking them over. Like most Corsican
families, they believed in intermarriage. Joseph, after meeting young Jerome in America, had written to Pauline to propose that the boy marry his younger daughter Charlotte. Now,
having seen Jerome, Madame Mère wrote agreeing with

Joseph that Jerome was the husband for Charlotte, who had gone to America to visit her father.

> Before this you will have embraced your Charlotte; she will be a great comfort to you. You were right to decide to marry her to Jerome's son. The young man has been here two months. I am amazed at him. It is hardly possible to find so much *aplomb* and good sense in one of his age. There is no doubt that Charlotte will be happy.
>
> You will find enclosed copies of the letters from his father and Catherine; they will show you their desire to see this union effected. I have written to you, as Pauline did also, that she has promised, in the event of this marriage, 300,000 francs to be paid at her death. If you are of the same opinion, it will only be necessary to write to Jerome to return to America at once.

Bo's Uncle Louis also approved of the match. One day Madame Mère suggested the idea to Jerome's mother.

"What would you think of it, Elisa? We like Jerome, for himself and on account of the name. In that way, Joseph's money will remain in the family."

Betsy was so delighted, her joy scarcely permitted her to speak. "I should be—highly honored—" she stammered.

Through Betsy's mind flashed the thought that her son would be marrying royalty, the daughter of the ex-King of Spain, the niece of the Queen of Sweden. This was the kind of marriage she had always hoped Jerome would make. Her money problems would be over. Joseph, who was reported to have smuggled out a million dollars from Switzerland in jewels alone, was said to be planning to give his daughter $100,000 as a marriage settlement. But more important to Betsy was the recognition of her own marriage this alliance would mean. She had hoped to have her son mentioned in his grandmother's will. This was infinitely better. A marriage with a Bonaparte cousin would declare to the world that Jerome's legitimacy was acknowledged by his father's family in a way that could never be disputed.

But Jerome's feelings must be considered. At sixteen, the boy was naturally romantic. What would he say to a marriage arranged for him by his family in the European manner?

"I'm not forcing you into this, darling," Betsy said wistfully, "but surely you realize what it would mean for both of us—" Jerome was old enough to have been told the truth, that because the validity of her marriage had been questioned in France, there was some doubt of his right to the Bonaparte name.

"All right, I'll go to America and look Charlotte over," he agreed, "that is, if I can take Le Loup with me."

Betsy, congratulating herself on having such a docile son, would have been dumbfounded to know that Jerome was so homesick he would even marry a cousin he had never seen to get back to America. Happier than he had been for a long time, Jerome wrote on January 7, 1822, to his grandfather:

> I have been now seven weeks in Rome, and have been received in the kindest and most hospitable manner possible by all my relations who are in Rome. My father is expected, but I don't know whether he will come. My grandmother and my aunt and uncle talk of marrying me to my uncle's, the Count of Survillier's daughter, who is in the United States. I hope it may take place, for then I would return immediately to America to pass the rest of my life among my relations and friends. Mama is very anxious for the match. My father is also, and all of my father's family, so I hope you will approve of it.

It was arranged that Jerome should leave on the *White Oak,* in February, 1822; and while he was at Leghorn, waiting to sail, he again wrote his grandfather:

Mama is still in Rome, and is not decided whether she will embark in the spring for America or not. I should rather think not, as the climate does not suit her, and her health is bad in the United States. I am very glad that I shall soon have the pleasure of seeing you and all my relations and my country; but, on the other hand, I am going to leave Mama and my relations on my father's side, who have been so very kind to me during my stay in Rome.

Betsy had set her heart on this match. But she was too thrifty to go to the expense of crossing the Atlantic, until the engagement was actually announced. Her father could look after Jerome's interests as well as herself. She wrote him to be shrewd with Joseph Bonaparte over the marriage settlement. And she cautioned him not to tell any of the family, Aunt Margaret, Aunt Nancy, or her brothers George and Henry, a word about this arranged marriage. They would be shocked and might talk Jerome out of it.

Betsy also reminded her father that the examination at Cambridge took place on the 26th of August. After her own unhappy experience, she was skeptical of any verbal promises the Bonapartes might make. Betsy had decided, if the marriage with Princess Charlotte fell through, rather than go to the expense of bringing Jerome back to Europe, he might as well enter Harvard, as his grandfather wished. That would be a calamity, though, Betsy hoped she would never have to face.

A few weeks after her son sailed, Mme. Patterson began to pack to return to Geneva. The King of Westphalia was expected in Rome. Since Napoleon's death, the Bonapartes were allowed to travel about Europe more freely, and Jerome was coming to Italy to visit his family. Betsy wrote her father:

They expect the K.W. and his wife here on a visit to his mother. I fancy he is coming to get money out of her . . . I shall not see the K.W., nor would he like it himself, after the unhandsome way in which he has always conducted himself. I shall hold my tongue, which is all I can possibly do for him.

Holding her tongue when Jerome's name was mentioned wasn't easy. Saying spiteful things about him seemed to ease the ache in Betsy's heart. More than anything in the world she longed to see her ex-husband. So Betsy went about Rome saying that nothing would induce her to remain in Italy *one moment* after the King of Westphalia arrived.

Otherwise, she was glad to be leaving Rome. Pauline, ill with the cancer that would kill her in a few years, made everyone's life miserable with her caprices. There was a quarrel over a dress that Betsy thought the Princess had given her, and Pauline declared had only been lent. The Princess Borghese retaliated by telling friends she hadn't invited the American Bonapartes to Rome, they had come and forced themselves on her. As for Jerome Junior, she would "give him nothing, either during her life or after her death." Betsy, sick at heart, after catering for weeks to the Princess' whims, wrote her father:

She has treated him exactly as she has done all her other nephews—that is, promised and then retracted. She makes a new will every day . . . and will finally leave her property to strangers. All that has been said of her is not half what she deserves . . . it is impossible not to believe her mad.

Lady Morgan and Mr. Astor had warned her. She might have expected it. Still, to be snubbed by Pauline, who at first had been so friendly, was humiliating to Betsy's pride. She was "continually vomiting," she wrote home to Baltimore, her stomach troubling her, as it always did when she was emotionally upset. Though "if I hear of his (Jerome's) safe arrival and his marriage, I shall be quite well again." Rome was "horribly dear," so Betsy decided to return to cheaper Geneva with her friends the Packards.

On the way, they stopped over in Florence to do some sight-seeing. Betsy was inspecting the paintings in the Pitti Palace, when she felt someone looking at her. She turned and, to her consternation, found herself staring into the startled eyes of her ex-husband.

It was nearly seventeen years since that morning in Lisbon when Jerome had kissed away her tears and ridden off to face Napoleon. But as he stood across the room with his second wife and a group of friends, Betsy saw the soft light of remembrance come into his eyes.

The handsome prince of her youth had grown stout. He was losing his hair, she noticed with satisfaction. The years had been kinder to Betsy. At thirty-seven, she still had the beauty that had won Jerome in the first place, and could win him again, if she so much as crooked a finger. The eagerness in his eyes told her, plainly enough, that he would be willing to pick up where they had left off.

But did she want to revive a love that for each of them had never really died? "I'm not going to so much as speak to him!" Betsy quickly decided. Their eyes, a kiss in them, had met across the crowded room. There was no need for words. Let each of them keep their illusions. It was better that way.

The King of Westphalia left his wife's side. He reached out a hand and took a step in Betsy's direction. But the woman he had spurned started quickly for the door. As she passed her ex-husband, though, vanity made Betsy fling her coat open to let him see her smooth white throat, her still slim and graceful figure, and compare her with his dowdy Catherine, she hoped.

Jerome turned to his aide. "That's the only woman I ever really loved, my American wife," Betsy heard her old-time lover say, as she walked past him, head high, and out of the room.

15. Jerome Sows Some Wild Oats

JEROME, arriving in New York on April 21, 1822, with his dog Le Loup, longed to go straight to Baltimore, he was so eager to see his grandfather. But Bordentown, New Jersey, was on the direct route south. He knew his mother would wish him to call on his Uncle Joseph. His conscience troubled him. Freed for the first time from Betsy's domination, the sixteen-year-old boy, before sailing from Leghorn, had recklessly bought six hundred cigars—and told the tobacco merchant to send his mother the bill. Jerome dreaded to think what she would say; he mustn't provoke her further. So from New York Jerome wrote his grandfather he would pass a few days in Bordentown on the way home.

> Mama has written to you the object of my journey. I left her in Rome. She intends to go thence to Geneva, there to remain, her health being too delicate (as she thinks) to support the American climate.

Until now, Jerome had been too happy, just being back in America, to think of anything else. But on the boat ride from New York to Amboy, he began to wonder for the first time what Princess Charlotte was like. A girl brought up in Europe, would she be willing to live in America? Well, she'd have to! He hated Europe, nothing would induce him to live there.

Jerome remembered the white mansion, perched on the Jersey bank of the Delaware River, that he had visited with his mother three years ago. But when the stage dropped the young man and his dog off in Bordentown, at the gate to Bonaparte Park, he hardly recognized the place. Two years ago, the big house had burned. The Count of Survilliers had converted his stable into a cottage, easier on his rheumatic limbs. But the smaller house was furnished as the old, with the loot Joseph had brought from Europe and the Napoleonic relics rescued from the fire.

The ex-King of Spain met his nephew at the door. "How is your lovely mother?" he asked, embracing him. "Jerome, meet your Cousin Lolotte—" So this was the girl he was to marry? Jerome looked at her furtively, as he followed his uncle into the parlor. She was a pale, mousy little person he saw, neither pretty, nor homely.

There were other guests, two titled Frenchmen visiting America. At dinner, seated across the table from Princess Charlotte, Jerome watched her between the candles and wished they could get acquainted. But the meal over, the Count took his guests into his library and showed them the Spanish Crown jewels Jerome remembered seeing as a boy. He turned from the group of men examining one of Napoleon's treaties to speak to Charlotte. She had disappeared.

Next day, the girl proved as elusive. After breakfast, the Count of Survilliers took his nephew on a long horseback ride. He showed him the house by a lake he was building for his older daughter, Princess Zenaide, who was to marry her cousin, Prince Charles Bonaparte, Lucien's eldest son, in Brussels, in June.

Charlotte hardly spoke at lunch and excused herself as soon as they returned to her father's study. The Count, placing an album on the table, told Jerome to draw up a chair. He opened the book, filled with engravings of Napoleon's life and, pausing at every page, described at length the scenes pictured. It was late in the afternoon, when his uncle finally went to take a nap before dinner, before Jerome was able to escape and take Le Loup for a walk.

"Where's Charlotte?" her reluctant suitor raged. "What kind of a courtship is this? How can I woo a girl I can't even talk to?"

In a summerhouse overlooking the Delaware, he came upon his cousin sketching. Jerome sat down beside her. He wanted to put his hand on Charlotte's reassuringly and say, "Don't be afraid of me, I don't want to marry you any more than you want to marry me!" Instead, he asked cheerily, "May I see your drawings?" He looked at the sketch in her lap, of a ship's cabin in which a man sat reading a book. Under the drawing was written, "Capt. Mickle."

Charlotte blushed. "That's the captain of the ship on which I came from France." She showed him her sketchbook, filled, Jerome saw, with pictures of handsome Captain Mickle of Camden, New Jersey.

An hour later, when they walked back to the house, Charlotte and Jerome had become sufficiently good friends for her to confide to him that she had given the young American seaman a diamond pin when they parted. Jerome suspected Charlotte was in love with him. Yet he realized, shocked and full of pity for the poor girl, that she was reconciled never to see Captain Mickle again and resigned to marry whatever Bonaparte cousin her father selected for

her—himself; Napoleon, Louis' son; or Achille Murat, Caroline's boy, who, Jerome learned, was coming on a visit to
Bordentown.

He also discovered that, in the European manner of arranging a marriage, it wasn't Princess Charlotte he must court,
but her father. Jerome was expected to ride with his uncle
mornings, to listen by the hour to the Count's stories about
Napoleon and to admire his art treasures. Bo was thankful
enough when, after two days, he found an excuse to leave.

"You must come and see us again," his uncle said.
"Zenaide and Charles will be with me in a few months, and
your other cousins, Napoleon and Achille."

Jerome drove away with the feeling that the Count of
Survilliers had deliberately mentioned Napoleon and Achille
to let him know that Charlotte had other suitors. Well, he
couldn't compete with Napoleon, the ex-Crown Prince of
Holland, or with Achille Murat, the ex-Crown Prince of
Naples! Jerome felt strangely lighthearted about it. With
Le Loup gamboling beside him, the young man danced a
jig on the deck of the boat that carried him down the Delaware to Philadelphia. If he thought of his mother's disappointment, he put it quickly out of his mind.

Never had Baltimore looked so good to Jerome as when
he and Le Loup bounded over the threshold of his grandfather's house on South Street. Nancy Spear, with a cry of
joy, jumped up so quickly to embrace him she knocked over
her tapestry frame.

"Jerome Napoleon Bonaparte! Well, for mercy's sake! We
didn't expect you for days. I told your grandfather you'd
stay in Bordentown at least a week. What happened? Was
your cousin so homely you couldn't stand her?"

"Oh, Charlotte was all right."

"Is that Le Loup? What a handsome dog! Oh, your grandfather will be glad to see you! He's been so lonely without you, Jerome. He carries your letters in his pocket and reads them to everyone he meets. He'll be home any minute from his counting-house. Run up, dear, and wash your hands. It's almost time for dinner. We're having roast beef. Isn't that lucky? You wrote us how you missed roast beef and steak in Europe."

Up to his old room—everything unchanged, although Jerome felt he had been away for a thousand years. Then he must dash all over the house and out into the garden, searching out every nook and corner of which he had memories, to show them to Le Loup. The big black dog bounded along, as excited as Jerome.

In the kitchen, Mammy Lu was sitting by the table, shelling peas. She gave a leap and a shout when Jerome threw his arms about her. "Mercy me, if it ain't de Young Massa! Come a'runnin', Moses, Homer, Magnolia, he's home agin! Praise be de Lord!"

They all gathered about him, the devoted servants he had known since childhood, admiring him, asking him questions. Do people die of happiness? Jerome wondered. He was back in dear old Baltimore, so happy he wanted to cry.

Zeke hurried in from the stables. Jerome was asking him about Frisky, who was living contentedly out at Springfield, when he heard the front door slam. A few minutes later, Bo was in his grandfather's arms.

"My boy, I've missed you! I don't know what I'd have done without your letters. We'll have to ride out to Springfield tomorrow and introduce Le Loup to Frisky, won't we, Jerome? And this fall we'll go duck hunting."

Now they were sitting around the dinner table, eating Mammy Lu's juicy roast beef, her crisp oyster patties and flaky cherry pie, of which Jerome had dreamed in Europe. Moses kept urging another helping on him.

"Well, do we drink to your engagement?" William Patterson asked, lifting his glass of Madeira.

His grandson grinned happily. "No, I haven't a chance in the world with Charlotte. Uncle Joseph never mentioned a word about the reason for my visit. I found I've other rivals—Napoleon, Uncle Louis' son, and Achille Murat, Aunt Caroline's eldest. I was merely being looked over as a possible son-in-law."

"Good! Then we can plan on your going to Harvard." Mr. Patterson looked as pleased as though he had made another million. "Frankly, I never approved of that match."

Nancy Spear spoke up, tartly. "Don't look so happy, Bo. I don't envy you having to break the news to your mother. She's going to take it hard."

Betsy was in Paris, ready to sail if she could be of any help to her son. When she read Jerome's letter, telling her that his marriage with Princess Charlotte wasn't likely to come off, and so her coming to America was unnecessary, Betsy was crushed. Yet she hadn't been unprepared for the blow. "Nothing can, or ever will, surprise me in that family," she wrote of the Bonapartes. From the first, she hadn't dared to hope for this marriage that, as Betsy told her father, "Would exactly meet my wishes, and they have ever been woefully disappointed." How thankful she was that she had cautioned him not to say anything about it in Baltimore! It was best in life not to admit one's failures.

She was sorry now that Jerome's studies in Geneva had been interrupted. But since he was in America, his mother was reconciled to his going to Harvard. Betsy, who was saving in everything else, repeatedly said in her letters to Balti-

more that upon Jerome's education no money should be
spared. Still, she hoped he wouldn't be recklessly extravagant
like his father. She couldn't forget that bill for six hundred
cigars!

So in the summer of 1822 Jerome went to Lancaster, Massachusetts, to be tutored in Greek by a clergyman, the Reverend Joseph Willard, for the Harvard entrance examination. The authorities refused to let him take his dog to
college. Le Loup, the animal who, Betsy declared, was "superior to half the persons one meets in the world," had to
be left behind in Baltimore. She sent her father detailed
instructions as to his care.

> "I regret excessively that his dog could not go with him,"
> Betsy wrote in September, "not only because he would de-
> fend him from dangers at night, but because he could amuse
> him during his hours of relaxation, and he is a safer com-
> panion than many others he will meet . . . I hope he (Le
> Loup) has a warm place to sleep in, as the cold would cer-
> tainly kill him, having been in the habit of sleeping on a
> mattress with sheets and blankets, with his head on his mas-
> ter's pillow."

In February 1823, having passed the oral entrance examination for Harvard, Jerome arrived in Cambridge. He
furnished his room with a pine bedstead, washstand, a table,
some chairs and a threadbare carpet, bought from a secondhand dealer for the outrageous sum of ten dollars. Then,
with his books arranged, his candles, flint, steel and tinder
box handy on the table, the freshman stood looking for-
lornly out of the window at the Yard, eager for friends.

His classmates began dropping in—most of them Yankee
boys—to admire Bonaparte's feather bed and worn carpet.
"Only a Southerner could afford such luxuries," they said
enviously. (All Southerners being reputed to be fabulously

rich.) But Jerome made friends, as he generously passed around his Italian cigars.

He learned the college taboos. Undergraduates in 1823 must wear all black. Not even a white waistcoat was allowed. And it was regarded as a crime by his class for a student to enter a recitation room before the bell rang or to remain to ask a question of an instructor.

Jerome would have liked to stay after his Spanish class and chat with Professor George Ticknor, who had studied in Europe. But that would have made him a "fisherman," unpopular in his class, and Jerome wanted his classmates to like him. He was older than they were, seventeen, while the average Harvard freshman was fifteen, some only thirteen; a Southerner in a Northern college; a Frenchman, among Americans; a Roman Catholic in a Protestant institution.

His Class of 1826 was an unusually turbulent one, even for those roistering days. With no organized athletics in which to vent their energy, the playing of practical jokes and rioting were the only ways the undergraduates had to work off their high spirits.

The college owned a little fire engine that the students trundled out whenever there was an alarm of fire. But since they made it a custom to stop at Porter's Tavern on the way, to strengthen themselves for the fire-fighting with several mugs of blackstrap, a rum and molasses drink, the boys usually arrived at the fire after it was out.

The food at commons, in University Hall, run by one Cooley, was notoriously bad. When the meat was tough, the soup watery, the bread half-baked, a sophomore would take out his ill-humor by hurling a plate at a freshman. A battle, in which much crockery was smashed, would result.

Jerome, accustomed to bountiful Maryland meals (Betsy declared that a Baltimore dinner would feed a family in

Europe for a fortnight), went to board with a professor at three dollars a week. But eager to be known as a "good fellow," he gave frequent convivial dinners at Porter's for less-wealthy friends, obliged to eat at commons and starve.

One of these parties that, unfortunately, ended with the merrymakers dancing on the Common, with resounding Indian war whoops, and smashing rum bottles against the Washington elm, caused Jerome to be summoned before President Kirkland for a severe scolding. But such lavish hospitality made him popular with the other students. By his sophomore year, young Bonaparte could take his pick of the Harvard clubs—the Hasty Pudding, the Porcellian, the Med. Fac. Society and the Institute of 1770. One night, before a cheering crowd, he was initiated, with other candidates, into the mysteries of the Institute, after pushing an apple across the Yard with his nose.

It was a happy, carefree life in which Jerome, no longer under his mother's watchful eye, found he could study just enough to get by, play cards most of the day, go to the theater in Boston several nights a week and get back to college at dawn, and no one seemed to mind. His conscience troubled him only on the days when he heard from Europe. His letters were addressed to "Edward Percival" because Betsy had seen the passengers on the packets beguiling the tedium of the long Atlantic voyage by reading the letters in the mailbags.

Her son was always in Betsy's thoughts; she wrote him reams of advice. Jerome must be economical and live on the $1,200 a year allowance she gave him, his mother told him. But when he had been at Harvard for fifteen months, there came the day of reckoning. Nancy Spear, who helped John White see to Betsy's American investments, informed her niece that, during his first year at Harvard, Jerome had spent $2,150.

Betsy was shocked and, remembering those six hundred cigars, was sure her son was turning into a spendthrift like his father. She wrote Jerome's grandfather bitterly that she had not skimped and saved for years, to have Bo fling her money away.

> After reflecting last night upon the $2,150, I have come to the resolution of insisting on Bo's spending $1,100 dollars annually. I will not on any pretext allow one farthing more. It is ample and even more than my fortune authorizes me to allow him. I have economized in every way myself, perhaps more than my position in society allowed, that I might leave him above want, but although disposed to grant him every reasonable indulgence, I am resolved not to permit him to suppose that I was born only to minister to his extravagant fancies. I may as well spend my income myself, as see it squandered by him.

Jerome wrote his mother he was sorry. He was going every Saturday into Boston, to have his portrait painted by Gilbert Stuart, but otherwise he didn't see how he had spent so much money. He promised to reduce his expenses and live "as economically as I can, and at the same time maintain the appearance of a gentleman."

Knowing that his grandfather was also displeased with him, Jerome wrote Mr. Patterson, defending himself. "The expenses of Southern students vary from $900 to $1,200 a year, and even more. I know a student who spent $2,300 during his freshman year." In order to reduce his expenses, Jerome suggested he take a roommate, thus save half the cost of firewood, candles and rent, although living with another boy would interfere with his studies. His only indulgence was a horseback ride twice a week. Jerome offered to give that up, if his grandfather thought it extravagant. In the future, he would try to live on $1,000 a year; but if he did, he reminded Mr. Patterson, it would be impossible for him to come to Baltimore for vacations.

Nor could he go to Philadelphia. Jerome, hurt and angry over letters from his mother and grandfather "teeming with reproaches," let Mr. Patterson know that his Cousin Charlotte had invited him to spend his two weeks' summer vacation at Bordentown, and he had declined, although he knew it was the one expense that would have pleased Betsy. "I would not wish to go as far as Philadelphia without going to Baltimore, and the vacation is too short to do both; moreover," he added virtuously, "it would cost a good deal of extra money, which is well saved."

Jerome meant to give his mother and his grandfather no further cause for complaint. But by summer he was again in trouble. This time, with the Harvard faculty.

That August of 1824, the Marquis de Lafayette came to spend a year in this country as the guest of the American government. He landed in New York, then came to Boston, on August 24, to be greeted with banquets, parades and an address by the Governor in "the new State House," as it was in those days; and to attend Harvard's Commencement, held, at that time, in August.

Lafayette "was very civil to Mama when she was in Paris," Jerome informed his grandfather, "therefore I called on him while in Boston."

When he entered the house, number 9 Beacon Street, where the Marquis was staying, Jerome beheld a man wearing a brown wig and limping on a cane, plainly dressed in buff trousers, blue coat and no decorations. "The papers say that he (Lafayette) is only sixty-eight years old, he looks nearer ninety-eight," was Jerome's comment. But he knew that, to the people filled with emotion who, from morning to midnight, swarmed into the General's house and filed in line before Lafayette to shake his hand, the aged hero was still the red-haired youth of nineteen who had come to help them win their independence, for many of the Marquis' visitors were veterans of the Revolution.

General Lafayette seemed to grow young and spry again as he talked of those old fighting days. He told Jerome how, in Baltimore, his Grandfather Patterson had helped to feed and clothe his ragged army.

He would see him at the Harvard Commencement, Lafayette assured Bonaparte on parting. But the next day, when the Marquis arrived in Cambridge with his military escort, driving between houses gay with French and American flags, the streets lined with cheering people, Jerome was not at the gate where President Kirkland, the faculty and students waited to greet Harvard's distinguished guest. The sad truth was that he had come to call upon General Lafayette, not from Cambridge, but from Lancaster, Massachusetts, where Jerome was again studying with Joseph Willard, his clerical tutor, while on a three months' suspension from college.

He had done nothing wrong, Jerome hastened to write his grandfather, but had been punished, most unjustly, with several of his friends. His club, the Institute of 1770, had met on Friday, the 29th of July, to choose a librarian. The group had been meeting regularly for fifty years, not in secret, the notice of their gatherings always being published on the college bulletin board, with a social hour of punch and cake after the business of the club was transacted. The faculty had never objected before. Nor had there been any horseplay that evening, Jerome declared. So the members were astonished when, the next day, they were called before

President Kirkland and told they were being sent home for three months.

The college was in an uproar of indignation. The rest of the students escorted the expelled boys out of town, cheering them as they went. They then returned to the Yard, assembled around the Rebellion Tree, where they voted to go on strike and cut classes all day. That night, President Kirkland was burned in effigy.

In the midst of the excitement, to make matters worse (if they could be, Jerome thought), his mother arrived from Europe to see about her American investments.

16. Panic and a Cry for Help

MME. BONAPARTE WAS SHOCKED to find her son "rusticating," as being expelled was elegantly called at Harvard, his studies interrupted for three months.

"Jerome's marks aren't to blame. He's a fair student," President Kirkland assured her. "I'm merely punishing the clubs with suspension for the playing of practical jokes, the broken windows, the smashed furniture, the gunpowder set off in the chapel recently. The Institute of 1770 boys have been especially unruly. I'm making an example of them."

"Apparently everyone who has been educated at Harvard has found himself in the same predicament at one time or another," Betsy informed her family. Somewhat relieved, she went to Lancaster to spend her son's enforced vacation with him.

She blamed herself for having left Jerome alone in America. She must stay with him and see that he applied himself to his studies. "If Bo takes a good education and continues handsome," Betsy told her father, "there is always a probability, with his name, of my marrying him advantageously." She meant in Europe, of course. A marriage with Princess Charlotte might be out of the question, but there were other Bonaparte cousins, Louise Murat and Jeanne, one of Lucien's daughters. Betsy felt especially drawn toward Lucien's family. His wife had also never been recognized by Napoleon.

Betsy's dream was that Jerome, by marrying into the Bonaparte family, might legitimize himself and her marriage. But if that was impossible, she hoped he would marry some titled European. As ambitious for her son as she had once been for herself, Betsy kept reminding Jerome that he was the son of a king and the nephew of an emperor and preaching the advantages of a "good" match to him, until he grew sick of the subject.

"Jerome's not like other boys, he doesn't seem to care much for girls," his mother told people complacently. "Oh, how I wish he did! I'd so like to see him happily married." Then Betsy went into a panic if Jerome so much as looked at a girl.

Her constant fear was that, on one of his vacations with his grandfather, Jerome would fall in love with someone in Baltimore. It would delight the old gentleman, Betsy knew, to have his favorite grandson marry a local girl and go into the family business.

For fear such a thing might happen, and because she was lonely without him in Europe, Betsy went back to Cambridge with her son when he returned to Harvard on November 2, 1824. She had been happy in Lancaster. She loved the quiet evenings she sat sewing, while Jerome studied his lessons. Betsy forgot all about Europe then, as she ran her needle in and out of the strands of silk across her darning egg. Goodness, how could Jerome get such huge holes in his socks!

Her intention was to live near her son for the next two years, until Jerome graduated from Harvard, and keep an eye on him. But the college authorities objected. Mme. Bonaparte was informed that the students' mothers were no more welcome at Harvard than their pets. So, after a winter in Baltimore with her father, Betsy sailed for France in June, 1825, with her brother Edward. She believed she would only be abroad a year. But it was nine years before she again saw her native land.

It hadn't been a pleasant winter. A week at home, and Betsy and her father were on each other's nerves. There were the usual angry words, the furious silences. Then Baltimore wasn't the same without Robert. He had died in October, 1822. His widow lost no time in joining her sisters, Louisa and Elizabeth, in England.

That didn't surprise Betsy. But it was startling to find William, a staid old bachelor of forty-five, boyishly in love with pretty Anne Gittings. Heavens, Betsy never thought Willie would get married! And she worried about Edward, her favorite brother. He was plodding along in his father's business, married to Sydney Smith and bringing up a large family of children, but his face was strained. He complained of stomach trouble.

Betsy recognized the signs of her own frustration. "Why don't you come to Europe with me?" she suggested.

She never thought Edward would do it. But to her surprise, when she sailed in June, he came along. "Just a short business trip," Edward explained, "to see our London agent."

On the way to Havre, brother and sister had twenty-eight long days at sea during which to become acquainted again. One day, Edward burst out, "I wish I wasn't going to England, but to Germany, to study music. I've never given up that idea, but when I think of telling Papa—Oh, Betsy, you're the only one in the family who has always done what you wanted to in life! I wish I had your courage."

Betsy remembered how afraid she had been to tell her father she was going to leave home. "If you want to do something badly enough, Eddie, you can do it. Even when Papa's against it."

"Possibly I could have, once. Now, with Sydney and the babies, it's too late. Why can't I be like Willie and Joseph? They get along all right with Papa, because they always give in to him. Betsy, do you love Papa?"

"Yes, when I'm in Europe. Not when I have to live with him in Baltimore."

"I wish I did. But when he tells me constantly what to do—"

"Oh, don't I know! And locks up at nine o'clock and sends you to bed, as though you were a child. I'm forty, Eddie, but Papa still hardly lets me out of the house alone. He always insists I wear a hat. I've resented not being able to go bareheaded in Baltimore, as long as I can remember."

"He doesn't realize any of us have grown up."

"I suppose so. Poor Papa, he probably thinks he has been the best parent in the world. Perhaps it's our fault. Jerome loves his grandfather. When he talks about him, my son seems to be talking about a man I don't know."

"Jerome caters to him. Let him, just once, go against his grandfather's wishes, Bo'll find out! Papa's a hard man, Betsy, and vindictive. He has it in for you especially, because you married against his wishes and left him to live in Europe. He threatens he'll disinherit you. But don't worry, I think in your case Papa's bark is worse than his bite. He has always loved you more than any of us, Betsy. That's why you have the power to hurt him so deeply."

Edward looked at peace and rested when they landed at

Havre. From London, he promised his sister he would go to Cheltenham for the cure. But he had almost forgotten about his stomach trouble.

While Betsy was at Havre, General Lafayette returned from his tour of America. She had seen the Marquis the year previous in Baltimore. William Patterson had entertained America's distinguished guest at Coldstream and had been so active on the Baltimore reception committee that Jerome wrote anxiously to his grandfather: "I'm glad to hear you've gotten through with General Lafayette. I fear that you must be very much fatigued with the noise and disorder which accompanies him wherever he goes." But Lafayette could stand any amount of military reviews, parades and speeches. For fifteen months he traveled all over America's twenty-four states. Colleges, towns, streets and children were named after him. He received ovations wherever he went.

The day he arrived in Havre, the General, looking rejuvenated by his arduous trip, called on Mme. Patterson, to tell her of the honors he had received in America—his sixty-eighth birthday celebrated by President Adams at the White House; $200,000 and 24,000 acres of land voted him by a grateful Congress for the services he had rendered; and from private citizens, gifts of furniture, Indian tomahawks and war bonnets; stuffed animals and live ones, snakes, a raccoon, an opossum, even a grizzly bear!

Betsy wrote her father of the parties for Lafayette she attended in Havre. "The Marquis is delighted with your present of the cows. He wants me to come to La Grange and see them." The General had personally chosen the four full-bred calves of the celebrated Coke Devon breed out of the Patterson herd. No other present he received in America pleased Farmer Lafayette as much as those cows from Coldstream.

Betsy's same letter informed her father that the Princess Borghese had died. Two years ago, there had been a reconciliation between Pauline and her husband. She was taken to Prince Borghese's Villa Strozzi, in Florence, where her health grew worse; and on June 9, 1825, at forty-five, Pauline died as dramatically as she had lived. Knowing the end was near, the Princess, with a flash of her old spirit, asked to have a red velvet cloak draped about her shoulders. Her haggard face was rouged and powdered. Decking her wasted neck and arms with jewels, she passed away looking at herself in a mirror for the last time.

Jerome was the only member of her family with Pauline at the last. The bulk of her fortune of two million francs, she left to her brothers, Louis and Jerome. But Betsy informed her father that she saw by the newspapers that the Princess had left 20,000 francs to Jerome, Junior. That was only $3,500, but Betsy was delighted to have her son's name mentioned in the will with others of the Bonaparte family.

Money was becoming increasingly important to her. Not for herself, although Betsy loved beautiful clothes and jewels, but so Jerome could make a fine marriage. In Europe, she let her father know, it was impossible to marry well without money, as the Gallatins had found out. Their pretty daughter Frances was unmarried, Betsy declared, only due to the fact that her father was too poor to give her a proper dowry.

Albert Gallatin, unable to struggle along on the small salary Congress gave him, had resigned from the diplomatic service. The family had gone back to America, to live in Baltimore. And Betsy thought it would take all of John Jacob Astor's money to marry off his daughter.

"Mr. Astor and his daughter are here," she wrote from Paris. "He seems, poor man, afflicted by the possession of a fortune which he had greater pleasure in amassing than he

can ever find in spending. He is, too, ambitious for his
daughter, to whom nature has been as penurious as fortune
has been the reverse. She may marry . . . but any idea of dis-
posing of her except to some ruined French or Italian noble-
man would be absurd. She is not handsome, and sense cannot
be bought; therefore they will wander from place to place
for a long time before their object is accomplished."

The Caton sisters, financed by their wealthy grandfather,
were having better success. But even Mary, Louisa (who
became a widow in 1819) and Elizabeth, Betsy let Baltimore
know, "are not yet married, which considering their per-
severing endeavors, rather surprises me." Mary Patterson's
friendship with the Duke of Wellington was the talk of
Europe, though. "He follows her everywhere," according
to James Gallatin's diary. Betsy, who had gloried in a mild
flirtation with Wellington (he gave her a little lap dog,
July, 1820), found to her chagrin that her sister-in-law had
stolen her most distinguished admirer. Young Gallatin
wrote:

> Mme. Bonaparte dined with us yesterday. She is really
> more brilliant than ever, a little embittered perhaps, par-
> ticularly against the Catons; they are her *bête noire* for the
> moment. Her sister-in-law, Mrs. Robert Patterson, *née*
> Caton, came in for her full share. It seems that the Duke
> of Wellington writes to her every week, and there is much
> scandal about their relationship.

There was little chance of Mary Patterson becoming the
Duchess of Wellington. Kitty, the present duchess, an invalid, clung tenaciously to life. Betsy, who, although a
woman beautiful and alone, had maintained in Europe an
amazing reputation for virtue, watched, shocked, as the hero
of Waterloo trailed the much-admired American widow all
over Europe.

Mme. Bonaparte was famous for her wit. She could have said plenty. It is amazing that Betsy curbed her tongue as well as she did. James Gallatin, who found Mme. Bonaparte "a most delightful and entertaining person," repeatedly reports how, at the American legation in Paris, she kept "the whole table alive with her witticisms." Yet Betsy's fun was seldom malicious. "I rarely heard her say an ill word of anybody," Gallatin states, "with the exception of the Catons and of her husband. She certainly has reason in that quarter after the treatment she has received at his hands."

Her jibes at Jerome were to cover up her love for him. Secretly, too, Betsy admired the Catons; and endured tortures comparing herself with her old school friends in Baltimore, who had everything—looks, family, wealth. Now to see them, thanks to Grandpapa's money, achieve without effort the social success in Europe that she had struggled so hard to attain was hard for Betsy to bear. Her pen ran away with her, as she wrote home about Mary:

> You would be surprised if you knew how great a fool she is, at the power she exercises over the Duke; but I believe that he has no taste *pour les femmes d'esprit,* which is, however, no reason for going into extremes, as in this case. He gave her an introduction to the Prince Regent, and to everyone of consequence in London and Paris. She had, however, no success in France, where her not speaking the language of the country was a considerable advantage to her, since it prevented her nonsense from being heard.

But James Gallatin, when Mrs. Robert Patterson dined at the American legation, found that she was "really beautiful and has a wonderful charm of manner."

> Her one topic of conversation is the Duke of Wellington. They say he allows her 100,000 francs a year; at least, so says Mme. Bonaparte. Her jewels are very fine. Mme. Bonaparte

says they are mostly imitation, but I think it is a case of sour grapes.

It was; Betsy was consumed with jealousy. She was pleased when she could write her father of Wellington giving Mary "a cool reception" on her second visit to England.

The Duke is said to be tired of them (the Catons); but, tired or not, they pursue him, live on his estate, and until he gets them husbands, he will never get rid of them . . . they are considered *mere* adventurers and swindlers.

Mr. Patterson, shocked, reminded his daughter that her letters might be opened and read by the passengers aboard the Atlantic packets. He cautioned her to be more discreet.

"I quite agree with you, that abusing the Catons can do me no good," Betsy replied, "and I have resolved not to speak of them again."

But by November, 1825, she broke her silence, to inform her father of what may have been a judicious "out" for the Duke—Mrs. Patterson's engagement to Wellington's elder brother, Richard Wellesley, Earl of Mornington. From Lady Morgan, who was in Dublin, Betsy heard enough about Mary's fiancé to give her an upset stomach for days. In 1797, Sir Richard was Governor of India, and for his services there, George III had made him Marquis of Wellesley. At the time he met Mary Patterson, the Marquis was Lord Lieutenant of Ireland. They were to be married at the vice-regal castle in Dublin.

James Gallatin's comment on the engagement was, "Mme. Bonaparte will burst with envy." But Betsy, making the best of it, wrote her father of Mary's success:

She has made the greatest match that any woman ever made . . . The Marquis of Wellesley is Lord Lieutenant of Ireland. He is sixty-five. He married an Italian singer, by whom he had a family of children. She is dead. He has no fortune. On the contrary, he is over head and ears in debt. His salary is 30,000 pounds per annum as Lord Lieutenant of Ireland.

The Catons, I suppose, will be enchanted at the match, and with reason, too, for it gives them a rank in Europe; and with Mr. Carroll's money to keep it up, they may be considered the most fortunate in the United States of America. Of course old Mr. Carroll will strain every nerve to maintain his grandaughters, now that they have connected themselves so highly. Mary's fortune is reported in Europe to be 800,000 pounds cash. It has been mentioned in all the papers at that sum.

There, she had let Papa know that, instead of objecting to a foreign marriage, Mr. Carroll, whom he so admired, was *proud* to support his granddaughters in European society!

Prince and Princess Alexander Galitzin, a former Russian diplomat and his wife with whom Betsy boarded in Geneva, to cut down expenses, thought it a fascinating coincidence that two Baltimore girls, sisters-in-law, and the first Americans to make sensational international marriages, should marry brothers of two of the great generals at Waterloo, Napoleon and Wellington.

"Oh, Betsy, how exciting!" Princess Caroline exclaimed. "What will you wear to the wedding?"

Betsy, opening her wardrobe, looked discontentedly at her dresses, sacques and bonnets. Having economized for years to build up a fortune for Jerome, she hadn't a thing fit to be seen in at Dublin Castle. She would have to get some new dresses, if only to impress Mary's maid.

Getting ready for the trip to Ireland, actually going shopping again, was an event for Betsy, she had denied herself anything new for so long. "My friend, Lady Morgan, will be so disappointed I can't stay with her in Dublin," she boasted to friends, "but my sister-in-law will, of course, insist I stay at the castle over the wedding." Each day, Betsy searched the mail for the invitation. It never came. Too many of her caustic remarks had reached Mary's ears.

"Oh dear, my stomach! I don't feel well enough to go to Dublin," Betsy finally said and, as the day of her intended departure approached, took to her bed. Princess Galitzin pretended to believe her. After that, they never spoke of the wedding again.

Betsy's letter to Ireland was gay. She had been ill and missed all the festivities. Lady Morgan must write her about the wedding. "Was the Duke, the Great Bollingbroke, there?" she asked wickedly. Then, the letter sealed, Betsy put her head down on her arms and cried. She was frightened, as she looked into the future. Everyone now would compare her with Lady Wellesley. Mary was beautiful, younger and richer—how could Betsy, on her own financially, as she had always been, compete with the Carroll millions?

For the first time, she felt herself alone and defenseless in Europe. "Jerome—!" Betsy called to her son across the wide Atlantic, aching with loneliness for him. She couldn't wait several months more, until he graduated from Harvard. She needed him. Only Jerome, by making a brilliant marriage, could restore her prestige in Europe.

That night, Betsy did what she had never thought she would do again, interrupt her son's education. So great was her desire to have him with her that she wrote her father to ask the Harvard faculty to let Jerome leave college and come to her in Europe, at once.

17. *Young Man with a Great Name and a Slender Purse*

"WELL, where is this boy of mine you all like so much?" King Jerome had asked his family on arriving in Italy.

"He has just sailed for America," Madame Mère replied. "Too bad you missed him. He's a son of whom to be proud."

The King of Westphalia had always longed to see his child by Betsy. He wrote to his first-born in America of his disappointment that they had failed to meet. King Jerome and Queen Catherine decided, since the family assured them the boy was really outstanding, to make an effort to contribute $1,200 annually toward his expenses. And all during Bo's college years at Harvard, the King kept up a loving, fatherly correspondence with the son he had never seen. He repeatedly expressed the wish they could meet and urged Jerome to visit him, if he came to Italy.

In the summer of 1825, when Bo was twenty and a junior at Harvard, his father wrote him that, since his Cousin Char-

222

lotte was probably going to marry Achille Murat, he would try to find another bride for him. He asked Jerome, if a marriage was arranged, what his mother could do for him.

Jerome replied that his mother was too poor to settle anything on him. Then, after mailing off the letter to his father in Rome, he wrote asking his grandfather's advice.

Mr. Patterson was glad to express his views, so different from daughter Betsy's. After his graduation, Jerome should settle in Baltimore, he said, and go into the family shipping business. He didn't think, after Jerome's three years in America, he would enjoy living in Europe again. Besides, he thought him too young at twenty to marry.

The old gentleman was fighting with Betsy for the boy they both loved, as he begged his grandson not to go to Europe and connect himself with the exiled Bonapartes.

> Your father's family cannot get clear of the notion of what they once were and the brilliant prospects they then had. Their fortunes cannot now be very considerable. They are living in idleness on what they have, and when that property they now possess comes to be divided among their children, it will scarcely keep them from want. The next generation will in all probability be beggars. What prospects, then, would you have by marrying into such a family? Should you remain in this country and make a good use of your time and talents, you may rise to consequence; but in Europe you would be nothing.

Jerome, who wished to remain a bachelor for a while longer, was only too happy to forget about getting married and enjoy his last year at Harvard. He never completed it. In April, 1826, he was surprised to learn that his grandfather had written to President Kirkland, asking permission for him to leave college in order to join his mother in Europe.

It was at his daughter Betsy's urgent request, Mr. Patterson explained. Though he did not approve, he asked President Kirkland whether Jerome's degree might be conferred *in absentia?*

On the 18th of April, 1826, the President and Fellows of Harvard voted as follows:

> In consequence of an application from William Patterson, Esq., requesting leave of absence for his grandson Jerome Napoleon Bonaparte during the last term of his Senior Year without a forfeiture of his Degree:—
>
> Voted: that for the Reasons stated in Mr. Patterson's Letter, his request be granted.

The next evening Jerome was busy packing. Friends dropped in to say good-bye. Around him the bare walls, the stacked furniture, the half-filled trunks made Bonaparte realize this was the last night he would sleep in these rooms. His three happy years at Harvard were over.

He looked wistfully at his classmates, who would be present at Commencement, in August, to receive their diplomas. But what could Jerome do but obey his mother's plea to join her in Switzerland? Betsy had always said that nothing must interfere with his getting an education. Was she ill? Otherwise, why had she sent for him in such desperation?

While at Harvard, Jerome Napoleon Bonaparte, as his parents had done, sat for his portrait by Gilbert Stuart. In ill health, and busy at the time painting Daniel Webster and John Quincy Adams, Stuart had only finished young Bonaparte's head, when, as usual, he put the portrait aside. It was unfinished when Jerome sailed for Europe in May, 1826, on the *William Penn* from Philadelphia.

On the 16th of June, the day after he landed in Rotterdam, Jerome wrote to ask his grandfather to try and get his portrait for him. If the artist's health was failing, as he had heard, and Stuart wasn't able to work, wouldn't it be better to take the picture as it was? Since the head was finished, the body could be painted by someone else.

I called upon him frequently for six months before I left Boston, to hurry him, but without success. Perhaps now that I am away he may be prevailed upon to finish it at once. When I left Boston I was on excellent terms with Stuart; but he is so capricious that he may possibly be offended at my having left the country without having given him any notice of it.

Betsy, remembering her own difficulties with Gilbert Stuart, could sympathize. She had only succeeded in getting her portrait from him after Robert Gilmor of Baltimore interceded for her.

Jerome and his mother met in Lausanne, Switzerland, after a year's separation. Betsy wasn't ill, Jerome was relieved to find, and as beautiful as ever, but her gaiety seemed forced. She looked unhappy. Could Lady Wellesley's marriage be the cause of her discontent? Lady Sydney Morgan, who frequently visited Dublin, kept Betsy informed of the splendors of the vice-regal court. Every letter, Jerome noticed, brought on one of his mother's stomach attacks.

"Mary has had great luck in life. I always was unlucky," Betsy sighed. And when Jerome reminded her of the Marquis' age, his debts and infirmities, she still insisted that, with all these drawbacks, he was the Viceroy of Ireland, wasn't he?

"I know, his salary is mortgaged, his carriage was seized for debt in the streets of Dublin, the silver on his table is hired, but the Marquis of Wellesley has made Mary the Queen of the British Isles, since King George of England has no queen. What if he is old and infirm? At his death, she'll get a pension of a thousand pounds a year. Meanwhile, Mr. Carroll can support them, which he's only too happy to do, now his granddaughter has married so well. He isn't like your grandfather, Bo."

Jerome hastily changed the subject. He loved both his mother and his grandfather. He wished they got on better. He agreed with Mama, it was a pity the old gentleman refused to help them as long as they lived abroad, but he hated to hear her criticize him.

His mother was bitter these days, Jerome knew, because Princess Charlotte had returned to Europe and married, not Achille Murat, but another cousin, Uncle Louis' son. Joseph had only daughters. Napoleon, the eldest child of the ex-King of Holland, was thus the pretender to the French throne and, if the Bonapartes were restored to power, would become emperor. Joseph had chosen wisely for his daughter, Betsy was forced to admit. But she was so disappointed Jerome hadn't captured Princess Charlotte that her ideal daughter-in-law was now described as "a hideous little creature," who had forced her cousin "by her perseverance into the match." Nor was Charlotte the heiress everyone thought. Betsy let people know that one of the Rothchilds of Paris had told her that King Joseph's fortune "was much over-rated."

"Thank goodness that girl's married, I hear she's a little vixen," she told Jerome. "It was a lucky escape for you, Cricket. You're much too good for her."

With her father, Betsy was more realistic. "I wish I could find a suitable wife for my son," she wrote, in utter discouragement. "Everyone is able to marry their children well, except me."

Even John Jacob Astor, whom Betsy never thought would find a husband for his homely Eliza, had captured for her Count Vincent Rumpff of Switzerland, minister from the German Free Cities at Paris.

"Rumpff is a handsome man of thirty-five," Betsy reported, "and we all think she has been fortunate in getting him, as she has no beauty. He has no fortune, but is well connected . . . Astor is delighted."

Rich Mr. Astor had been able to give his daughter $300,000 "to secure the match." If she had that much money to settle on Jerome, Betsy thought, many a poor princess would be pleased to get him. She ran over the names of several eligible girls in her mind. Unfortunately, the last Murat girl, Louise, and Lucien's Jeanne had recently married. Lucien's next daughter, Maria, was only eight years old. So Betsy, reluctantly, was forced to give up her dream of her son marrying into the Bonaparte family.

Betsy's next choice was one of the daughters of her two most intimate Russian friends, Princess Galitzin's Sophie or the Countess Schouvalov's Helène. Count and Countess Gregoire Schouvalov lived in Rome. The King of Westphalia, now living there too, was friendly with the Schouvalovs. It would be an ideal way to bring the young people together; and Betsy wrote her ex-husband to remind him of his suggestion, which she had always jealously opposed, that their son come to Italy and visit him.

After being paid for two years, Betsy had not received the $1,200 promised her annually by King Jerome for their son. The cost of the trip to Italy would come out of her own pocket. Still, it was worth it. So Betsy was pleased when the King replied that he would be at his Château of Lanciano, near Sienna, in the fall, and would expect Bo there the first of October.

It wasn't a very cordial invitation. King Jerome was afraid that any recognition of his American son might be misunderstood by the courts of Wurtemberg and Russia, who paid his wife Catherine her annuity. Bo, had he known of his father's feelings, would probably have called off his visit. As it was, he was pleased at the idea of going to Italy and seeing once more his grandmother, whom he remembered fondly. He was curious, too, to meet the father he had never seen, his half-brothers and half-sister, Prince Jerome, Prince Napoleon and Princess Mathilde.

Betsy decided to spend the winter in Florence, while Jerome was with his father. They set out for Italy, by way of Geneva and Aix in Savoy. From Aix, Jerome wrote his grandfather he planned to leave Rome by the 1st of April, 1827.

> So I shall probably return to America about the middle of next summer . . .
>
> I have seen a great many things since my departure from home, but the more I see, the more firmly I am persuaded of the superiority of my own country, and the more I desire to return to it and remain in it. This journey was absolutely necessary for me on many accounts, but when it is over I shall settle myself quietly in America.

Betsy knew nothing of her son's desire to live in America permanently. Jerome hadn't the courage to tell her. But she had promised that, if he would stay in Europe with her for a year, she would return with him to Baltimore in the spring, and live there, while he read law.

On the 25th of September, 1826, when Jerome left for Sienna, Betsy sent him off with detailed instructions. "Remember, darling, to tell your father how happy I am. Describe to him my handsome apartment in the palazzo of the Count and Countess Arrighetti. Let him know I'm immensely popular in Florence, that I go to balls every night, and my whole time is taken up with whist parties and returning calls."

"Shall I tell him about the Marquis of Douro?"

His mother blushed. "By all means!"

It made Betsy feel a little better about Mary Patterson's marriage that her latest conquest was the Marquis of Wellesley's nephew, son of the Duke of Wellington. What if people were saying that he was young enough to be Mme. Patterson's own son? Her women friends in Florence were green with envy. Only last night at a masquerade ball, a jealous rival had slipped a note into Betsy's hand.

> Ah, who is that languishing fair?
> *E bella—e bella securo;*
> In one hand a tabatiere,
> In the other, the Marquis of Duoro.
> Pretty Patterson ply every charm,
> Those charms will too soon be at zero.
> Get the *hand* if you can, not the arm,
> Of the heir of the Waterloo hero.

As Bo drove up to the Château of Lanciano, in Sienna, he wondered what his reception would be. The door was opened by a liveried servant, but King Jerome stood in the hall—a man of forty-one, still handsome, in spite of receding hair, pouched eyes and a stoutish figure. He had overcome his fears of the political repercussions of Bo's visit, and, as his father embraced him, the young American felt himself accepted by him as his eldest son.

"I would have recognized you anywhere," the King said. "You look like a Bonaparte. No wonder the Bourbons are afraid to let you into France. You're no more welcome there, I hear, than we are. Come and meet my family—" He led the way into the parlor. "Trinette, this is my American son."

Queen Catherine, stout and amiable, rose from her armchair and, taking Bo's face between her plump hands, kissed him. "My poor child, I am the innocent cause of all your troubles," she said tenderly.

Three handsome children came in from the garden with

their governess, Baroness de Reding. Princes Jerome and Napoleon, twelve and four, eyed their half-brother suspiciously. But Princess Mathilde, blonde and six, ran up to him and took his hand. "Did you bring Le Loup with you?" she asked. "Oh, I hope you did! I love dogs."

By dinner time, the French boys had overcome their hostility (or was it shyness?) and seemed friendly enough, as Prince Jerome, who was at the Lazarist College in Sienna, asked the American about Harvard.

Betsy, naturally, was in everyone's thoughts. It wasn't long before King Jerome asked, "How is your mother? As beautiful as ever? I'm surprised she hasn't remarried."

"Oh, I think she will—" Bo, coached in advance, mentioned some of Betsy's admirers, among them, Prince Gortschakov, the Russian chargé d'affaires in Florence, and the young Marquis of Douro.

"Wellington's son!" Jerome frowned. The idea of his discarded wife marrying anyone so distinguished, and so much younger than himself, as the Marquis of Douro, didn't seem to please the King. Yet he appeared fond of his Trinette. As for Queen Catherine, the discredited and almost penniless exile was as dear to her as ever the King of Westphalia had been. She told Bo, "I would give my three children for Fifi's little finger!"

A kind, jolly lady, Catherine did everything she could to make the child of Jerome's first wife feel at home. Bo spent October and November at Sienna with his father's family. In December, he went with them to Rome for the winter, where the King and Queen of Westphalia lived in a huge stone palazzo in great style, with a large staff of servants.

But whether at Sienna or in Rome, the life in his father's household, Jerome found, was the same lazy, extravagant existence. There were few guests, as Queen Catherine was suffering from dropsy. The family slept all morning. Breakfast was at one, dinner at seven, supper at midnight. Bo never got to bed before one-thirty in the morning. The family seldom went out. The King and Queen of Westphalia sat all day and half the night playing cards or talking endlessly about how glorious it would be if the Bourbons were overthrown, the Bonapartes restored to power in France. Jerome found it impossible to read or study. He escaped when he could to pour out his disgust of this idle life in long letters to Grandfather Patterson.

Bo enjoyed most the days when his Uncle Lucien, an amateur archeologist, took him walking in the Forum, among the old Roman ruins, and the hours he spent with his grandmother. She was living now on the corner of the Corso and the Piazza Venezia. Like most Roman palaces, the exterior of Madame Mère's palazzo was forbidding, but it was built about an inner courtyard fragrant with orange trees. Here the old lady, now seventy-eight, received the visits of the Cardinal, her children and grandchildren every afternoon. Since Napoleon's death, she refused to see anyone but the family.

Madame Mère was to survive the son she mourned for more than fifteen years. Her last days were sad, though from the Pope down, Napoleon's mother was regarded by everyone in Rome with the greatest sympathy and respect. She was growing blind and infirm. Yet she went every day on foot to hear Mass at Santa Maria in Portico and took an occasional drive in her carriage with the Imperial arms on its doors to the Pincian hills, to spend an hour walking under the ilex trees. But most of the time Signora Letizia, dressed in black, her dark eyes full of sorrow, spent her lonely hours knitting, surrounded by portraits of her children who had sat on the thrones of Europe.

She could no longer see the face of her American grandson, when he came to see her. But as Jerome knelt before her, Madame Mère passed her hands over what she called his "Bonaparte features."

"Listen carefully," she said, "for I want to say something you must tell your mother—something I've had on my conscience for a long time—my deep remorse for the wrong I did her. It was I who robbed Elisa of her right to be Jerome's queen. I let Napoleon persuade me to sign that paper. How I've lived to regret it!"

For months, Madame Mère had refused to put her name to the document which stated that Jerome's marriage, without her consent, was illegal. At last, only Napoleon's threat that, if she didn't, he would banish Jerome to America, and she would never see him again, had won Letizia over. But a very religious woman, she had felt ever since that she had sinned in helping annul a marriage blessed by the Church.

From her armchair, Signora Letizia still ruled what was left of the Bonaparte clan. She gave to them generously, but she never ceased to preach economy to her children, who found it hard to give up the habits they had acquired during their years of prosperity. They incessantly pestered the old lady for money, Jerome being the worst offender.

"Retrench! This extravagance is sinful," his mother scolded him. But her remonstrances were ignored. The King of Westphalia found it impossible to economize. He couldn't forget he had once been a king. Catherine received $15,000 a year from Russia and Wurtemberg. Jerome spent twice that amount. The difference had to be supplied by his mother, whose fortune had shrunk in five years from one million to $300,000.

Bo, brought up by Betsy to count every penny, was shocked. All his foreign relations, except his grandmother, were living beyond their means. He saw that it was unlikely that his father could help him financially, or in other ways, even if he wanted to.

"I'd like to do what is right by you, my boy," the King said. "But Queen Catherine's cousin, the Czar of Russia, and her father, King Frederick, who give us the income on which we live, would never allow me to recognize you, thus making the children of my marriage to Catherine illegitimate."

All King Jerome's hopes were centered in the Bonapartes' return to power. In case of an Imperial restoration, his children by Catherine were next in line of succession after Louis' sons. Nothing must hurt Prince Jerome's chance of mounting the French throne. But the King urged his first-born to live with him always; and if Bo wished to marry and settle in Europe, he would find just the right girl for him.

"The Queen and I are giving a ball at Carnival time," his father told him. "At it, you can look over the prettiest girls in Rome and take your pick."

In February came the Roman Carnival, with the Corso thronged with carriages and masked pedestrians, bombarding one another with confetti; with races between riderless horses, pricked by nails under their ornaments, that galloped through the emptied streets; with fancy-dress balls at the theaters and in the palazzos.

The King and Queen of Westphalia, in spite of debts and dunning creditors, gave a ball attended by all the great Roman families. On the night of the dance, their home was a beautiful sight, glittering with the jewels and medals of the aristocratic guests who thronged the rooms hung with paintings by Gerard of the Imperial family. Queen Catherine was too ill to appear. King Jerome received his guests alone and introduced them to the short, dark-haired young man beside him, his American son.

Bo dutifully danced repeatedly with a girl with whom by now he was well acquainted, the daughter of Betsy's close friend, the Countess Schouvalov. Countess Helène was dark-eyed, vivacious and, Jerome had to admit, very pretty. He knew how such a marriage would delight his mother. But the idea of marrying except for love revolted Jerome more and more. Nor did he care about living in Europe and being an Imperial prince. An American citizen was good enough for him. He wanted to get back to Baltimore and start preparing himself to practice law. In a fit of homesickness, Jerome wrote a letter that so pleased his grandfather when he received it, Mr. Patterson went about Baltimore showing it to everyone he met.

> I am exceedingly tired of living at my father's. I am glad I came to Rome to see my family, but their mode of living and thinking is so entirely different from my habits of living and thinking, that I do not enjoy my residence at Rome. I feel that I am living a type of life to which I'm not entitled, and to which, not being able to support it, I do not wish to become accustomed. You've no idea how anxious I am to return home. I was always aware that America was the only country for me. Now I'm more firmly persuaded of it than ever.

When in March Jerome rejoined his mother in Florence, he found her going to parties all day and half the night, her head quite turned by the attentions she was getting from the Marquis of Douro and the diplomatic corps. Betsy had been presented at the Court of Tuscany, where she had been so cordially received by the Grand Duke, she told her son, she almost burst into tears.

"Only the thought that I might ruin my red velvet gown, if I cried, steadied my nerves," Betsy declared, "and I was able to go through the ceremony with proper dignity."

Louis Bonaparte was now living in Florence. Jerome met his two sons by Queen Hortense—Napoleon, who had married Charlotte, and his younger brother Louis, about Jerome's age, who lent him a horse. The two young men rode together every afternoon.

Jerome was as bored in Florence as in Rome, but for three months he dutifully escorted his mother to dinners, receptions and balls every night. Betsy's heart swelled with pride as everyone complimented her on her son. "With his famous name, your boy ought to be in the diplomatic service," Prince Gortschakov pleased her by saying.

A diplomat! Betsy's eyes shone. Jerome wanted to be a lawyer, but diplomacy was an even more distinguished career. Why hadn't she thought of it herself?

She would have liked to have Jerome stay in Europe and court Countess Helène. But Helène's father, Count Gregoire Schouvalov, a former Russian ambassador to Paris, would surely prefer a rising young diplomat for a son-in-law. So Betsy became eager, in fact insistent, that Jerome return to America as soon as possible. He must be presented to President John Quincy Adams, and have his grandfather and his Uncle Sam Smith use their influence to get him a diplomatic appointment.

Jerome reminded his mother of her promise to go with him.

"Oh, I'm too ill to make a long ocean voyage at present," cried the lady who could play whist and dance half the night. "Besides, you know the climate of Baltimore disagrees with my health. No, darling, you go, I'll join you in a few months."

What Betsy really meant was that she couldn't face living in South Street with her selfish, irritable, opinionated old father. But that wasn't anything she could explain to her son. So on June 4, 1827, when Jerome left for England, to sail from Liverpool for New York, he went alone.

It was Betsy's second great mistake. She would have done better to have gone home and put up with Papa. For the rest of her life, she would regret that she remained in Europe.

18. Love at First Sight

By 1827, when Jerome Napoleon Bonaparte returned from Europe, Baltimore had become the third largest town in America, partly because of a road west, the National Pike.

George Washington had been over the Alleghenies and seen the fertile lands beyond. It was he who first suggested that a turnpike be built from Baltimore to the Ohio Valley. In 1806, Jefferson laid out the road. Soon stagecoaches, herds of cattle and sheep being driven to market in Baltimore, and pioneers moving into Ohio, Indiana and Illinois, by wagon or on horseback, traveled over the National Pike. It opened up our Middle West, as George Washington had hoped it would.

Conestoga wagons, the freight cars of those days, brought tobacco, grain and other western products to Baltimore, the eastern terminal of the pike. But land travel was slow. People preferred water transportation. Jerome, living with his grandfather while he studied law, had returned to America at a time when Baltimore's prosperity was threatened. A canal was being planned along the Potomac River, for the purpose of getting the trade from the West. Meetings were held at William Patterson's home, when George Brown, Evan Thomas and other men discussed with him how to keep the western trade coming to Baltimore.

Jerome, yawning over his Blackstone and Coke, was more interested in the men's conversation. "That canal along the Potomac will carry Baltimore's western trade to Washington," he heard his grandfather say. "That is, unless we can think of a quicker means of travel."

Evan Thomas had been to England. One evening, he told of seeing an experiment there with cars on rails.

"That's our solution!" William Patterson exclaimed. "Let Washington have their canal. Baltimore's going to build a railroad to the Ohio Valley!"

Patterson and his friends had the Maryland legislature pass a charter for the Baltimore & Ohio Railroad, although people laughed at the building of such a startling innovation. Few people in America had ever seen a railroad. To compete with the National Pike and Washington's Chesapeake & Ohio Canal, the railway would have to go over the Blue Ridge and the Allegheny Mountains. Nobody had ever tried to build a railroad up a grade or one longer than a mile. People thought Patterson crazy; they wrote protesting letters to the newspapers.

Jerome admired his grandfather's courage. The stubborn old man ignored the abuse and ridicule showered upon him. He kept on telling people how the B & O would benefit Baltimore, until enough money was raised to build the first section of the first railroad in America, to Ellicott's Mills, thirteen miles west of Baltimore.

July 4, 1828, was a great day for seventy-six-year-old William Patterson. The first stone on which the first rails of his railroad would be fastened was to be laid. No one had thought of the modern ceremony of driving the first spike.

In a gaily-decorated wagon, the corner stone was carried out to Mount Clare, two miles west of Baltimore, followed by a parade of floats and military and civic organizations. Up Charles Street came the marchers, with bands playing. In a carriage rode Mr. Carroll, ninety-one, the last surviving Signer, who was to have the honor of turning the first spade of earth. Behind him rode Philip Thomas, president of the new B & O, William Patterson and other directors. At Mount Clare, the parade wound up in a field where a tent had been erected. The exercises opened with a prayer, followed by a reading of the Declaration.

Jerome sat in the front row of the flag-draped platform. At his side his grandfather, the last man in Baltimore to wear the old-fashioned powdered wig and knee-breeches of the Revolution, wagged a finger to the lively strains of the band playing the *Carrollton March,* composed for the occasion.

While the Hon. John Morris delivered the oration, Jerome looked over the audience, thinking how the women all looked alike in enormous bonnets that hid their faces. Then he saw her, half concealed by a plumed bonnet, worn by a large woman in orange satin. A slim girl without a hat, the blue ribbon in her brown hair matched her blue cape. Her eyes met Jerome's in the midst of Mr. Morris' speech. She smiled. Jerome's heart pounded under his frock coat. She was pretty. He must meet her.

Jerome turned to James Gallatin, seated behind him with his wife Josephine. On coming to Baltimore, James had fallen in love with Josephine Pascault, Henriette Reubell's younger sister, and promptly married her. "Who is she? Next to the one in orange, with the plumes," Jerome asked.

James stretched his neck almost out of his tall stock to see. "In orange? With the plumes? Oh, that's Mrs. Williams."

"Mrs.!" Down went Jerome's heart. "Is that young girl married?"

"Young? Oh, you mean *behind* Mrs. Williams? That's her daughter, Miss Susan."

Up flew Jerome's heart. Susan! What a lovely name! "Do you know her? Will you introduce me?" Gallatin, looking at Jerome with amused amazement, promised he would. Odd! Bonaparte usually showed little interest in girls.

The rest of the exercises seemed endless to Jerome. Mr. Morris finally concluded his speech, amid applause. The wagon on which the stone rested was driven up. All eyes (except Jerome's) were on the venerable Mr. Carroll, as, taking a spade, he made the gesture of turning the earth. The stone was then put in place, while the band played *The Star-Spangled Banner*.

With the last note, Jerome leaped down from the platform and, followed by Gallatin, made his way through the crowd. Mrs. Williams gave the young men a finger. Miss Williams blushed. Jerome could not guess the color of her eyes, her lashes were long and black against her cheeks.

The crowd was moving toward the refreshment tables. "Will you—could you—eat?" Jerome's eyes pleaded for Mrs. Williams' consent. At her regal nod, he began steering the two ladies toward the oysters, the soft-shelled crabs, the terrapin and canvasback duck. Mr. Carroll passed by; Mrs. Williams, to Jerome's delight, darted after him. James Gallatin went back to his Josephine. Jerome and Susan, at the refreshment table, found themselves alone. They drank claret. Miss Susan nibbled crab Imperial. Jerome had no appetite. How old was she? Sixteen. He was twenty-three. Just right!

"Do you live in Baltimore?" he asked.

She did. On the corner of Charles and Pleasant. "Don't you remember me, Jerome Bonaparte? You danced with me three years ago, at the Assembly."

She had grown up while he was abroad, and become so pretty, he hadn't recognized her. "Then we're old friends!" Jerome grew bold. When might he be allowed to call? "Tomorrow?" She smiled and nodded. But that was twenty-four hours away! So long to wait, her eyes said, returning his ardent look.

"Susan!" a voice called.

"Yes, Mama—" Jerome bent to kiss Miss Williams' hand. He wished he could have kissed her lips, as red as cherries and as tempting.

Next morning, people awoke to the fact that there was much work ahead before Baltimore's railroad west could be built. William Patterson, at the breakfast table, announced glumly to his grandson that yesterday, on the very afternoon Mr. Carroll was turning the first shovel of earth for the B & O, President John Quincy Adams, near Washington, was doing the same thing for the Chesapeake & Ohio Canal. Canal and railroad promoters were in a bitter race to open the way west for freight and passenger travel to the frontier. Everybody thought the canal would get there first.

Jerome, reading a letter Moses had handed him, hardly heard what his grandfather said. He was stunned. Miss Susan wrote, her mother thought it best for Mr. Bonaparte not to call. Then she added a few lines—Jerome was sure, unknown to Mrs. Williams. Miss Susan hinted she liked to walk afternoons in Howard's woods. If she should, by chance, see Mr. Bonaparte there—

Later that day, Jerome anxiously paced a forest trail on a

hill north of the town. And as his father had forgotten all about Napoleon and his career in Europe on seeing Betsy, so their son no longer remembered how much his mother wanted him to marry Princess Sophie Galitzin or Countess Helène Schouvalov. Jerome was in love. Would Susan come? He doubted if she could escape from her stern mama. But Susan did, chaperoned by Judy, a little Negro maid who kept her distance and had been bribed with a red hair-ribbon not to report what she saw.

"Oh, I can't stay but just a minute! If Mama finds out I've seen you, I'll be put on bread and water, Mr. Bonaparte—"

"Don't call me, Mr. Bonaparte."

"Prince Bonaparte then, *mon prince.*"

Hers? Oh, he was, if she would have him!

"Susan, darling, I'll go crazy if I don't kiss you. Please get rid of your maid! I can't kiss you with that girl looking at us." He drew her behind a bush. There, hidden, they kissed. "Sue, I love you!" breathed Jerome. "Will you marry me?"

There, he's said it, Susan thought, her heart racing. What would Mama say now? She had warned that Mr. Bonaparte never would propose, that he'd go back to Europe and abandon her, as his father had jilted his mother. "That's why he's not to call, do you hear me, Susan? That young man needn't think he can trifle with your affections." But Mama had misjudged Jerome Bonaparte. He loved her and wanted her to marry him. She loved Jerome too, Susan whispered. Yes, she would marry him. Her head was in a whirl. Mrs. Jerome Napoleon Bonaparte! How impressed Baltimore would be!

"Why can't I call, Sue? What has your mother against me?"

"Nothing against you. It's—" Miss Williams' voice dropped to the merest whisper—"your mama."

"Mama! What has she to do with it?"

"What is she going to say when she hears you're marrying a Baltimore girl? Mama says your mother wants you to live in Europe and marry a princess."

Wasn't Susan an American princess, the daughter of the late Benjamin Williams, who had been one of Baltimore's merchant princes? "Mother will love you, Sue, when she meets you," Jerome vowed. With all his heart, he hoped Betsy would.

But the thought of asking the formidable Mrs. Williams for her daughter's hand paralyzed Jerome with fright. His grandfather would have to do it. That night, over a glass of port, he told him about Susan.

"Ben Williams' daughter? I knew her father, from the time he first came here from Roxbury, Massachusetts, and opened a store on Bowley's wharf. Ben's death was a great loss—" Mr. Patterson was delighted. To have his grandson marry and settle in Baltimore had always been his fondest wish. Pouring them both another glass of wine, he promised to call on Susan's mother.

Since the death of her husband, fifteen years ago, Mrs. Williams had devoted her life to her only daughter. Benjamin Williams had left a large fortune. His little girl, only a year old when he died, would be wealthy. Mrs. Williams reared Susan carefully. But, at sixteen, she was her mother's despair. The girl was beautiful, with her slim figure and big brown eyes, but her small head was filled with the most absurd notions. She talked of her duty to the poor; she was forever visiting the slums and wanted to found an orphanage. Recently, Susan had expressed the wish to go to New York and study social work. Mrs. Williams was horrified. Was ever a girl more difficult? She must get Susan married quickly and put an end to this. Dear God, Mrs. Williams prayed, send us some suitable young man.

And then, from Heaven, came a proposal of marriage. From Heaven, by way of Moses, who brought to the Williams house on Charles Street Mr. Patterson's letter. He wrote that his grandson had fallen in love with Miss Susan. Might he call that afternoon and formally ask for her hand?

At first, Mrs. Williams was elated. Jerome Bonaparte! In all of Maryland, there wasn't a finer family than the Pattersons. She replied, requesting Mr. Patterson to call, then remembering what she had heard about his grandson, that the young man was going into the diplomatic service and returning to Europe to live, Mrs. Williams' joy subsided. She firmly made up her mind to let the affair go no further. She didn't want to lose her only daughter.

That afternoon, Mr. Patterson's letter in her hand, Mrs. Williams went into the room where Susan sat at the dressing table, while Judy brushed the girl's heavy, dark hair that hung to her waist.

"Darling, if you want to go to New York—" her mother began. But Susan, her eyes on the letter, replied, "No, Mama, I've changed my mind. I'm staying in Baltimore, to marry Jerome Bonaparte. Has his grandfather written to you?"

Could Sue have been seeing Bonaparte behind her back? Mrs. Williams looked at her daughter suspiciously. "You'd better think this over," she warned. "If I were you, I wouldn't want Betsy Bonaparte for a mother-in-law."

"Oh, I'll handle her!" Susan jumped up and threw her arms about her mother. "Mama, I think Mr. Patterson has arrived. Please go down and be sweet to Jerome's grandfather."

Mr. Patterson had indeed arrived a few minutes before, and now he waited in the parlor below, wishing with all his heart that Benjamin Williams was alive and they could have talked this matter over, man to man, at the Exchange. He didn't know Ben's wife. Mr. Patterson's nervousness increased when a big, fearsome lady in green taffeta, a frilled cap perched atop her brown wig, came rustling into the room.

After a few remarks about the weather, Mrs. Williams turned the conversation to the reason for Mr. Patterson's call. Was it true, as she had heard, Mrs. Williams asked, that Jerome was going into the diplomatic service? He would carry Susan off to Europe. She might never see her child again.

"My daughter, would like to have Jerome get a foreign post, Mrs. Williams," admitted Mr. Patterson, who had in his pocket a letter from Betsy on the very subject. Still in Florence, she demanded what had he and Uncle Sam done about getting Jerome appointed to London? "But I assure you there's little chance of Betsy's getting her wish. After the trade war that's been going on between Baltimore and Washington over our railroad and their canal, those fellows down in Washington aren't going to grant William Patterson any favors, or Sam Smith, either." The old man chuckled. "My grandson is reading law and, on being admitted to the bar, will handle the court business of our firm, I hope. I promise you, Madam, Jerome is in Baltimore to stay."

That removed Mrs. Williams' last objection to Jerome Bonaparte. Otherwise, he was the greatest catch in Baltimore, almost equal to what his princely father had been. She graciously requested Mr. Patterson to invite his grandson to call upon her daughter, that very day if he wished.

The young man lost no time in doing so. Under Mrs. Williams' gimlet eyes he sat evenings listening fondly while

Sue sang at the pianoforte. They were engaged, but when Jerome tried to name the wedding day, Mrs. Williams demanded sternly, "When is your mother coming to America? Well, the wedding won't take place until she's present." His future mother-in-law's firm decision plunged Jerome into despair. What did he know of Betsy's plans!

Expecting her son to return to her, for he didn't dare write her otherwise, Betsy lingered on month after month in Europe. In the summer of 1828, she had made a fainthearted attempt to take passage for America, then canceled it. The *Don Quixote,* Betsy wrote, was "a ship in which nothing would induce me to sail." Since then, either her health was bad, or the weather was too stormy to cross the Atlantic.

Month after month passed, and when Susan had been engaged to Jerome for a year, she finally lost patience. "Write your mother she'd better get here by November, because we're going to be married then," she told him.

Jerome promised he would. He couldn't keep Susan waiting any longer. He informed his father, his grandmother and all the rest of the Bonaparte family of his approaching marriage—and let Susan and Mrs. Williams think that he had written to his mother. They decided to have the wedding on November 3, 1829. The Reverend James Whitfield, Archbishop of Baltimore, who had succeeded John Carroll, was asked to perform the ceremony. Jerome wrote to invite his ushers—Colonel J. Spear Nicholas, Charles Tiernan, William Donnell and the elegant Pierce Butler of Philadelphia, who later married Fanny Kemble.

Letters came from his father, his grandmother, his uncles and Princess Charlotte—the girl Jerome might have married—wishing him happiness. No letter came from his mother. Mrs. Williams expressed herself forcibly about Betsy's silence. But it was too late by then to postpone the wedding. Susan didn't let it trouble her too much.

The wedding day came, and the bride was in a daze. She stood on a sheet, crinoline and petticoats were lifted over her head, then the wedding gown.

"Breathe in, Susan," Mrs. Williams begged. "And don't breathe out again or every hook will pop!"

Judy arranged the veil of Spanish lace over Sue's dark hair and fastened the brooch and necklace the King of Westphalia had sent as his wedding gift. Then the little maid was sent to peep over the bannisters. From the hall below came the buzz of voices.

"Oh, all the best people in Baltimore are here, Miss Susan, the Bishop waiting to marry you, and Mr. Jerome and his ushers looking so handsome!"

Susan went out into the hall and, on the arm of her brother George, started down the stairs. Keep your eyes down, Mama had said. But Susan took a peek and, looking at the throng of guests waiting below, saw only Jerome, grave and dignified, standing beside the Bishop.

After that, the bride's eyes were veiled by her long lashes, her voice was almost too low during the ceremony to be heard, and her prayer book shook in her hands. But the wedding supper was gay. Mrs. Williams saw to it that there was plenty of champagne, for, to her joy, Joseph Bonaparte had come to the wedding and brought as a gift two busts by Canova of the bridegroom's grandparents, Charles and Letizia Bonaparte. The ex-King of Spain made a speech. So did the French consul at Baltimore. There was a wedding cake, toasts, kisses and tears. No one mentioned Betsy.

The wedding trip was a ride on the new railroad. It was the latest craze. Everyone wanted the thrill of speeding along at ten miles an hour. Of course, the car was drawn by a

horse. The cars were mounted on rails only to make it easier
for the horses. No one imagined anything but horse-drawn
cars would ever be used on a railroad.

"It's odd you don't hear from your mother," Susan said, as
Betsy had remarked to another Jerome. To Sue's shocked
surprise, her husband admitted, sheepishly, that he hadn't
written his mother about the wedding. His nerve had failed
him. So his grandfather had broken the news to Betsy too
late, on purpose, for her to object.

19. Live for Today

BETSY STAYED ON in Florence, not to escape from Papa, she convinced herself, but because it was in Europe that she could best promote her son's career. At the balls and concerts given at the Tuscan court, she discussed Jerome's future with her diplomatic friends.

"You should try to get Jerome made secretary of your American legation in London," Lord Burghersh advised her. The Swedish minister said, "From England, your son should go to Stockholm, where his Bonaparte name will help him with the King, who was one of Napoleon's marshals."

London was expensive. Betsy couldn't support both Jerome and herself there. She would remain in cheaper Geneva, she decided, economize in every way she could and be able to send Jerome most of her income. She wanted him to live well in England, and was willing to make any sacrifice, if only Jerome could be a success.

Why did he stay so long in America? He'd had smallpox, but wasn't likely to be marked, Jerome had written her; also that he was trying to get the appointment to London from the State Department, largely to please her. Diplomatic life didn't appeal to him very much. Meanwhile, he was studying law, which would always come in handy.

There was never any mention of girls in Jerome's letters, for which Betsy was thankful. Hadn't James Gallatin fallen in love with the first pretty face he saw in Baltimore? American girls were dangerous, Betsy thought, not for the first time.

By October, 1829, she had left Count Arrighetti's palazzo as too expensive, and was living in a shabby section of Florence, in tiny furnished rooms, dark, cold, under the roof, but cheap. Betsy was putting every penny she could save aside for Jerome. He would need it in London.

Detesting needlework, she was sewing one morning, making over her old red velvet ballgown, hoping it would look well enough to wear through the winter. She refused to buy a new dress and was recklessly ripping the silk braid from her winter coat to cover the bad spots, for the sake of her own pride. The mother of a future diplomat mustn't look shabby!

Giovanna, the maid, dirty and incompetent, but all Betsy could get for the wages she would pay, handed her a letter from her father. She hadn't heard from Papa or from Jerome for months; she ripped it open eagerly. Had Jerome, at last, been appointed to London? She saw him already American minister, hung with decorations, his mother hovering proudly in the background, repaid for her years of self-denial—

They heard her cry of anguish. The maid and Betsy's Geneva friend, Princess Alexander Galitzin, who was also in Florence and had come that morning to see her, met in the hall, outside Betsy's room.

"What's happened to Mme. Bonaparte, Giovanna?" the Princess demanded. "She is in there, sobbing as though her heart would break."

"She had a letter from America, *Princesse*. Perhaps her son is ill or dead?"

Betsy wept on the bed, her face buried in a pillow, while Princess Caroline hung over her, murmuring sympathy, and tried to dab cologne on her temples. "*Chérie*, what's happened? Something to your dear Jerome?"

She lifted a tear-stained face. "He's engaged to an American girl, Susan May Williams, someone in Baltimore I never heard of! Oh, I can't believe it! I had such wonderful plans for him—" Betsy fell back weeping on the pillow. Suddenly she sat up. "I won't have it. I'll put a stop to the wedding!"

Giovanna was sent running out, to inquire when the first ship sailed for America. Then Betsy began to cry again, for she found that there wasn't a boat leaving Italy that would get her to Baltimore in time to prevent the wedding.

"They did it on purpose," Betsy wailed. "How Papa must have enjoyed writing that letter!"

She was deeply hurt, not only by Jerome's marriage, but by the deceit practised on her by her father and son. Waves of misery and despair swept over her. For days Betsy lay prostrate on her bed, a pitiful figure, heartsick and utterly exhausted. She did nothing but weep and refused to eat, being unable to keep down even a cup of soup.

Over and over Betsy asked herself, how could Jerome have done such a thing? He knew how she wanted him to marry into the Galitzin or Schouvalov families and live near her in Europe. Instead, Jerome preferred to remain in America, with *that girl!* In the future, separated by the wide Atlantic, his mother would seldom see him. Oh, Betsy wailed, her heart was broken! If only Prince Gortschakov hadn't suggested that Jerome go into the diplomatic service! If only she hadn't let him go to America alone! If only she had sailed on the *Don Quixote!* If only he had never met Susan! If only—

For days Betsy never left her room and bed. Finally, though tears still came often, she was able to inform Lady Morgan, "I'm less in a weeping mood than when you saw me." But it was months before Betsy could trust herself to write to Baltimore. Even then, she didn't write to Jerome, but to her father. Because she knew he had encouraged the match, she reproached him bitterly for what he had done.

> I never can forget the treatment I have been made to experience in the conduct of this marriage. It is a recollection which will haunt me through life, and prevent my ever knowing an hour of happiness. I hope that your conscience will not trouble you for your conduct, which has been even more unnatural than that of my son. I have not been able to write to the latter about his marriage since it took place. The subject always brings on the most dreadful feelings, and makes me ill for days.

Betsy had never before confided her defeats in life to her friends, but tried to hide them. Now, indulging in self-pity, she poured out her woes to anyone who would listen. Countess Guiccioli, coming to call to reminisce about her tempestuous friendship with the poet Byron, was annoyed to have to listen to Mme. Bonaparte's troubles instead.

"If your son can be satisfied with living in Baltimore, forget him," exclaimed the Countess Teresa, to whom all of America was a wilderness inhabited by savage Indians.

That was exactly what Betsy planned to do. For years she had economized on food, heat, light and clothing, and gone without things she wanted, in order that Jerome should be well educated. In future, she would spend every penny of her income of $4,000 a year on herself. There was no longer any incentive to save. Betsy stopped Jerome's allowance of

$50 a month. But an epidemic of cholera was sweeping Europe, and, in case she should die, she made a will leaving her entire fortune to her son at her death.

It didn't mean Betsy had forgiven him. "I feel that no parent has a right to disinherit a child," she let her father know. "And I should have done exactly the same thing, if Jerome had tried to cut my throat and failed in the attempt."

Betsy was forty-five when she became a grandmother on November 5, 1830. Jerome wrote to inform his mother, his father and all his European relatives that another Jerome Napoleon Bonaparte had been born in Baltimore.

"I hope the dear child will grow up to be a great comfort to you," his father replied. "I love to think that one day I may be able to hold him in my arms. The Queen sends congratulations . . . Jerome, Mathilde, and Napoleon send their love." King Jerome had reason to be pleased. This marriage solved one of his problems. If his first-born was content to remain in the United States and become an American citizen, he eliminated himself as a rival to Catherine's sons, in case of a Bonaparte restoration.

Betsy ignored her son's letter.

Determined now to live but for herself and "make as good an appearance as I can," she wrote home to Nancy Spear to send her linen, silver and jewels to her, in care of the American minister at Paris, to save duty. When they arrived, Betsy had her jewelry made over. A diamond solitaire ring and the diamonds from a pin the Princess Borghese had given her, she added to her earrings. All her emeralds and other diamonds, with twenty large pearls, three white topazes and her turquoise ring, she turned into a magnificent tiara that could also be worn as a necklace.

Everyone thought her white topazes were diamonds. No

one had them in Europe. They looked as if they had cost a million dollars. The first time Betsy wore her white topaz necklace she created a sensation. The men could scarcely find words to express their admiration or the women their envy. Betsy smiled to herself and wrote for more topazes for a belt buckle, and for some for Princess Galitzin, who liked false jewels and was as economical as Betsy.

With her flashing tiara in her dark hair, and wearing a favorite black lace gown that lay bare the creamy smoothness of her shoulders, Mme. Bonaparte was the belle of Florence and, after May, 1831, of Geneva, when she returned to Switzerland to board with the Galitzins. Betsy was forty-six—still one of the loveliest women in Europe, but there were lines of discontent about her lips and, embittered as she was by her second crushing disappointment, an added sting to her wit. "She charms by her eyes and slays with her tongue," people said of Mme. Bonaparte.

At a dinner given by a "rich idiot, whose menu and wines were first rate," the Hon. Mr. Dundas asked her, maliciously, if she had read Captain Basil Hall's book on America? And did Mme. Bonaparte notice he called all Americans vulgarians?

"Yes," Betsy replied, "and I'm not surprised. Were the Americans the descendants of the Indians and the Eskimos, I should be; but being the direct descendants of the English, they're naturally vulgarians."

The listening guests twittered; and the Englishman, his face scarlet, turned his back on the beautiful American for the rest of the meal.

Princess Caroline scolded on the way home. "Why do you have to be so disagreeable, Betsy? I know you don't mean it. You've been terribly hurt. It makes you, at times, want to lash out at people. But being hateful won't ease the ache in your heart. It only makes enemies. And you frighten men away. They loath a sharp-tongued woman. Don't be nasty to them. Be sweet. Oh, I do want to see you get married again!"

Betsy laughed. "Perhaps I will, to an English duke this time, instead of a Corsican blackguard! Even quarrels with one's husband are better than the *ennui* of living alone."

But she had broken with the Marquis of Duoro, persuaded Wellington's son to fall in love with a girl his own age. Betsy had yet to find the man that could fill Jerome's place in her heart. She might speak scornfully of her ex-husband, but she was too loyal to tell the Duchess d'Abrantes anything discreditable about him, when, at Balzac's suggestion, Laure Junot d'Abrantes came to Mme. Patterson to gather spicy anecdotes for her book on the Bonaparte family.

"You've already said enough ill of Jerome," Betsy squelched the gossipy Laure, "and more good of me than I deserve."

Betsy liked to talk literature with Lamartine, the French writer who represented Charles X at the Tuscan court. She flirted with the Duke of Dino, Talleyrand's nephew, and sometimes fancied she might marry Prince Alexander Gortschakov, the Russian chargé d'affaires in Florence, if only to spite Jerome.

Betsy had always longed for a title and a smart turnout, not a shabby hired hack. Rich Prince Gortschakov could provide her with both. Betsy saw herself riding about Florence, a crest on the door, behind two satiny horses, two men in livery on the box. "That's the Princess Gortschakov, wife of the ablest diplomat in Italy," people would say. There, wouldn't that show Jerome that others appreciated the woman he had cast aside!

But Prince Alexander Gortschakov's title was recent. Ambitious to increase his social position by marrying into one of the old princely families of Russia, he was cautious. Nothing came of the romance.

In a frenzy of restlessness, inspired chiefly by the desire to flee from herself, Mme. Patterson roamed Europe—Aix-les-Bains in the summer, Paris in the winter. She had dreamed for years of coming to France. Well, now she was here. Betsy had longed for beautiful clothes when she first came abroad, but saving for her son, she hadn't gone into a Paris shop. Now she bought recklessly, hats, gowns, furs, jewels, a red silk parasol to guard her still-lovely complexion. Betsy was so used to living economically, the high prices shocked her. She had little pleasure in her purchases.

By October, 1833, even Paris bored her. Where should she go next? Not back to Florence. The King of Westphalia, expelled from the Papal States, was living there, entertaining lavishly in the Orlandini Palazzo. "I never wish to see him again," Betsy snapped, when Lady Morgan tried to bring them together. The truth was that, twenty-eight years after he had kissed her good-bye in Portugal, Betsy still couldn't trust herself to meet Jerome casually. Had she cared a little less passionately, been able to establish friendly relations with her ex-husband, they might at least have talked over the problem of their son together.

At forty-eight, bored and unhappy, Betsy began to think of herself as old. She wrote Lady Morgan, one of the few persons allowed a glimpse behind the mask:

I am dying with *ennui,* and do not know in what way a person of my age can be amused. I am tired of reading and of all ways of killing time. (She was reading Walter Scott's novels.) I doze away existence; I am too old to coquet, and without this stimulant I die with *ennui.* The Princess (Caroline Galitzin) tries to keep me up to the toil of dressing by telling me that I am a beauty. I am tired of life, and tired of having lived . . . It is a bore to grow old.

What, Betsy asked herself, was the good of being beautiful, if the two Jeromes weren't there to admire her?

Once she had her son to plan and save for; but life, without him, had lost its meaning. Betsy was sick of Europe; weary of living among strangers; and satiated with freedom. She had longed to escape from home and live her own life. Now, after years of wandering about Europe, from one dingy hotel to another, deprived of a real home and household cares, she was finding that to live for yourself alone is an empty existence. As her father had said, long ago, "People must look at home for real happiness."

Longing for the sight of someone from Baltimore, Betsy decided to go to England and visit the Wellesleys. They were at Windsor Castle. The Marquis had been appointed Controller of the royal household of William IV; his wife, lady in waiting to Queen Adelaide.

Louisa, too, had made a brilliant second marriage, to the Marquis of Carmarthen, eldest son of the Duke of Leeds. He was no old man, like Mary's husband, but handsome and twenty-eight. "The Duke of Leeds is very angry at his son's marriage," Betsy was pleased to hear from Sydney Morgan. Still, at his father's death, the Marquis would be a duke. And Elizabeth, the third sister, was said to be engaged to Baron Stafford. With titles captured for three of her four daughters (Emily, the youngest, had married in America), ambitious Polly Caton had reason to congratulate herself.

Betsy decided she would write to Lady Wellesley, recall the old days and hint for an invitation. Lately, she had curbed her tongue about Mary. And, after all, they had been sisters-in-law. Mary couldn't very well refuse her. She would at least ask her out to Windsor for a weekend.

Then a letter came from Jerome, who was living at Mt. Pleasant, a plantation at Reisterstown, near Baltimore, that his Grandfather Patterson had given him as a wedding present. Betsy hadn't heard from her son in four years, not since she ignored his letter announcing the birth of a child.

Reading what he wrote, Betsy forgot all about going to England. In her heart she knew that this appeal from Jerome to return to America and see his son was what she had been waiting for. Her grandson! A thrill raced through Betsy, as when in Camberwell she had first held the child's father in her arms. "He's a fine, healthy boy," Jerome said. His grandmother experienced a blinding rush of pride. Jerome Napoleon Bonaparte III. How she longed to see him! Then bitter memories swept back and dulled the moment of exultation. Nothing would induce her to go to America. Her presence there would indicate her approval of Jerome's unfortunate marriage. He needn't think because of the child she would forgive him.

"He begs me to come home," Betsy said to herself, re-reading Jerome's letter. "He doesn't yet admit that he should have asked my advice before he married. He says a man's love alone should guide him in choosing a wife. I had hoped— yes, I admit it—that their marriage wouldn't last. But Jerome writes that he and Susan are very happy. He doesn't sound the least bit repentant. But he signs himself"—her eyes softened—"your very affectionate son." Betsy's head lifted. "Very well, I'll go to America. But"—her lips tightened into a severe line—"for only a brief visit, to see about my investments."

A letter that Betsy had received some time ago from her father gave her the excuse she needed.

"I won't be able to go to England; I'm sailing for America," she told the Galitzins. "Papa writes, there's been a financial panic, that I'd better return to Baltimore and look after my business affairs. The sooner the better, he says."

Princess Caroline smiled. "And you're not going home to see that grandchild of yours? Oh, Betsy, why aren't you honest with yourself, just once!"

"Oh, I might possibly see him—" was all Betsy would admit. Still insisting she was returning to America purely for business reasons, she sailed in the summer of 1834, taking with her enough Paris finery, including twelve bonnets, to last her, Betsy thought, all the time she was in America, which wouldn't be very long.

20. Rebuke from the Grave

WILLIAM PATTERSON'S AMBITION had always been to outlive that other Baltimorean of Irish descent, old Carroll of Carrollton, and be the richest man in Maryland. Mr. Carroll died in 1832, at ninety-five. Two years later, a month before Betsy returned from Europe, her father, eighty-two, took to his bed.

"There's nothing much physically wrong with Papa, Doctor McKenzie thinks," Edward said, on meeting his sister at the boat, "but he's in a bad way and may be dying, because—well, Papa has had his wish. He has outlived Mr. Carroll."

Seeing her father lying weak and helpless in bed stirred Betsy's remorse. For the first time in her life, she wasn't afraid of him. "Papa, I'm home now, you'll be all right." She bent to kiss his cheek. But the old man turned his face away, his eyes stern and reproachful. All these years Betsy hadn't come home to be a companion and nurse him. She had only come now, because he'd written her she had better see to her American investments.

There would be no quick return to Europe for her, Betsy

saw. She settled down in the big brick house on South Street, filled for her with bitter memories, and, at this late date, tried to do her duty by her father. Nancy Spear gave up her visits to the Samuel Smiths in Washington, where she liked to attend Congress and listen to the debates, to nurse her brother-in-law. Old Moses fed him, bathed him like a baby.

Betsy's brother William had died, two years after he married. But John, Joseph and Edward came to tell their father any news about the business they considered cheerful. Their wives came to hover over Dear Papa and brought their children to see Grandpa. But it was his errant daughter old Patterson wanted, and asked and asked for, although when Betsy came to sit beside him, half the time he called her Dorcas.

On his better days, when he was clearheaded, William Patterson's mind reverted to the past. He liked to talk of his early struggles—how as a boy in Ireland, he had peddled berries from door to door, raised chickens and sold the eggs, to help support his parents and a large brood of brothers and sisters. Unlike Mr. Carroll, whose wealthy father had sent him to college in Europe, William had never had time for an education. In Philadelphia, a fourteen-year-old shipping clerk, he had bought books with every cent he could save and read them by candlelight, after a long day's work. He had always wanted to go to college. But he must earn enough to send money back to Ireland. By the time he was independent and had ships of his own, he also had a wife and children, and it was too late for a formal education.

Feeling the lack of it, William Patterson had tried to make up for not going to college by being a good citizen of Baltimore. He was proud he had helped to build the Baltimore and Ohio Railroad, the first railway west, and had served as its president. "I guess that's as good as being able to read

Greek and Latin, as Mr. Carroll could!" William chuckled.

Since July 4, 1828, the day six years ago when President Adams had started digging the Chesapeake and Ohio Canal at Georgetown, and Charles Carroll had laid the corner stone of the railroad at Baltimore, every mile of canal and track had been built as fast as possible. The race to the Ohio Valley was still undecided. The canal was ahead. The B & O had only reached Harpers Ferry. But eighty-two-year-old William Patterson still believed in his dream.

"Let the canal get to Cumberland first, Peter Cooper's *Tom Thumb* gave us the answer, Betsy. Now that the B & O has decided to use steam engines instead of horses, we'll get Washington's trade away from them. Imagine hauling goods at the speed of fifteen miles an hour. No canal boat can compete with that! Think what it will mean for Baltimore. When I came here, as a young man, I found the place a village. Now look at it."

Gracious, he loves Baltimore like his own child, Betsy thought, ashamed of herself. Her father had his pride, too. How she must have hurt him, when she scoffed at the town he had helped to build! But why hadn't Papa opened his heart to her like this before?

They also talked about Jerome. Mr. Patterson was glad that there had been a reconciliation and Betsy liked Susan. The afternoon of February 7, 1835, after she had been home six months, Betsy came into her father's room at sunset. She had been out to Mt. Pleasant, Jerome's home at Reisterstown.

"How's my great-grandson?" William asked.

Betsy remembered how, when she first saw the boy, she had tried to harden her heart against him. But who could resist Jerome Napoleon Bonaparte III, astride his pony, both of them so young and plump? Certainly not his grandmother.

He was four now and had been ice-fishing that afternoon,

with old Jake, the gardner. From the window, Betsy had watched her grandson come trudging up the lane, a tiny fishing pole over his shoulder. She told her father how, when he came bursting into the house, wet, dirty, but his face radiant, crying, "Look, Granny, what I caught for your supper!" she had hugged him, fish and all.

But Betsy was still determined to appear indifferent. "Jerome looks more Patterson every day. He'll never be mistaken for Napoleon. Too bad his ears stick out like yours, Papa. Susan ought to *do* something."

At his whoop of laughter, Nancy Spear came running, shocked, disapproving, saying, "William, you'll exhaust yourself. You must rest!" She chased Betsy away. Aunt's jealous, her niece thought. Papa's getting better, he looks quite like himself tonight. But next day William Patterson was worse. He didn't know it, though, and was full of plans for what he would do when he was on his feet again.

"I want to take you out to Hampstead Hill, Betsy. You know that cow pasture of mine where your Uncle Sam stopped the British advance? I've always felt that saved Baltimore, more than the fort holding out. Well, I've given that land to the city for a public park, so the children, down at the docks, will have somewheres to play. . . . As a child, I never had a chance to play . . ." His voice trailed off, his head sank back on the pillow, he seemed to doze.

When Nancy Spear tried to make him eat his supper, William wouldn't eat. That cold winter night, to his family's consternation and grief, he died in his sleep.

On the day of William Patterson's funeral, all Baltimore mourned its First Citizen. Bells tolled dismally through the river fog. There were miles of carriages. People stood outside the First Presbyterian Church, unable to get into the crowded building.

Mr. Patterson had been connected with so many activities that had made Baltimore great—shipping, railroads and real estate—that in the days that followed, a stream of people, from rich merchants to rough sailors, came to his house to offer condolences.

The lawyer appeared with the will and read it to the family, assembled in the parlor. Mr. Coster, knowing what was in the document, didn't like the disagreeable task before him. William Patterson's sons were all left equal shares in the business, large legacies of cash, choice Maryland real estate besides. Now he must come to the part about Mme. Bonaparte. Poor old Coster, darting a glance at Betsy's attentive face, wished with all his heart he didn't have to do what he had to do.

The lawyer, his face red, cleared his throat. It was an old will, he said, made while Miss Betsy was in Europe. Recently, Mr. Patterson had indicated he would make another, when he got well. He hadn't done so, for, as the family knew, their father didn't expect to die. Then, in an embarrassed voice, Mr. Coster began to read:

"The conduct of my daughter Betsy has through life been so disobedient that in no instance has she ever consulted my opinions or feelings; indeed, she has caused me more anxiety and trouble than all my other children put together, and her folly and misconduct has occasioned me a train of expense that first and last has cost me much money. Under such circumstances it would not be reasonable, just, or proper that she should inherit and participate in an equal proportion with my other children in an equal division of my estate. Considering, however, the weakness of human nature and that she is still my daughter, it is my will and pleasure to provide for her as follows . . ."

There followed a list of four small lots of real estate, which her father gave Betsy for her lifetime,

"and after her death I give, devise and bequeath the same to my grandson, Jerome Napoleon Bonaparte."

Because of her "disobedient" conduct, Papa had left her, out of his large fortune, only four small houses and the wines in his cellar—worth in all about $10,000—Betsy couldn't believe her ears! There was a moment of pained silence. When she recovered from the shock, she turned, eyes swimming with tears, lips quivering, to ask her brothers, "What have I done that this should happen to me?"

"You went off to Europe and left him, while we stayed home and gave up our lives to please him," John reminded her. He had been left his father's estate of Atamasco, in Baltimore County, and property in Virginia. "I know, I did, I hate the business. I've never gotten over wanting to be a doctor."

"Or I a musician," Edward sighed.

But Papa hadn't disinherited George, who hadn't liked being in Patterson & Sons and had become a farmer. His father left him Springfield. It was only against his daughter that William Patterson had discriminated, as he threatened he would, if she went abroad. After Betsy defied her father to marry the man she loved, he was always harsh on her.

"Papa never forgave you for not staying in Baltimore and keeping house for him, after Mama died," Henry told his sister.

"He softened toward the end, Betsy." Edward came and put an arm about her. "I'm sure, had Papa lived, he would have made a different will."

Nothing her brothers could say healed the hurt. They couldn't bear to look at Betsy's despairing face, that she was trying to control, biting her lip to hold back the tears.

Her father had never shown any sympathy for her suf-
ferings, nor for her ambitions, but had continually reproached her for her long absences from home. Betsy realized
now how Papa had nursed his resentment through the years,
as he denounced her in his will as "undutiful" and of his
enormous wealth left her but a small share. Even from
beyond the grave, William Patterson struck a final blow at
the one child he had never been able to curb. In bitter words
that could be read by anyone who wished to go to the Court
House and look them up, he had let all Baltimore know
how unforgiving he felt toward her. Betsy's cheeks burned.

"I don't care about the business," she told her brothers,
"and that I have only those few miserable houses—while you
have Springfield, George, and you have Coldstream, Joseph,
and the rest of you the best land in Baltimore and all that
money—but the humiliation of what Papa said about me!
How could he do that to his own flesh and blood? When I
die, I've left Bo every cent I have, although he broke my
heart when he married. I told Papa, often enough, a parent
has no right to deprive a child of his rights, no matter what
he does. Oh, it isn't fair! To practically disinherit me—"
Betsy burst into tears and, utterly crushed, sobbed into her
handkerchief. Most of all she wanted Coldstream, where she
had spent her honeymoon with Jerome. Now it belonged
to Joseph.

As Mr. Coster continued to read the will, Aunt Spear wept,
too. Brother William had repaid her years of devotion to
him by leaving Nancy a small legacy, but only on condition
that she give up attending the sessions of Congress, her one
pleasure.

In the past, Betsy had been able to endure her poverty
with courage. She took Papa's threats he would disinherit

her to be just that, mere threats, and had looked forward to being, after his death, a rich woman. Her disappointment seemed more than she could bear. Betsy's brothers wished to share their inheritance with her, but she refused. "No, the will must stand. We must carry out Papa's wishes," Betsy insisted. She would not accept charity.

Again humiliated before all Baltimore, her first thought was to get out of town as fast as possible. She couldn't endure having people, knowing about the will, whisper behind her back. It would be easier to hide her wounded spirits in Europe, among strangers.

Much as she hated leaving Jerome and his family, Betsy had made arrangements to sail, when she went one day to inspect the property her father had left her. Until now, she had been too scornful of the four small houses and lots even to look at them.

Disdainfully, she inspected her meager inheritance—two brick houses on Gay Street, near Griffith's bridge; three adjoining brick houses on the corner of Market and Frederick Streets; two houses near the Market Street bridge; and a house at number 18, South Street. This last bit of real estate was a white cottage, beyond the Patterson garden, that Betsy had passed for years with hardly a glance. Now that it was hers, the small house interested her. It was where her parents had lived when they were poor, before William and Dorcas built the brick mansion at number 20. In this cottage Betsy had been born.

It was a dear little house, with frilled curtains at the windows and hollyhocks growing by the door. The cottage seemed to typify all the domestic joys Betsy had missed in life. A longing came over her to live there. It was occupied by Mr. Duncan, the shoemaker, but he could be persuaded to move elsewhere. Why should she go abroad? Live again that nomad life of hotels and boarding houses? At fifty, Betsy had lost her taste for Europe. Here, she would have a home, the joy of being near Jerome and of watching her grandson grow up.

Betsy threw back her head. "Nothing will make me leave. It would be running away."

It took courage to stay on in Baltimore, but Betsy had always had plenty of that. She moved out of 20 South Street, that now belonged to Joseph, and went to live in the cottage next door.

"Courage," Betsy murmured as, ignoring the pitying glances that followed her, she went about town with a smile. The past was finished, she would forget her mistakes. But the future! She could meet it bravely. And she would, by building at fifty a new life for herself, here in America.

It was a momentous decision that would have a far-reaching effect on Betsy's life. She didn't know it, but, as that year of 1835 drew to a close, Jerome would also know bereavement. In Lausanne, Switzerland, where he had taken Queen Catherine for her dropsy, the King of Westphalia sincerely mourned his devoted wife who died in November, as Mathilde and her two brothers knelt at their mother's bedside.

"Good-bye, what I most loved in this world was you, Jerome," were Catherine's last words, as she lifted his hand to her lips.

Had Betsy returned to Europe, instead of remaining in Baltimore, who can tell what might have happened? Jerome was free to marry again, and Napoleon was dead.

21. Another Public Slap in the Face

JEROME WAS A GOOD HUSBAND to Catherine, after his fashion. She told everyone how happy he made her. When she lay sick in Lausanne, the King nursed his wife tenderly and never let her suspect how ill she was. He read to Catherine by the hour, until the Queen fell asleep, her hand in his, soothed by his assurances she was getting well.

So on that last night, when the doctor warned him his wife was dying, Catherine was surprised when Jerome brought their children to her bedside to receive her blessing. She understood what it meant. "I'm not afraid to die," she said bravely, melting away before their eyes. Jerome could not believe it yet, but Catherine was gone.

His sorrow made a new trouble almost unimportant, at first. The two annuities on which they had been living ceased with Catherine's death. Her brother, who had succeeded his father on the throne of Wurtemberg, refused to continue Catherine's life pension. Her allowance from her cousin, Czar Alexander, also stopped.

The King of Westphalia moved to a small house at Quarto,

near Florence, that for five lean years was all he could afford. But Jerome was always lucky. In 1840, two marriages rescued him from poverty. His daughter Mathilde married Count Anatole Demidov, the son of the fabulously rich Count Nicholas Demidov whom Betsy had known in Geneva and Florence; and that same year, Jerome, who couldn't be long without feminine companionship, took a wife for the third time, a Florentine widow, the Marchesa Bartolini-Badelli.

The Marchesa was wealthy, handsome and only forty, but Jerome, sixteen years her senior, while he graciously allowed his bride to pay off his debts, wouldn't agree to anything but a morganatic marriage, for he was to be allowed to return to France. In September, 1847, Jerome Bonaparte, at sixty-two, was back in Paris, from which he had been banished thirty-two years ago, living at the Invalides with his new wife and his son Napoleon, his eldest boy by Catherine having died.

Jerome's money worries were over. Mathilde, separated from Count Anatole Demidov with a large marriage settlement, was able to give her father 40,000 francs a year; Louis Philippe made him governor of the Invalides, at a salary of 45,000 francs.

In contrast, the year of 1847 that saw the King of Westphalia's honors restored to him, found Jerome's ex-wife living quietly in Baltimore. Betsy, making a new life for herself in America, had been abroad, only once, in 1839, when she went to Paris with her son. Madame Mère died in Rome in 1836, leaving her savings to her children. But Cardinal Fesch left Jerome a small legacy. The American Bonapartes went to Europe to collect it.

Since then, Betsy had hardly left Baltimore. She lived alone, spending her time managing the real estate her father had left her and keeping an eye on her investments. Betsy saw a great deal of Jerome and his family. Otherwise, she went out little socially. Occasionally though, Mme. Bonaparte might be seen at the theater, wearing one of her Paris dresses, usually a low-cut, black velvet gown, and her white topaz necklace that puzzled Baltimore—were they diamonds?

Summers, Betsy spent a few weeks at Rockaway Beach, Long Island, or at White Sulphur Springs, in Virginia. Her tongue was as glib as ever, and fascinated groups gathered about Mme. Bonaparte in the hotel parlor, to hear her tell of the famous people she had known in Europe. At White Sulphur, Betsy refused to step into the pool. Where so many people bathed together, the water was unhealthy, she said. She wrote to Lady Morgan, describing herself as having "grown fat, old and dull." Betsy wasn't, of course. She was still lovely, but though only in her fifties, sensitive about her age. She was enjoying the compliments of a Kentucky colonel one day, until he made the mistake of asking her how old she was. Mme. Bonaparte curtly replied, "Nine hundred and ninety years, ninety-nine days and nine minutes." She never spoke to him again.

Betsy, who had always expected to inherit money from her father, realized now that she had no one else to depend upon but herself. But when had she ever been anything but alone in life? Forced to fight her own battles? Over fifty, she was not only making a new life for herself in America, but a fortune.

Her lean years in Europe, when Mme. Bonaparte had been compelled to be extremely careful with money, had made her miserly and warped her naturally generous nature. But having to count for every penny had also made Betsy as shrewd and cautious a financier as her father. Her business acumen was remarkable for a 19th century woman. By frugal living, she had been able to save a little of the pension Napoleon gave her until the fall of the Empire. This, and the four small bits of real estate her father left her, that became valuable due to Betsy's careful management, formed the start of the fortune she was adding to each year by investing, not in risky stocks, but in safe U.S. government bonds.

By 1840, Betsy wrote Lady Morgan that she had an income of $10,000 a year. She spent only $2,000 of it; and in those days before income taxes, money accumulated. What was she saving for? From habit, Betsy said. Jerome, with a wealthy wife, didn't need it. He and Susan were living on a beautiful new plantation, Bella Vista, where Jerome was leading the country life he loved—farming, shooting, foxhunting—and in Baltimore, running the exclusive Maryland Club, of which he was the first president. But with no one to plan and save for, her days seemed to Betsy at times to be empty and pointless. She longed for some glorious cause on which to expend her energies, she didn't know what.

Then, in 1848, the Bonaparte dynasty was restored in France, and Betsy knew why she had been hoarding her money. Her spirits soared, her ambitious hopes revived, hopes that had been dormant for nineteen years, since Jerome's marriage. King Louis Bonaparte's son, Princess Charlotte's husband Napoleon, had died during a revolution in Italy, leaving his brother Louis heir to the Empire. With the Prince's election as president, then as emperor of the French Republic, the future looked bright again for the Baltimore branch of the family.

"You knew the Emperor in Florence," Betsy reminded Jerome. "Don't you remember, your Cousin Louis lent you a horse, you used to go riding with him? You must go to France. He's sure to give you some great honor."

Jerome had a new boat. He would rather have gone cruising on the Chesapeake that summer. But his mother was insistent, so he went to France, taking his twenty-three-year-old son with him. They arrived in Paris in July, 1854, and were invited to dine at St. Cloud. Betsy was elated when Jerome wrote home how cordial Napoleon and his bride, the Empress Eugénie, were to him. Jerome was to be declared a French citizen, for the Emperor wished to create his American cousin, Duke of Sartène.

"My son, the Duke of Sartène—" Betsy let people know. She thought how proud she would be to help Jerome live up to a title. But two years passed, nothing happened, and Jerome wrote that, although Princess Mathilde was nice to him, he was having trouble with Prince Napoleon, who was jealous of his half-brother.

It was as Betsy had always said. As long as the American Bonapartes remained quietly in Baltimore and asked no favors of them, her husband's family were "lavish with kind words." But when Jerome asked to be recognized as the eldest son, his father was no longer so loving, his brother Napoleon became an enemy.

A Prince Imperial was born in 1856 to Napoleon III and Eugénie. Still, only the baby's frail life lay between the King of Westphalia, his children and the throne of France. It was imperative that Prince Napoleon get rid of his American half-brother. If Jerome was declared legitimate, being older, he would have precedence over him. A family council was held, at which Prince Napoleon induced his father to demand that Jerome leave Paris and stop using the name of Bonaparte, "which does not legally belong to him."

A French lawyer, Berryer, represented the Baltimore Bonapartes. But he stood little chance against the prestige that Prince Jerome, "the hero of Waterloo," had acquired in the Second Empire as the last living brother of the great Napoleon. Napoleon III had created his Uncle Jerome a marshal of France, president of the Senate and a prince. Victor Hugo describes him as living in style at the Palais Royal—a dignified, gray-haired gentleman, still with a charming smile and exquisite manners, the Legion of Honor on his breast.

Nor did Napoleon III, whose right to the name of Bonaparte was also in doubt, dare to oppose his uncle, for fear the old Prince might question his own birth. So the family council decided that the descendants of Mme. Elizabeth Patterson, being legitimate, might call themselves Bonapartes, but not being of royal rank, they were not entitled to rule France.

Jerome returned to Baltimore indignant at the injustice done him. "Did the Emperor create you Duke of Sartène?" his mother demanded.

"Oh, that was only to get me to give up the name of Bonaparte and my rights as the eldest son," Jerome replied, "so I declined the title."

The light died from Betsy's face, but she understood. Years ago, she had risked Napoleon's wrath by refusing also to give up the name of Bonaparte.

On June 24, 1860, King Jerome Bonaparte, at seventy-five, died at his Château of Villegenis, near Meudon, with Napoleon and Mathilde at his bedside. The Marchesa had long ago been sent back to Italy. There was a State funeral; and the King of Westphalia was buried with great pomp in the Invalides, near his famous brother. Weeks later, the Marchesa Bartolini, cast off by him like Betsy, yet unable to forget the man who had treated her so badly, came to kneel at Jerome's tomb and cry her heart out.

His death brought sadness and a sense of bereavement to Betsy, too. She wept and for days could eat scarcely a thing. She had not only lost the great love of her life, but with Jerome she saw disappearing a part of her youth. Something had gone she could never recapture. For over fifty years, Jerome had seldom been long out of her thoughts. And Betsy clung to the belief he still loved her. She liked to remember how Henriette Reubell had said that, after Jerome's second marriage, he had an artist paint a portrait of Betsy from a miniature he had, which he kept hidden from Catherine.

"Jerome loved me to the last," Betsy said, after his death. "Many people live and die without ever knowing what love means. It brought me suffering, but I'm glad I knew one great love. There has never been a day since Jerome and I parted in Lisbon that I haven't been lonely for him. And I'm sure he was always lonely for me."

So she was hurt and indignant to learn that Jerome had failed in his will to make any provision for their son, who had been declared legitimate. In fear of Prince Napoleon, who dominated his father completely, he had left everything to this son born of his second marriage. Jerome's namesake, his first-born in America, wasn't even mentioned.

This second slap from the grave was as crushing to Betsy's pride as her father's will had been. One of her attacks of nervous indigestion laid her low for several days. Then she crawled out of bed to face the situation with her usual determination.

Jerome, coming to see his mother, found her swinging a pair of dumbbells. He opened his eyes in amazement.

"Mama, what on earth are you doing? Becoming one of those new athletic women we hear about?"

"Dr. McKenzie says that exercise will make me young and strong again," Betsy replied haughtily. "I'm in training, preparing myself for the long journey."

"But, Mama, what journey?"

"To Paris. Jerome, you and I are going to fight your father's will!"

Betsy's brothers heard of her plans with consternation. Joseph arrived, frowning, to protest. Was she mad? A woman of seventy-six going abroad to engage in a bitter lawsuit in a strange land! Betsy must be out of her mind.

Too old to go? Did Joseph mean to insult her? Look at her. Was anyone in the family as strong? The eldest daughter, she had outlived her sisters, Augusta, Peggy, Caroline and Mary Ann Jeromia; her brothers, William, Robert, John, Henry and Octavius. What if she was nearly fourscore years, didn't she still hold herself upright? Wasn't her courage burning as brightly as ever? Betsy's ambition was to live to be a hundred.

Nothing Edward, Joseph and George said could quell her reawakened energy. Betsy was going to France and fight that hateful Prince Napoleon. She couldn't trust Jerome to be forceful enough. So, at seventy-six, the unconquerable old woman went. The result, in February, 1861, was one of the world's most famous lawsuits.

Through Berryer, Mme. Bonaparte, who called herself the widow of the late Prince, again appealed to the French court, this time for a share in his estate. However, it was not the money Betsy was fighting for, but for the recognition of her marriage and Jerome's rights as the eldest son. For since the King of Westphalia had made his will, his child by Betsy had been declared legitimate.

The eloquent plea of the famous French lawyer, who had also appeared before the family council in her behalf, made all Europe pity Elizabeth Patterson, as, standing before the judges of the Palais de Justice, on February 15, 1861, Berryer told of her romantic marriage to the First Consul's brother, and how, a devoted mother, Betsy had fought for half a century for her son's name. Her rights, he said, were incontestable, based on the validity of her marriage, performed by the Archbishop of Baltimore, and her marriage settlement.

Listening, Betsy remembered that contract her father had insisted upon, and how she had scorned it. "Our marriage annulled? For heaven's sake, why? Jerome says, nothing but death can part us again." Those were her foolish words. And Papa had been so wise and cautious. Betsy remembered him with gratitude.

But not even William Patterson's foresight could help his daughter now. Prince Napoleon's counsel replied that Miss Patterson and her late father had been informed before the marriage, by the chargé d'affaires at Washington, of the French law, that no minor under twenty-five could be married without the consent of his parents. Yet they had gone ahead with the ceremony. The wording of the contract showed they knew the marriage would not be considered binding in France.

The judges agreed that the Pattersons had acted in defiance of the French law, and since no legal marriage existed, the child born of the union was illegitimate. Napoleon had said the same, fifty years ago.

It had been a losing battle from the start. The granting of Betsy's appeal would have angered the Italians. Prince Napoleon's marriage to Princess Clothilde, daughter of Victor Emmanuel of Savoy, had been a political move, to cement an alliance between France and Italy. A verdict in Betsy's favor, recognizing her son as heir to his father, would have given the throne, not to King Victor Emmanuel's son-in-law, but to the American line—Jerome and his two sons—in case of the death of the Prince Imperial.

The American Bonapartes, having lost even the concession of legitimacy they won five years earlier from the family council, returned to Baltimore dejected. Coming home, on one of the new, iron steamboats, at fourteen knots—a vast improvement in speed and comfort upon the slow sailing ships and clumsy wooden paddle-wheelers by which Mme. Bonaparte had previously crossed—the ocean was rough. Betsy hardly left her berth. Her illness wasn't due to seasickness, though, as much as to the realization that she had gained nothing by this trip to Europe. Her last hope of getting her marriage declared legal was gone. She must pay the heavy cost of the trial; and as a crowning humiliation, the court had ruled that Betsy and her descendants must hyphenate the names of Patterson and Bonaparte.

Jerome, his arm about his mother, tried to comfort her. "Stop torturing yourself. Forget about Europe," he begged.

Surely, there was trouble enough awaiting them at home. They found Maryland, at the outbreak of the War Between the States, divided on the slavery question. Families were divided, too. Jerome, his wife and mother were in sympathy with the Union cause. George Patterson, Jerome's uncle, sided with the South.

The Federal forces sent raiders to Springfield, to burn the plantation, carry off slaves, food and horses. George Patterson met the cavalry at the door. He demanded on what authority his home was entered. The officer in charge, his hand on the hilt of his sword, snapped, "My authority is here." George, by nature a gentle soul, drew his revolver. "Cross that threshold then, and I'll kill you!" The Federals knew the owner of Springfield meant what he said. They turned their horses and galloped away.

With bands playing *Maryland, My Maryland,* with Union and Confederate armies fighting on Maryland soil the famous battles of South Mountain and Antietam, Betsy lived through another war in Baltimore, this time not under bombardment, but in a city largely Southern in its sympathies, occupied by Northern forces. Her heart was with the Union cause. But she cooked food for the Federal troops and made surgical dressings, her thoughts far away with Jerome Napoleon Bonaparte III, a young soldier in Italy.

Betsy's ambitions still would not let her rest. But she was no longer planning for her son. With a clarity of vision that had come to her with old age, she realized that she had been as selfish and domineering as her father in trying to force Jerome II to live his life as she wished.

"I used to think Papa was horrid, and all the time I was being just as bossy and hateful to you, darling." Betsy patted her son's hand. "Will you forgive me for being such a bad mother, if I promise in the future to leave you alone?"

"You're incorrigible, Mama, and I love you—" Jerome laughed. He knew why he was being cast aside. By the gleam in Betsy's eyes, he could tell that her mind was teeming with new plans, for the next generation, her grandson.

22. *Baltimore's First Lady*

J EROME III was better material for Betsy's ambitions. He was handsomer and more aggressive than his
father. And he loved France. From early childhood, when
he had listened eagerly to his grandmother's stories about
Napoleon, the boy had wanted to be a soldier. After one
year at Harvard, Jerome III had entered West Point, where
he was graduated in 1852, with his proud grandmother, his
parents and one-year-old brother Charles in the audience.
There was twenty-one years' difference in age between the
two boys.

"He's another Napoleon," Betsy said to herself, pleased
with Jerome's new military bearing. She no longer noticed
his Patterson ears.

Jerome must have the career in Europe his father scorned.
It would take money, and, saving for her grandson, Betsy
was happy as she hadn't been happy since she stopped piling
up a fortune for her son. She had never enjoyed spending
on herself.

If Jerome III had money enough, he might some day oc-

cupy the Tuileries as emperor or as president—at least, marry
a princess. To make such a thing possible, Betsy insisted that
the new second lieutenant resign, August 16, 1854, after serv-
ing two years with the United States Third Cavalry in Texas,
and accept a commission in the Seventh Dragoons of the
French army.

"Don't worry about money," she told him. "I'll see that
you can live up to being the grandson of a king."

Betsy could well afford to do so. She was now a very
wealthy woman, with an income of $100,000 a year. The
greater part of the million and a half dollars Mme. Bonaparte
left at her death, she accumulated during the last thirty years
of her life, by strict economy and shrewd investments.
Stingy with herself, she was generous to her grandsons, especially to Jerome in the French army, sending him checks
for $5,000 to $10,000 at a time.

When on July 17, 1870, Jerome II, at sixty-five, died of
cancer—the disease that killed so many Bonapartes—leaving
his Bella Vista plantation to his sons, Betsy bought out the
share of her grandson in Europe and gave it to his younger
brother. She sent Charles to a French school in Baltimore
and tried to make a French boy out of him. But Charles had
little interest in Europe. Like his father, he loved Baltimore.

Charles Bonaparte entered Harvard as a junior in 1869.
He was a serious young man. Betsy was more interested in
his dashing older brother, who shared her love for France.
In order to be able to lay aside a large part of her fortune for
Jerome's future use, she rented her cottage on South Street
and lived for the last eighteen years of her life in a succession of down-at-the-heels boardinghouses.

In 1871, Betsy's small furnished room was a fifth-floor
walkup, a hundred tiring steps above the street, at Miss
Peter's, on the corner of St. Paul and Lexington Streets.

With an income of $100,000 a year, Mme. Bonaparte refused to pay more than $25 a week for her board; objected to gas, because of the expense, and burned candles; wrote notes on the backs of letters to save the price of paper; suffered from cold to conserve fuel; and lived frugally on plain food. She refused to own a carriage and did her own laundry, shocking Baltimore by hanging her red flannel petticoat and other "unmentionables" out of the window.

A spry little old lady in a black velvet bonnet with orange feathers, carrying the red silk umbrella from Paris that, in sunshine or rain, she was never without for forty years, Mme. Bonaparte was a familiar figure in the business section of Baltimore that she visited almost daily to bank her money. Betsy invested her income in various ways, but she preferred real estate. To save his commission, Betsy refused to employ a real estate agent. She hardly gave herself a day of rest— inspecting houses, asking the price of property that caught her attention and taking notes on improvements she intended to make. And as she went from house to house, collecting her rents, Betsy grew to know Baltimore well, and to love the town, as her father had done.

One day, standing on Hampstead Hill which he had given the city, now called Patterson Park, Betsy looked out over the town. Her cheeks burned to think she had ever disliked Baltimore. She would always be grateful to the place, for, thanks to Baltimore, she was amassing the fortune that might make possible her dream of seeing her grandson ruler of France.

How proud she was of him! Betsy's happiest days were when she received a letter from Jerome. In the Crimea, he was a hero at Sebastopol. He was decorated by Queen Victoria; by the French, with the Legion of Honor; and by the Turkish Sultan, with the Order of Medjidie. In 1856, Jerome

III was in the French Algerian campaign. During the American War Between the States, he was fighting in Italy, where he was decorated by the King of Sardinia.

In 1867, he was transferred to the Dragoons of the Empress. Betsy, reading every foreign paper she could get her hands on, was thrilled to learn that, when Napoleon III went to the front in 1870, at the start of the Franco-Prussian War, he left Colonel Jerome Bonaparte in command of the Tuileries and the Empress in his care.

After Sedan, when Eugénie escaped to England, the American colonel rushed to her side, to help settle the Empress at Chislehurst, in Kent. Then Jerome returned to France, to nearly starve during the siege of Paris. Peace came; and in April, 1871, Betsy was surprised to hear that her grandson was returning to America. Susan went to New York to meet him at the boat.

Betsy awaited their return impatiently. Why was Jerome coming to America? Then she remembered that, with Napoleon III's death, her grandson had moved closer to the throne. No one wanted Prince Napoleon, who had disgraced himself by fleeing the Crimea when cholera broke out among the troops. An exciting thought came to her. Was the Third Republic, also cool to the Prince Imperial, thinking of an American for president? Hadn't Napoleon III made himself president, then emperor? It was not improbable that, if the Empire was restored, the next Emperor of France might be Colonel Jerome Napoleon Bonaparte of Baltimore.

Nor was Jerome's doting grandmother the only one who thought that he could become ruler of France. Betsy cherished a clipping from the *Baltimore Sun* of January 19, 1870:

The troubled conditions in France may yet afford the Baltimore Bonapartes an opportunity, and a Patterson occupy the Tuileries as Prince President, just as Louis, a Beauharnais, occupied the palace in 1849. Jerome Bonaparte acted badly enough to Miss Patterson. Nor has his family done much better. It would be a piece of justice if Time should balance the account.

Happy to be needed again, Betsy converted her securities and mortgages into cash, ready to hand them over to her grandson for any *coup d'état* he planned. This was why she had saved; this was the proud moment for which she had been living.

Susan returned from New York alone. "Where is Jerome?" Betsy demanded. Had something happened to him?

"Jerome is in New York, Mama."

Ah, then he was all right! There was nothing to be worried about. But what ailed Susan? Her glance met Betsy's, then fell. Somehow Betsy felt her daughter-in-law was afraid to meet her eyes. But why? "Jerome isn't ill?" she asked anxiously. Susan turned away, her eyes evasive.

"He's engaged, Mama. He remained in New York with his sweetheart."

"Engaged? To whom? To one of the princesses he wrote us of knowing in Paris? How odd! Why didn't Jerome write me about his engagement?"

"I fancy, because he knew you'd be angry," Susan replied, for Jerome had fallen in love with Mrs. Newbolt Edgar, a young American widow he had met in Paris.

An American had won a second Jerome Bonaparte! In an instant all Betsy's hopes of seeing a descendant of hers on the French throne vanished. Jerome had thrown away the chance she had given him, wrecked his whole career, for a woman who would complicate things in case of a return of the Empire. It was the final blow to Betsy's proud, ambitious spirit. She turned deathly pale, her eyes flooded with tears.

"Caroline is well-born," Susan tried to console her. "She is the granddaughter of a great American, Daniel Webster."

Betsy, in a trance, seemed not to hear. At last she spoke. "I'll cut off Jerome's allowance. I never want to see him again!" In that moment, renouncing forever her dreams of a lifetime, Betsy's face grew suddenly wrinkled and drawn. Her shoulders sagged. She seemed to age. Susan reached for her hands. They were cold and lifeless, like Betsy's face. Her heart aching for her mother-in-law, Susan put her arms lovingly about the broken old woman.

In spite of the fact that his grandmother almost had a stroke because she was so hurt and upset over it, Colonel Jerome Bonaparte married Mrs. Edgar, born Caroline Le-Roy Appleton, on September 7, 1871, and brought her to Baltimore to live.

"The Princess Mathilde writes Jerome," Susan came to report, "that the great demonstration of the people at the funeral of Napoleon III shows that the Empire may yet be restored. During the minority of the Prince Imperial, Jerome may be made co-regent with the Empress."

Betsy lifted her head proudly. "I believe he will be. I shall yet live to see a descendant of mine ruling France!"

She hadn't recovered from her crushing disappointment. The scars were slow to heal. Repeated blows in life, however, had taught Betsy to put the best face on things. She never forgave Jerome, but, in spite of her threats to cut off his allowance, she continued to be generous to him. It was his grandmother who sent the Colonel and his wife the money that made possible their home on fashionable Charles Street, their servants in olive livery with red waistcoats and the elegant carriage, with the Bonaparte crest in silver on the door panels, that drove past Betsy's shabby boarding house.

The old lady looked out of her dormer window under the roof at the carriage and pair she had always wanted and sighed. But as the years dragged on, Betsy found that her most comforting thoughts did not dwell in the present. As for the future, she no longer gave it a thought. She lived in the past. Her small, uncarpeted room, with its dingy whitewashed walls, was piled high with twenty trunks, filled with things she had brought from Europe. Betsy liked to open them and show her treasures to friends. She dearly loved her possessions, for they recalled the romantic days of her youth.

"This is my husband's purple satin wedding coat. Here is the pink dress Princess Borghese gave me. This red velvet gown I wore at the Court of Tuscany. This one, at the Pitti Palace, the day I met Jerome and his German wife—"

Betsy no longer wore her costly Paris frocks. Baltimoreans saw her on the street in a shabby plaid shawl, a cheap alpaca dress and an old-fashioned bonnet. She had not bought a bit of clothing in twenty years.

Indoors, Mme. Bonaparte wore a black velvet ribbon across her forehead—"A mark of royalty," she explained—and a lace cap. She sat at her desk evenings, writing up the diary she had kept for forty years, or working on her recollections of the famous people she had known in Europe. It was rumored that Mme. Bonaparte was also engaged in composing a more sensational story of her life, in the form of conversations between her father and her husband in Hell, to be entitled, *Dialogues of the Dead.*

Betsy was still vain of her beauty. She would sit for hours, admiring her portrait by Gilbert Stuart. "I like it the best of my pictures," she said, "because Jerome held my hand while Stuart painted me."

In 1875, Betsy moved back to Miss Elizabeth Gwinn's

boardinghouse, on the corner of Cathedral and Richmond Streets, where she had formerly lived. There, in a plainly furnished room on the second floor, facing Cathedral Street, she spent the last four years of her life.

Everyone told Mme. Bonaparte how remarkably young she looked for a woman of ninety. Her figure was still trim, her skin smooth, her eyes bright. But due to the fact that she kept large sums of cash in her room, Betsy had grown fearful and suspicious. In constant dread of being murdered for her wealth, she would no longer receive visitors in her room, and if called down to the parlor to see anyone, she took with her a bag containing her jewels and money and hung it on the back of her chair.

Her most distinguished visitor was General Bertrand, Napoleon's Grand Marshal, who had been with the Emperor at St. Helena.

"Napoleon often spoke of you with admiration, Madame," he said, "and regretted he ruined your life. He heard you thought kindly of him and one day exclaimed to me, 'Bertrand, those whom I wronged have forgiven me, while those I loaded with kindness have forsaken me.' "

Baltimore, that had never liked young, bewitching Betsy Patterson, grew proud of the odd old lady, strong-willed and sharp-tongued, she had become. Mme. Bonaparte was a great reader of the Bible in her old age and knew long passages by heart. She wanted to turn Roman Catholic. "It's the faith of kings and queens," Betsy said. But she remained a Presbyterian, explaining to her pastor, "Reverend Leftwich, I was baptized a Presbyterian, and I shall die one, I cannot give up the stool my ancestors sat on."

Neurotic in middle-age, due to unhappiness, Betsy was now proud of her energy and longevity and refused to become an invalid. She was a remarkably spry old lady up to the age of ninety-two. Then her health began to fail. Her mind remained as keen as ever, but Betsy's stomach had always troubled her when she was emotionally upset, and, during the last two years of her life, her digestion was so bad she lived almost entirely on brandy (which she disliked) and milk. Feebly, with the help of a cane, she managed to get downstairs on Christmas day, 1878. Five days later, she was taken ill with bronchitis and never left her room again.

On February 6, 1879, Betsy spent her ninety-fourth birthday in bed. Dr. McKenzie knew that this illness might be her last. She didn't demand to get up and allowed him to find a woman to look after her, a suggestion Mme. Bonaparte had always fought before, because of the expense.

"Doctor, I've an illness no medicine can cure—old age," she said. "Can I live until my grandson returns from France? I'd like to kiss Jerome once more."

He returned on March 26th. Betsy knew him, then gradually fell into a stupor. But her remarkable vitality continued to the end. She became unconscious, then lay for over two days, still and composed as an effigy on a tombstone, with the life silently ebbing away within her.

Dr. McKenzie spoke in a low voice to the nurse. "I think she has left us, Mrs. Clark."

Hearing him, the gallant old lady, a fighter to the last, sat up in bed and announced tartly, "I'm not dead. What's more, young man, I intend to live to be a hundred!"

From that moment Betsy began to improve. She was better for a few days, then grew worse. On the last day, she asked Mrs. Clark and Miss Gwinn, her landlady, to pray for her. The Reverend Leftwich, of the First Presbyterian Church, came to see her. Betsy said his prayers comforted her. During the night, Miss Gwinn heard her distinctly say, "The blood of Jesus, His Son, cleanseth us from all sin; that's in the Bible." These were Betsy Bonaparte's last intelligible words. She died at 1:15 P.M., on Friday, the 4th of April, 1879, at ninety-four, six years short of her goal, having outlived her son, and the last of her generation in the family, her twelve brothers and sisters.

Betsy had a great fear of being buried alive. During her last illness, she asked Doctor McKenzie to have a post-mortem done on her body or, better yet, to shoot her through the head. He promised Mme. Bonaparte he would see that she wasn't buried alive, so the funeral didn't take place for several days. Then her body was carried from Miss Gwinn's humble boardinghouse to the home of Mrs. Susan Bonaparte, at 85 Park Avenue.

As she lay in her silver-trimmed, walnut coffin, standing between two pillars in the marble-tiled entrance hall, it was noticed how, at Mme. Bonaparte's advanced age, her face was still beautiful. It was a small family funeral. There were no flowers; at the head and foot of the coffin, only two lighted candles. But Park Avenue, outside the house, was lined with throngs of curious people, gathered to see the woman who had become a legend in her lifetime carried to the grave.

The carriages moved out to Greenmount Cemetery, where the mourners stood about in the chill April rain, under a huge oak tree, as the Reverend Leftwich read the burial service. Then there sank into the earth the last remains of the American sister-in-law of the great Napoleon.

There Betsy lies, not in the Patterson family plot at Coldstream with her parents, her brothers and sisters. By her own request, Mme. Bonaparte was buried by herself, in a small, triangular lot she had purchased seven years before her death, large enough for only one grave. Her dying request was, "As I've been lonely in life, I wish to be alone in death." Her long and eventful life had been a constant struggle against overwhelming odds. Betsy was tired. Death would be a good sleep, she hoped. And she asked to have carved on her tombstone the words from Macbeth: *After life's fitful fever she sleeps well.*

Afterword

In June, 1879, with Betsy Bonaparte but two months in her grave, the twenty-three-year-old Prince Imperial, only child of Napoleon III and the Empress Eugénie, was killed fighting the Zulus with the British army in South Africa. A warship carried his body back to England, where the Empress Eugénie was living in exile, and to the funeral in Kent of the young man who called himself Napoleon IV there hastened all that remained of the European descendants of the great Napoleon.

Would the American Bonapartes join their royal cousins at the funeral? Baltimore was agog to know, and reporters trooped out to his home to interview Betsy's younger grandson. He had never visited Europe and never would, Charles J. Bonaparte curtly informed the press; and he issued a statement to the *Baltimore Sun* that, not being members of the Imperial family, he and Jerome would not attend the funeral.

Thus, in a four-line release, did Betsy's grandson relinquish his Imperial rights and those of his brother, and by meekly accepting the verdict of the Paris Tribunal of 1861, announced to the world that the American Bonapartes were no longer heirs-presumptive to the French throne. Charles, especially, cared nothing about being a prince. Like his father, he preferred to be a useful American citizen. But what would his militant old grandmother have said to him?

The Empress Eugénie had never forgiven Prince Napoleon for opposing her marriage to Napoleon III. When the will the Prince Imperial left in England was opened, it was found that he had expressed his dislike and his mother's for King Jerome's son by skipping over Prince Napoleon and naming Prince Napoleon's son, Victor Napoleon, as his successor. The American Bonapartes were also ignored, and the precedent was established that, in the future, the pretenders to the Imperial throne of France would come from the descendants of King Jerome's European son.

One can imagine how Betsy would have fought any such decision, that the succession should descend through the cadet line, rather than the senior, and Prince Victor Napoleon become the possible Napoleon V. The indomitable old woman would surely have made another trip to Europe to make life miserable for Prince Napoleon and his son. But Betsy was dead. And neither of her grandsons cared enough about their Imperial rights to continue her long struggle for them.

So the Bonapartist pretenders to the throne of France have ever since come from the European branch of the family. Victor Napoleon married Princess Clementine of Belgium, daughter of Belgium's late Leopold II, and great-aunt of the present King Baudouin. Their son, Prince Napoleon, King Jerome's great-grandson, a prosperous chemist in his forties, is the current Bonapartist pretender.

Jerome and Charles ignored the ruling of the French

court that they must hyphenate the names of Patterson and Bonaparte. But, after Betsy's death, the American Bonapartes never again pressed their Imperial claim. The Colonel and his wife went to Paris in 1878 and, after living abroad for six years, returned to their homes in Washington and in Newport. Jerome Bonaparte III died from cancer (the Bonaparte disease) at Pride's Crossing, Massachusetts, on September 4, 1893, leaving a daughter, Louise Eugénie, who married Count Adam de Moltke-Hintfeldt of Denmark, and a son, Jerome Napoleon, born in Paris in 1878.

Betsy's marriage was annulled by Napoleon's order, but the Pope always refused to sanction the decree, and in the eyes of the Catholic Church, the only legitimate heirs to the Imperial throne of France, on the death of the Prince Imperial, were the Baltimore Bonapartes. Many still considered them to be of royal rank, and in 1921, a visiting delegation from Albania suggested to Jerome Napoleon Bonaparte IV that he become king of Albania. But no formal offer was made, and Mr. Bonaparte was content to remain an American citizen, prominent in New York, Baltimore, Washington and Newport society. He married Mrs. Blanche Strebeigh of Boston. They had no children, and with the death of Betsy's great-grandson in 1945, there passed away the last person to bear the Bonaparte name in the branch of the family that stemmed from the romance of the belle of Baltimore to the brother of an emperor, for in 1921 Mr. Bonaparte's Uncle Charles had died, also without heirs. He did, however, leave behind him a reputation at the Maryland Bar and in politics that made Charles Joseph Bonaparte the most famous of Betsy's descendants.

Charles, in contrast to his brother Jerome, who frequently visited Europe, took pride in being an American and lived all his life in Baltimore. He never went abroad, but traveled extensively in the United States, even visiting Alaska. Charles graduated from Harvard in 1872, attended Harvard Law School, then returned to Baltimore, where he became known as a fighter for civil service reform. His activities attracted the attention of the then Civil Service Commissioner, Theodore Roosevelt, who had known Bonaparte at Harvard. When Roosevelt became President of the United States, he appointed Betsy's grandson Secretary of the Navy, in 1905, and later Attorney General. While Attorney General, Charles J. Bonaparte advocated a secret service in the Department of Justice. This was actually established by his successor and is now known as the FBI.

It is a pity that Charles, twenty-one years younger than his brother Jerome, had only graduated from law school, married Ellen Channing Day of Hartford, Connecticut, and been admitted to the Bar, when his grandmother died. Had she seen her grandson in Roosevelt's Cabinet, it might have satisfied Betsy's ambitions, and turned her interest from the Old World to the New.

There is no doubt of her love for Charles. With Jerome abroad a great deal, Betsy grew very fond of her younger grandson in her last years. She divided her money equally between the two brothers, but it was to Charles that she left the treasures dear to her: the Gilbert Stuart portraits of herself and King Jerome, Betsy's portraits by Massot and Kinson, the thirteen-volume story of her life, the diaries she kept for forty years (for which a Boston publisher offered Mme. Bonaparte $10,000), her letters and the *Dialogue of the Dead.*

Her diaries, memoirs and the famed *Dialogues* are not among Betsy's belongings that Charles J. Bonaparte bequeathed to the Maryland Historical Society in 1921. Charles and his brother Jerome must have had a bonfire after their grandmother's death. It is a pity, Betsy's sarcastic comments on the famous people she had known would make lively reading.

But Charles Bonaparte did leave the Society a whole roomful of his grandmother's personal things. From the wall, Betsy's lovely face looks out of the D'Alamine copy of the Stuart painting onto the possessions she cherished as long as she lived—the fan she carried to the Chase ball; her rouge pot and manicure set; a chest with games she liked to play; her crystal seal with the Imperial crown; a collection of visiting cards, on them the names of princes and princesses Mme. Bonaparte knew in Europe; and a pair of tiny slippers in which she must have danced many a night away.

There is the flower-painted trunk Betsy took to Lisbon when she sailed with Jerome, filled with her lace shawls, dainty undergarments and nightcaps. Several of her dresses are on display; and in a case, her books and jewelry. You can read on the clasp of the garnet necklace Jerome gave Betsy the word, *Fidélite.* How ironic that promise was but two years later! There is a tiara of pearls and amethysts in which Betsy must have looked like a queen. She is wearing that comb of garnets and pearls in her portrait by Massot on the wall. And how often she must have wept over this miniature of Jerome!

In a folder marked "love letters," there is a paper yellow from age and worn from being much read—Samuel Graves' poem, *Thoughts in Bed, the Same She had Once Occupied.* Betsy kept his tender sentiments, her whole life long.

The most amusing item in the collection is a copy of Du Casse's *Memoires du Roi Jerome,* annotated and underlined by Betsy herself. On the title page she wrote, "A tissue of lies, contradictions and nonsense." On other pages there are such caustic comments as: "A lie . . . Bah! . . . Stuff! . . .

True ... Fudge!" At one place, where the author states that Mr. Patterson sent his daughter South to get her away from Jerome, Betsy scribbled in the margin: "Where he ought to have kept her!"

Betsy's cookbook has in it a recipe for syllabub-under-cow. You're told to "put into a punch bowl a pint of cyder and a bottle of strong beer." Perhaps she made this heady concoction in her big china punch bowl, out in the hall. In another room is Jefferson's banquet table at which the Jerome Bonapartes were entertained at the White House. On it are arranged a selection from the 191-piece china dinner service that belonged to Mme. Bonaparte. This was presented to the Maryland Historical Society by Mrs. Andrew Robeson (Laura Dyer), great-great-granddaughter of Betsy's brother Edward.

William Patterson's South Street mansion has gone. So has Coldstream, his house on Kirk and Homestead Avenues, now in Baltimore, where the Jerome Bonapartes spent their honeymoon. Joseph Patterson, who became president of the Baltimore & Ohio Railroad in 1836, inherited the property. But Joseph preferred 20 South Street for a town house, and his Gothic villa, Evesham, in Govanstown, as a country place. His brother Edward, who was in the iron business with Joseph after their father's death, occupied the estate summers. This was convenient because Coldstream was near Montebello, the home of the Samuel Smiths, the parents of Edward's wife. He died there, in 1865. Joseph deeded the place to Edward's son, and at his death, it passed to a niece, Mrs. William Turner, and from her to her daughter, Mrs. Elisha Dyer.

The house, a tenement by that time, surrounded by factories, was torn down in 1920. But you can climb the hill north of the house site to the old burial ground of the Patterson family. Behind a brick wall are the graves of William and Dorcas Patterson and twenty-three of their descendants. But not Betsy. Andrew Robeson, husband of Laura Dyer, who died in 1939, was the last person to be buried here.

You can also visit Springfield, at Sykesville, twenty miles west of Baltimore, another suburban home the Pattersons went to in summer, to escape from yellow fever. The plantation was inherited by Governor Frank Brown of Maryland from his aunt, who married George Patterson. The Governor liked to tell how Mme. Bonaparte often came to Springfield in her old age and always went to look at some pecan trees she had planted as a girl, taking great pride in their growth. Governor Brown sold the property to the State in 1906. It is now the State Hospital. The house Betsy knew burned down in 1912, but the main hospital building is built on the old foundations.

In Baltimore, you can stroll through the park that grew from the five acres of cow pasture William Patterson gave the city. You can visit the Flag House, where lived Mary Pickersgill who made the original Star-Spangled Banner, and buy your groceries from the Center Market where Betsy shopped, now called Lexington Market. The big Spanish oak, trysting place of Jerome and Betsy, lasted until 1937, on the old site of the Samuel Ready School for Girls at North and Hartford Avenues, when, struck by lightning, it was taken down. Mr. Patterson's will, the longest and most amazing one ever filed in Baltimore, is in the Hall of Records, at Annapolis, Maryland, where it can be seen on request. And no reader of this book who goes to Baltimore should fail to visit Betsy's grave in Greenmount Cemetery, where she lies alone under a marble monument said to be a copy of Napoleon's tomb at St. Helena.

A child of the 18th century, born just after the Revolution,

Betsy lived on, in memory at least, into our own 20th century. There are still people living in Baltimore whose parents remembered Mme. Bonaparte going around town, collecting her rents in a little bag. Stephen Bonsal, writing in the *New York Times Magazine* of August 7, 1921, tells how, as a boy of seven, he often saw Betsy come out at dusk from her dingy boardinghouse on Cathedral Street, to sit in Miss Gwinn's neglected garden or hobble about its paths, leaning on her cane. The children in the neighborhood would stop their play to stare at the odd, arrogant old woman. She fascinated them because of her connection with Napoleon.

One day young Bonsal, in a rush of confidence, told her that "when my hand-writing improves" he was going to write a history of the Bonapartes. Betsy turned on the boy her sad, dark eyes. "It would be an interesting story," she replied. Stephen grew up; he went away to boarding school; and when he returned, the old lady was no longer in the garden.

Betsy had died, but the glamour of Baltimore's first famous international marriage remains, one of America's favorite love stories. Perhaps she is better remembered than if Jerome had not deserted her and Betsy had become Queen of Westphalia. The Bonaparte line in America is extinct. But while there is romance in the world, the story of the beautiful Baltimore girl who married the brother of an emperor will never be forgotten.

Alice Curtis Desmond

Bibliography

Doing research for this dramatized biography of Betsy Bonaparte was the excuse for two trips my husband and I made to Europe. We visited Camberwell, a London suburb that retains much of the quiet village charm it had when Betsy went there to give birth to her son. Nor has the English spa of Cheltenham, where we spent several days, changed a great deal since Mme. Bonaparte sought its gaieties as an escape form her harsh, self-righteous father.

We found many places in Paris that recall Jerome Bonaparte. There was the Palais Royal, where the King of Westphalia lived in style in his old age; and his tomb at the Invalides, near those of his brothers, Napoleon and Joseph. In the summer of 1955, we were fortunate enough to be in Paris when there was being exhibited at the Invalides a collection of furniture, clothing, jewels and art objects that had belonged to Napoleon and his brothers and sisters. These were lent mostly by Prince Napoleon, the present head of the Bonaparte family. Among them was a silver-fitted dressing case of Jerome's, as costly as the one he bought for 10,000 francs as a young man (and maybe the same one), and other personal belongings.

It was fun searching through London and Paris bookshops for secondhand books about the Bonapartes. Their titles, with the considerable research material I acquired in America, are listed below:

Interesting source material is the APPEL DE M. JEROME-NAPOLEON BONAPARTE ET MME. ELISABETH PATTERSON CONTRE S.A.I. LE PRINCE NAPOLEON, COUR IMPERIALE DE PARIS, 15 FEVRIER, 1861. Baltimore: James S. Waters, 168 Baltimore Street.

This brief, written in French, was used by Lawyer Berryer in behalf of the son and widow of King Jerome in their plea before the Paris Tribunal of February 15, 1861, for a share in the estate of the late Prince. It contains in full Jerome's letters to Betsy after he deserted her.

Didier, Eugene L. LIFE AND LETTERS OF MADAME BONAPARTE. New York: Charles Scribner's Sons, 1879.

These letters from Betsy to her father cover the years from 1815-1834, when she lived in Europe. They were published in 1879, the year Mme. Bonaparte died. Didier does not say how he secured them. Written after the humiliation of being deserted had turned a sweet girl into a sour, unhappy woman, this bitter correspondence is unfortunately the source material of too much written about Betsy Bonaparte. Her surly, critical father brought out the worst in her.

That hard, sure manner of Betsy's was to hide her being so wretchedly unhappy. James Gallatin remarked, "Mme. Bonaparte . . . does not allow herself to show too much of her true nature." Betsy, when she wrote these letters, was emotionally near the breaking point. To cope with her troubles, she tried to be as cold and cynical as she could. But no matter how hard the shell, there was still a woman's heart underneath, a heart that had been deeply wounded. That is why the author felt that a sympathetic biography of Betsy Bonaparte was needed.

Saffell, W. T. R. THE BONAPARTE-PATTERSON MARRIAGE AND THE SECRET CORRESPONDENCE ON THE SUBJECT NEVER BEFORE MADE PUBLIC. Philadelphia: 1873.

This correspondence, relating to Betsy's marriage, begins with Robert Patterson's letters to his father from Europe, in 1804, and concludes with Betsy's return from Europe, a deserted wife. It reads like fiction. All the ingredients of a thrilling romantic novel are here, even Robert's letters in cipher.

William Saffell writes in the preface that he bought the original letters from Houtine & Murdock, a Baltimore paper maker, who had contracted with Patterson & Sons to remove refuse from the basement of their warehouse on Gay Street. Thrown out, the chances were a thousand to one this correspondence would never have been heard of again had not one of the men in Houtine & Murdock, in sorting the waste paper, happened to glance over the bundle of letters and, suspecting they might be of value, offered them to Saffell, a Philadelphia publisher.

Mr. Saffell, inspecting his purchase, was intrigued by the material he found about Mme. Bonaparte's marriage. He goes on to say that, having copied the letters, he returned the originals to William Patterson's grandson, now head of the firm. Then realizing the interest there still was in the beautiful Baltimore woman whose romantic marriage linked America and Europe, he decided to publish his find.

Betsy was still living in 1873, and caution prompted him to send her the proof sheets of the book. Mme. Bonaparte made no objection to its being published. In fact, she replied that, to her, "the publication of the volume was a matter of perfect indifference."

It is probable that Betsy, at eighty-eight, far from being indifferent, was delighted to have her romance recalled to public notice. Her grandson Charles was not so well pleased. In January, 1873, with the book about to be published, he called upon Mr. Saffell to demand that it not be printed. Saffell refused to withdraw the book. But he agreed to say in the preface that it had been published against the wishes of Colonel Jerome N. Bonaparte and Mr. Charles J. Bonaparte.

Du Casse, edited by Baron. Memoires et Correspondence du Roi Jerome, Paris, 1861.

Sioussat, Annie Leakin. Old Baltimore. New York: The Macmillan Company, 1931.

Ludwig, Emil. Napoleon. London: George Allen and Unwin, Ltd., 1927.

Woodward, W. E. Lafayette. New York: Farrar and Rinehart, 1938.

Delteil, Joseph. Lafayette. New York: Milton, Balch and Company, 1928.

Barney, Mary, edited by. Biographical Memoires of Commodore Joshua Barney. Boston: Gray and Bowen, 1832.

Parton, James. Daughters of Genius. Philadelphia: Hubbard Brothers, 1888. Sketch of Lady Sydney Morgan.

d'Abrantes, The Duchess (Mme. Junot). Memoires of Napoleon, His Court and Family. 2 vols. New York: Appleton and Company, 1867.

Paine, Ralph D. Joshua Barney. New York: Century Company, 1924.

Whitley, William T. Gilbert Stuart. Cambridge, Mass.: Harvard University Press, 1932.

Roberts, Octavia. WITH LAFAYETTE IN AMERICA. Boston: Houghton Mifflin Company, 1919.

Parker, A. A. RECOLLECTIONS OF GENERAL LAFAYETTE ON HIS VISIT TO THE UNITED STATES IN 1824 AND 1825. Privately printed, 1879.

Woodward, E. M. BONAPARTE'S PARK AND THE MURATS. Trenton, New Jersey: Privately printed, 1879.

Kaessmann, Beta, Harold Randall Manakee, and Joseph L. Wheeler. MY MARYLAND. Baltimore: Maryland Historical Society, 1955.

Morris, Anne Cary, edited by. DIARY AND LETTERS OF GOUVERNEUR MORRIS. 2 vols. New York: Charles Scribner's Sons, 1888.

Williams, H. Noel. THE WOMEN BONAPARTES. 2 vols. New York: Charles Scribner's Sons, 1909.

Sergeant, Philip W. THE PRINCESS MATHILDE BONAPARTE. London: Stanley Paul and Company.

Scharf, Colonel J. Thomas. CHRONICLES OF BALTIMORE. Baltimore: Turnbull Brothers, 1874.

Mayer, Brantz. BALTIMORE PAST AND PRESENT. Baltimore: Richardson and Bennett, 1871.

Stockett, Letitia. BALTIMORE (A NOT TOO SERIOUS HISTORY) Baltimore: The Norman, Remington Company, 1928.

Smith, Margaret Bayard. THE FIRST FORTY YEARS OF WASHINGTON SOCIETY. New York: Charles Scribner's Sons, 1906.

Guedalla, Philip. WELLINGTON. New York: Harpers, 1931.

Beirne, Francis F. THE AMIABLE BALTIMOREANS. New York: E. P. Dutton and Company, 1951.

Sencourt, Robert. THE LIFE OF THE EMPRESS EUGÉNIE. New York: Charles Scribner's Sons, 1931.

Oddie, E. M. (Elinor Mary O'Donoghue) THE BONAPARTES

IN THE NEW WORLD. London: Elkin, Mathews and Marrot, 1932.

Maude, John. VISIT TO THE FALLS OF NIAGARA IN 1800. London: Longman, Rees, Orme, Brown and Green, 1826.

Wilson, R. McNair. NAPOLEON, THE MAN. New York: The Century Company, 1928.

ST. MARY'S SEMINARY OF ST. SULPICE, BALTIMORE, MD. 1791-1891 Centenary volume. Baltimore; John Murphy and Company, 1891.

Reniers, Perceval. THE SPRINGS OF VIRGINIA. University of North Carolina Press, 1941.

Wilstach, Paul. TIDEWATER MARYLAND. Indianapolis: Bobbs-Merrill Company, 1931.

Footner, Hulbert. SAILOR OF FORTUNE: THE LIFE AND ADVENTURES OF COMMODORE BARNEY, USN, New York: Harpers, 1940.

Brent, Harrison. PAULINE BONAPARTE. New York: Rinehart and Company, 1946.

Henderson, Daniel. THE GOLDEN BEES. New York: Frederick A. Stokes Company, 1928.

Quynn, Dorothy M. and Frank F. White, Jr. JEROME AND BETSY CROSS THE ATLANTIC. Baltimore: Maryland Historical Magazine, September, 1953.

MacCartney, Clarence Edward and Gordon Dorrance. THE BONAPARTES IN AMERICA. Philadelphia: Dorrance and Company, 1939.

The Berkeley Men. THE NAPOLEON DYNASTY. New York: Cornish, Lamport and Company, 1852.

Atteridge, A. Hilliard. NAPOLEON'S BROTHERS. London: Methuen and Company, 1909.

Ertz, Susan. NO HEARTS TO BREAK. New York: D Appleton-Century, 1937.

Various Contributors. HISTORY OF BALTIMORE. 3 vols. Chicago: Lewis Historical Publishing Company, 1912.

Smith, Ellen Hart. CHARLES CARROLL OF CARROLLTON. Cambridge: Harvard University Press, 1942.

Aubry, Octave. PRIVATE LIFE OF NAPOLEON. Philadelphia: J. B. Lippincott Company, 1947.

Richardson, Norval. MOTHER OF KINGS. New York: Charles Scribner's Sons, 1928.

Tschudi, Clara. NAPOLEON'S MOTHER. London: Swan Sonnenschein and Company, Ltd., 1900.

Crawford, Mary Caroline. ROMANTIC DAYS OF THE EARLY REPUBLIC. Boston: Little, Brown and Company, 1912.

Turquan, Joseph. THE SISTERS OF NAPOLEON. London: T. Fisher Unwin, 1908.

Guedalla, Philip. THE SECOND EMPIRE. London: Constable and Company, Ltd., 1922.

Bingham, the Hon. D. A. THE MARRIAGES OF THE BONAPARTES. 2 vols. London: Longmans, Green and Company, 1881.

Gallatin, edited by Count. THE DIARY OF JAMES GALLATIN. New York: Charles Scribner's Sons, 1916.

Pier, Arthur Stanwood. THE STORY OF HARVARD. Boston: Little, Brown and Company, 1913.

Carlton, W. N. C. PAULINE: FAVORITE SISTER OF NAPOLEON, New York: Harpers, 1930.

Bearne, Mrs. FOUR FASCINATING FRENCH WOMEN. Sketch of the Princess Mathilde Bonaparte. New York: Brentano's, 1910.

Passara, J. Magruder. MARYLAND: STORIES FROM HER HISTORY. Baltimore: Williams and Wilkins Company, 1905.

Sergeant, Philip W. THE BURLESQUE NAPOLEON. London: T. Werner Laurie, 1905.

Peacock, Virginia Tatnall. FAMOUS AMERICAN BELLES OF

THE 19th CENTURY. Philadelphia: J. B. Lippincott Company, 1901.

Brooks, Geraldine. DAMES AND DAUGHTERS OF THE YOUNG REPUBLIC. New York: Thomas Y. Crowell and Company, 1901.

Bishop, Joseph Bucklin. CHARLES JOSEPH BONAPARTE: HIS LIFE AND PUBLIC SERVICE. New York: Charles Scribner's Sons, 1922.

Didier, Eugene L. THE BALTIMORE BONAPARTES. Scribner's Monthly Magazine. May, 1875.

Caylus, Madame de SOUVENIRS. Paris: Libraire Colnet, 1822.

This pocket-sized book, the memoirs of the niece of Madame de Maintenon, belonged to Mme. Bonaparte, and was discovered by the author in a French bookshop in New York. Betsy was fond of marking up her books. The passages that she found of interest and underlined are most self-revealing. *"Il faut ne s'etonner de rien de mauvais,"* she comments bitterly. And after *"Les figures avoient un grand pouvoir sur l'esprit de Madame de Montespan,"* she writes, *"Sur le mien aussi."* EP, 1837. Betsy was fifty-two when she read this book, but she was still childish enough to like to scribble her name and initials in the margins. On page 136, she drew a funny caricature of a face. We wonder of whom?

Alice Curtis Desmond
Newburgh, New York.

ALICE CURTIS DESMOND

is the wife of New York State Senator Thomas C. Desmond. They spend their busy days between Albany and their home at Newburgh, New York, when they are not traveling.

Much of Mrs. Desmond's life has been passed in Europe, South America and the Orient. She has been to Alaska twice and made two trips around the world. Her first two books were travel books. Then Mrs. Desmond followed up her journeys to South America and to Alaska by writing for young readers five books with Peruvian, Argentine and Brazilian backgrounds and two juveniles on Alaska. Several of these books have been translated into Portuguese, Swedish, French or Dutch.

All of Mrs. Desmond's writings are based on her liking for travel and history, although she also lists as hobbies, painting and photography. She is a member of several patriotic societies, a trustee of the Society of Colonial History, and a Fellow of the Society of American Historians. Russell Sage College conferred upon Mrs. Desmond the honorary degree of Doctor of Letters in 1946. The same year, the Rochester Museum of Arts and Sciences made her an honorary Fellow for her historical writing.

Mrs. Desmond's three fictionized biographies—*Martha Washington: Our First Lady; Glamorous Dolly Madison;* and *Alexander Hamilton's Wife*—read like historical romances, but they are true stories, the result of careful research. Three years of hard work and two trips to Europe to gather material have produced another biography in this popular series, the romantic story of the beautiful Baltimore girl who fell in love with Jerome Bonaparte, dashing young brother of the great Napoleon, and married him in spite of her father's and Napoleon's opposition—*Bewitching Betsy Bonaparte.*